Y0-CAT-175

Fodor's Family

SAN FRANCISCO WITH KIDS

1st Edition

Where to Stay and Eat
for All Budgets

Must-See Sights
and Local Secrets

Ratings You Can Trust

Excerpted from *Fodor's San Francisco*

Fodor's Travel Publications New York, Toronto, London, Sydney, Auckland

www.fodors.com

FODOR'S FAMILY SAN FRANCISCO WITH KIDS

Editor: Michael Nalepa

Production Editor: Evangelos Vasilakis
Writer: Denise M. Leto
Editorial Contributors: Fiona G. Parrott, Natasha Sarkisian, Sharon Silva, Sharron Wood, Sura Wood
Maps & Illustrations: David Lindroth, Mark Stroud, *cartographers*; Bob Blake and Rebecca Baer, *map editors*; William Wu, *information graphics*
Design: Fabrizio La Rocca, *creative director*; Guido Caroti, *art director*; Ann McBride, *designer*; Melanie Marin, *senior picture editor*
Cover Photo: (top) Corbis/Punchstock; (bottom) Phillip H. Coblentz/SFCVB
Production Manager: Angela L. McLean

COPYRIGHT

Copyright © 2009 by Fodor's Travel, a division of Random House, Inc.

Fodor's is a registered trademark of Random House, Inc.

All rights reserved. Published in the United States by Fodor's Travel, a division of Random House, Inc., and simultaneously in Canada by Random House of Canada, Limited, Toronto. Distributed by Random House, Inc., New York.

No maps, illustrations, or other portions of this book may be reproduced in any form without written permission from the publisher.

1st Edition

ISBN 978–1–4000–0887–2

ISSN 1943–0159

SPECIAL SALES

This book is available for special discounts for bulk purchases for sales promotions or premiums. Special editions, including personalized covers, excerpts of existing books, and corporate imprints, can be created in large quantities for special needs. For more information, write to Special Markets/Premium Sales, 1745 Broadway, MD 6-2, New York, New York, NY 10019, or e-mail specialmarkets@randomhouse.com.

AN IMPORTANT TIP & AN INVITATION

Although all prices, opening times, and other details in this book are based on information supplied to us at press time, changes occur all the time in the travel world, and Fodor's cannot accept responsibility for facts that become outdated or for inadvertent errors or omissions. **So always confirm information when it matters,** especially if you're making a detour to visit a specific place. Your experiences—positive and negative—matter to us. If we have missed or misstated something, **please write to us.** We follow up on all suggestions. Contact the San Francisco with Kids editor at editors@fodors.com or c/o Fodor's at 1745 Broadway, New York, NY 10019.

PRINTED IN THE UNITED STATES OF AMERICA

10 9 8 7 6 5 4 3 2 1

Be a Fodor's Correspondent

Your opinion matters. It matters to us. It matters to your fellow Fodor's travelers, too. And we'd like to hear it. In fact, we *need* to hear it. When you share your experiences and opinions, you become an active member of the Fodor's community. Here's how you can help improve Fodor's for all of us.

Tell us when we're right. We rely on local writers to give you an insider's perspective. But our writers and staff editors also depend on you. Your positive feedback is a vote to renew our recommendations for the next edition.

Tell us when we're wrong. We update most of our guides every year. But things change. If any of our descriptions are inaccurate or inadequate, we'll incorporate your changes in the next edition and will correct factual errors at fodors.com *immediately*.

Tell us what to include. You probably have had fantastic travel experiences that aren't yet in Fodor's. Why not share them with a community of like-minded travelers? Share your discoveries and experiences with everyone directly at fodors.com. Your input may lead us to add a new listing or a higher recommendation.

Give us your opinion instantly at our feedback center at www.fodors.com/feedback. You may also e-mail editors@fodors.com with the subject line "San Francisco with Kids Editor." Or send your nominations, comments, and complaints by mail to San Francisco with Kids Editor, Fodor's, 1745 Broadway, New York, NY 10019.

Happy Traveling!

Tim Jarrell, Publisher

CONTENTS

ABOUT THIS BOOK

Our Ratings

We wouldn't recommend a place that wasn't worth your time, but sometimes a place is so experiential that superlatives don't do it justice: you just have to be there to know. These sights, properties, and experiences get our highest rating, **Fodor's Choice**, indicated by orange stars throughout this book. Black stars highlight sights and properties we deem **Highly Recommended**, places that our writers, editors, and readers praise again and again for consistency and excellence.

Credit Cards

Want to pay with plastic? **AE, D, DC, MC, V** after restaurant and hotel listings indicate whether American Express, Discover, Diners Club, MasterCard, and Visa are accepted.

Restaurants

Unless we state otherwise, restaurants are open for lunch and dinner daily. We mention dress only when there's a specific requirement and reservations only when they're essential or not accepted—it's always best to book ahead.

Hotels

Unless we tell you otherwise, you can assume that the hotels have private bath, phone, TV, and air-conditioning. We always list facilities but not whether you'll be charged an extra fee to use them, so when pricing accommodations, find out what's included.

Many Listings

★	Fodor's Choice
★	Highly recommended
✉	Physical address
✛	Directions
⌂	Mailing address
☎	Telephone
🖷	Fax
⊕	On the Web
✎	E-mail
🎫	Admission fee
☉	Open/closed times
Ⓜ	Metro stations
▭	Credit cards

Hotels & Restaurants

🏨	Hotel
⇘	Number of rooms
⌂	Facilities
❍	Meal plans
✕	Restaurant
⌕	Reservations
↘	Smoking
𝅘𝅥	BYOB
✕🏨	Hotel with restaurant that warrants a visit

Outdoors

⛳	Golf
⛺	Camping

Other

☺	Family-friendly
⇨	See also
✉	Branch address
☞	Take note

WHAT'S WHERE

1 Union Square. Hotel and shopping central.

2 Chinatown. You'll feel like you should have brought your passport.

3 SoMa. Heavy-hitter cultural institutions and Yerba Buena Gardens, a picnic-perfect downtown oasis.

4 Civic Center. Monumental city government buildings and performing-arts venues.

5 Nob Hill. Staid and elegant mansions; old-money San Francisco.

6 Russian Hill. Roller coaster–like driving possibilities.

7 North Beach. Small Italian neighborhood with sunny sidewalk tables, excellent bakeries, and quirky shops.

8 The Embarcadero. A lovely waterfront promenade, anchored by the exquisite Ferry Building.

9 The Northern Waterfront. Fisherman's Wharf, Pier 39, and Ghirardelli Square. Kids love it.

10 The Marina. Palace of Fine Arts and the absolute-must-see Exploratorium.

11 The Presidio. Wooded shoreline park with spectacular views.

12 Golden Gate Park. San Francisco's 1,000-acre backyard.

13 The Western Shoreline. Miles and miles of windswept Pacific shore.

14 The Haight. '60s souvenirs, great secondhand shops, and lovely Victorians.

Golden Gate Bridge

PACIFIC OCEAN

101

Golden Gate
National
Recreation Area

Baker
Beach

China
Beach

Lincoln
Park

Point
Lobos

Lake St.

Clement St.

Geary Blvd.

43rd Ave.

34th Ave.

25th Ave.

19th Ave.

Park Presidio Blvd.

8th Ave.

Balboa St

RICHMOND

Fulton St.

Golden Gate Park

Kennedy Dr.

Middle Dr.

Stow
Lake

Lincoln Way

Judah St.

28th Ave.

19th Ave.

Funston Ave.

41st Ave.

Sunset Blvd.

SUNSET

Lawton St.

Noriega St.

Ortega St.

Quintara St.

McCoppin
Square

14th Ave.

Taraval St.

Larsen
Park

Vicente St.

Stern Grove

Portola

Yer

Sloat Blvd.

Monterey

STONESTOWN

Harding
Park

Lake Mercea

Merced Blvd.

Font Blvd.

Junipero Serra Blvd.

Holloway Av

Garfield St.

Oce

Skyline Blvd.

Great Highway

Ocean Beach

The
Presid

The
11

15 The Castro. Friendly, rainbow-flag-waving neighborhood with trendy boutiques.

16 Noe Valley. Cute, pricey neighborhood favored by young families.

17 The Mission District. Latino neighborhood with kid-friendly food and lovely Mission Dolores.

18 Pacific Heights. Home to some of San Francisco's most opulent real estate.

19 Japantown. Good Japanese food and fun shopping.

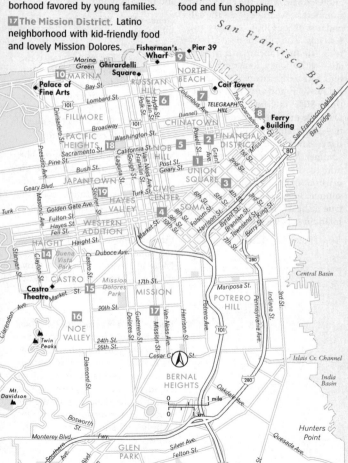

WHEN TO GO

You can visit San Francisco comfortably any time of year, but the best time is probably September and October, when the city's most summerlike weather packs the calendar with outdoor concerts and festivals. The climate here always feels Mediterranean and moderate—with a foggy, sometimes chilly bite. The temperature rarely drops below 40°F, and anything warmer than 80°F is considered a heat wave. Be prepared for rain in winter—especially December and January—and the city's famous fog in summer. Winds off the ocean can add to the chill factor, so pack warm clothing. That old joke about summer in SF feeling like winter is true at heart, but once you move inland it gets warmer.

San Francisco Temperatures

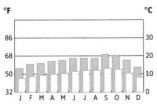

Among the hundreds of events on the city's annual calendar, the following stand out as kid-friendly and incredibly fun.

Chinese New Year, February. This celebration in North America's largest Chinatown lasts for almost three weeks. The grand finale is the spectacularly loud, crowded, and colorful Golden Dragon Parade, which rocks with firecrackers. Contact the Chinese Chamber of Commerce (☎ 415/982–3071 ⊕ *www.chineseparade.com*) for info.

St. Stupid's Day Parade, April. The First Church of the Last Laugh (⊕ *www.saintstupid.com*) holds this fantastically funny event in the Financial District on—when else—April 1.

Cinco de Mayo Festival, May. On the Sunday closest to May 5, the Mission District boils with activity, including a vibrant parade, Mexican music, and dancing in the streets.

Dance-Along Nutcracker, December. This fabulous holiday tradition—part spoof, part warmhearted family event—was started by the San Francisco Lesbian/Gay Freedom Band (⊕ *www.sflgfb.org*). You can join the dancers onstage for some free-form choreography, or simply toss snowflakes from the audience.

BAD-WEATHER PLANS

Soaked in San Francisco

Bay Area weather is usually moderate and pleasant, but in December and January we usually get a few stretches of heavy rain that put outdoor fun on the back burner. Here are some great rainy-day options for riding out a stormy day with your family.

Golden Gate Park. The park on a rainy day? Definitely. Two blockbuster sights within close proximity make this an all-day destination. The giant fish tanks, planetarium shows, and a three-story rain forest at the spectacular new California Academy of Sciences (⊕ *www. calacdemy.org*) that alone offers enough diversions to occupy kids of all ages for an entire day. The food is overpriced, though, so when it's time to refuel, either bust out your lunch bags or head across the music concourse to the café at the de Young Museum. Then head up the tower (free)—which has fantastic 360-degree views—and play spot the landmark.

Yerba Buena Gardens. The gardens themselves may not be welcoming during a rainstorm . . . but the rooftop attractions are, especially for those 10 and up. At hands-on technology space Zeum (⊕ *www. zeum.org*), kids can make their own Claymation videos and pretend they're newscasters. Then check out the skating rink (with great city views for the grownups), or head to the bowling alley. A glass cover protects the vintage carousel, so the little ones can take a spin in the rain. Kid-friendly dining options are close by, especially at the Metreon complex next to the gardens.

Exploratorium. Not even an entire day is enough to experience everything at the granddaddy of science museums (⊕ *www.exploratorium. edu*)—locals' traditional rainy-day pick. Located in a giant exhibition hall at the Palace of Fine Arts, the museum offers no shortage of room to roam and plenty for toddlers and teens alike. Little kids like to watch their shadows "stick" on the wall and play with magnetic black sand, while the older set may explore DNA, observe the dissection of a cow's eye, or climb through the utterly dark Tactile Dome (reserve ahead). The downside is the expensive, less-than-stellar food; pack some snacks, or plan to head over to Chestnut or Lombard afterward.

TOP EXPERIENCES

Ride the Cable Cars. Going to San Francisco and not riding a cable car is like going to Venice and skipping the gondola. Flag down a Powell–Hyde cable car along Powell Street, grab the pole, and clatter and jiggle up mansion-topped Nob Hill. Listen to the humming cable, the clang of the bell, and the occasional quip from the gripman. As you crest the hill, hold on for the hair-raising decent to Fisherman's Wharf, with the sun glittering off the bay and Alcatraz bobbing in the distance. It's an experience—and an adventure—that you shouldn't pass up.

Take a Trip to China . . . town. Live fish, frogs, and fowl wait in the shops to become dinner; the scent of vanilla, incense, and cigarette smoke mingles in the air; and the clack of mah-jong tiles and the hum of the cables provide the soundtrack for a foray into dense Chinatown. Visit a Buddhist temple and browse a Chinese market in the morning, try your luck choosing lunch from a restaurant's dim sum carts, then blow off steam at St. Mary's Square's welcoming playgrounds before giving yourself over to the most kid-friendly window shopping in town. Allow lots of time to take in chirping crickets, boxes of firecracker "poppers," elaborately carved tusks, lion masks, dragon kites, and scary-looking Ninja swords.

Uncover the Best of the Wharf. No matter what locals think of Fisherman's Wharf and Pier 39, kids—even those who live here—adore it. With a bit of planning you can uncover the gems hidden here and keep your wallet from taking too much of a hit. You can't miss the barking sea lions lolling in the water off Pier 39. Then head north to Fisherman's Wharf and steer the kids toward two of the best deals in town: the early-20th-century-arcade games at Musée Mécanique, and the gorgeous historic vessels docked at the Hyde Street Pier. Watch the grips turn the cable cars at Victorian Park's turnaround, then top off the day with a treat at the Ghirardelli Ice Cream & Chocolate Shop at Ghirardelli Square, where you can watch the chocolate manufactory in motion.

Set Sail on the Bay. San Francisco's greatest natural treasure is the bay, and the best way to experience it is by getting out on the water. Excursions to Angel Island and Alcatraz (which should be on your short list of sights to see) include short voyages that will show you a different side of the city. A cheaper option is to take a commuter ferry to Marin County or the East Bay (departing from the Ferry Building). You'll enjoy the same stunning skyline views and open-air seafaring at a fraction of the price, and have a chance to explore off-the-beaten-path gems like Tiburon, Sausalito, and Oakland.

Escape to the Rock. A shiver of excitement will run up your child's back—and probably yours, too—as the ferry approaches the dock at Alcatraz, America's most notorious federal prison. Husky-throated onetime inmates and grizzled former guards bring the Rock to life on the wonderful audio tour; you'll hear yarns about desperate escape attempts and notorious crooks like Al Capone while you walk the cold cement cellblock. But it's not all doom and gloom: you'll enjoy stunning views of the city skyline on the ferry ride to and from the island.

Play in the Park. Though parts of San Francisco feel like an urban jungle, the city is filled with wide (and wild) open spaces. Golden Gate Park, San Francisco's backyard, is home to iconic treasures like the Japanese Tea Garden, the Victorian Conservatory of Flowers, the wild western shores of Ocean Beach, and a herd of buffalo, not to mention the striking de Young Museum and the spectacular new California Academy of Sciences. And if you somehow run out of things to do in this vast park, you can head north to the Presidio to wander its wooded trails and enjoy its ocean lookouts—and views of the majestic Golden Gate Bridge.

Hunt and Gather in the Ferry Building. Roll out of bed and make your way to the magnificent Ferry Building—preferably on a Saturday—to join locals on a taste bud–driven raid. The restored historic building is stuffed to the brim with all things tasty, including cafés, restaurants, a farmers' market, and merchants peddling everything from wine and olive oil to oysters, mushrooms, and artisanal cheeses. Snag some takeaway food and some perfectly ripe fruit, and head outside to the promenade on the building's bay side, where you can enjoy a family picnic as you watch the arriving and departing ferries.

IF YOU LIKE

The Active Life. With its gorgeous natural setting, San Francisco draws even the most hard-core couch potatoes outdoors. Grab a pair of wheels and bike the Embarcadero, where you can take in bay views along the easy 3½-mi path, stopping at wharf attractions. Adventurous families can continue over the Golden Gate Bridge to lovely Sausalito; a sunset ferry ride back is a great way to end the day. At Stowe Lake in Golden Gate Park you can rent a surrey—quirky and easy for little ones—or tool around the lake in a paddle boat. The Coastal Trail out to Lands End in Lincoln Park is one of the most striking hikes around; watch at low tide for sunken ships and in winter for gray whales. Or hike the Filbert Steps up Telegraph Hill to Coit Tower for more gorgeous bay views, glorious gardens, and maybe an encounter with screeching wild parrots. And if all that activity tires you out, become a spectator instead: see hang gliders soaring over the water at Ft. Funston, on the southern end of Ocean Beach; watch windsurfers ride the waves at Crissy Field's East Beach; or catch the hardy surfers under the Golden Gate Bridge.

Ocean Life. The Bay Area is a mecca for budding marine biologists. Some worthy activities are expensive, full-day excursions outside the city that require advance planning, such as whale-watching trips, a visit to the elephant seals at Año Nuevo, or an outing to the justifiably famous Monterey Bay Aquarium. But there's plenty to see—and touch—in town, too. The California Academy of Sciences is an absolute must, with its giant octopuses, blacktip reef sharks, and stingrays; touch pool; and frolicking colony of African penguins. If your kids just can't get enough, head over to Pier 39's Aquarium of the Bay where a cool motorized walkway transports you through underwater tunnels. Kids have an opportunity to get their hands wet at the touch pool; you have an opportunity to buy them stuffed sea creatures at the store here, but consider heading to the Marine Mammal Center Store instead. Purchases here benefit the Sausalito center, which rehabilitates ailing marine mammals. You can learn about sea lions here, too—then follow the barking toward the back of the pier to see the resident colony flopping on floating docks.

Culture Hopping. Its wealth of immigrants has always made San Francisco a richly diverse town, the perfect place for pint-sized globetrotters to experience into other cultures without a passport. Duck into an incense-filled, red lantern–hung Buddhist temple, then choose dim sum off the cart for lunch in dense, bustling Chinatown. Visit

Clarion Music Center to see elaborate lion dance costumes and try to spot the Buddhist altar at the back of any storefront. In Japantown, check out the Peace Pagoda, cherry trees, and cool Japanese souvenirs—puffy family photo stickers, kid chopsticks, and tiny everything. Most kids get a kick out of restaurants' plastic food displays; lunch on noodles or let the kids choose sushi off little boats. At the Asian Art Museum downtown, compare art from those two countries. In the Latino Mission visit Mission Dolores, the city's oldest standing structure and an important remnant of Spanish culture, and grab a burrito for lunch. Keep your eyes open for the neighborhood's famous murals; some are funky, some humorous, and many contain Mexican and Central American history lessons. In espresso-fueled, garlic-scented North Beach, eat your way through Italy. Take your tiramisu or gelato to Washington Square Park. These days you're more likely to see tai chi than bocce here, but you'll be doing it under the spires of the neighborhood's Catholic church. (And for more Italian experiences, head over to Lake Merritt in Oakland, where you can take a ride on a gondola guided by an Italian-trained gondolier.)

Things That Go. Have kids who would just as soon watch a fire truck go by as see the sights? From cable cars climbing the hills to ferries plying the bay, San Francisco has lots to keep the Thomas the Tank Engine set entertained. Definitely ride the city's rolling historical landmarks—the cable cars—even though the price is as steep as Russian Hill. Get more bang for your buck and take the top off the system at the free Cable Car Museum, a perennial favorite. The immensely popular historical trolleys of the F-line and the free San Francisco Railway Museum make another vehicle/museum twofer. And be sure to get out on the bay, whether on an Alcatraz visit, bay tour, commuter ferry, or one of the amphibious car tours; if you can't get enough check out the yachts along the Marina Green. More for bargain lovers: the free San Francisco Fire Department Museum (655 Presidio Ave.), complete with vintage, horse-drawn trucks; also drop by Pier 22½ to see the fire boats.

FOR FREE

Despite—or perhaps because of—the astronomical cost of living here, San Francisco offers loads of free diversions.

Museums & Galleries That Are Always Free

Chinese Culture Center

Creativity Explored

Fort Point National Historic Site

Octagon House

Randall Museum

San Francisco Cable Car Museum

San Francisco Railway Museum

Tattoo Art Museum

Walter & McBean Galleries at the San Francisco Art Institute

Wells Fargo History Museum

Museums & Galleries That Are Sometimes Free

Asian Art Museum, first Sunday of every month

California Academy of Sciences, third Wednesday of every month

Cartoon Art Museum, first Tuesday of every month is pay-what-you-wish

Chinese Historical Society of America, first Thursday of every month

Contemporary Jewish Museum, watch for quarterly free days (18 and under are always free)

de Young Museum, first Tuesday of every month

Exploratorium, first Wednesday of every month

Legion of Honor, first Tuesday of every month

Museum of Craft and Folk Art, first Tuesday of every month

San Francisco Museum of Modern Art, first Tuesday of every month

Yerba Buena Center for the Arts (galleries), first Tuesday of every month

Free Concerts

Stern Grove Festival concerts, Sunday afternoons from June through August, are a long-standing city tradition.

The Golden Gate Park Band plays free public concerts on Sunday afternoons, April through October, on the Music Concourse in the namesake park.

Yerba Buena Gardens Festival hosts many concerts and events from May through October.

Exploring San Francisco

WORD OF MOUTH

"A number of mornings we took the cable car from the Union Square area, then switched to the California line and rode it to where it ends near the Ferry Terminal Building. That would be a great place for breakfast with kids— lots of choices, and big tables to eat at—some outside overlooking the Bay bridge."

—elberko

By Denise
M. Leto

SAN FRANCISCO MAKES IT WONDERFULLY easy to tap into the good life. Between the hot arts scene, the tempting boutiques, the awesome bay views, and all those stellar, locally focused restaurants and wine bars, it's the perfect place to indulge yourself . . . and it's also a surprisingly great destination for a family vacation.

Snuggled on a 46½-square-mi tip of land between San Francisco Bay and the Pacific Ocean, San Francisco is a relatively small city of about 744,000 residents (5% fewer than during the dot-com heyday in 2000). San Franciscans cherish the city, partly for the same reasons so many visitors do: the proximity of the bay and its pleasures, rows of Victorian homes clinging precariously to the hillsides, the sun setting behind the Golden Gate Bridge. Longtime locals know the city's attraction goes much deeper, from the diversity of its neighborhoods and residents (trannies in the seedy Tenderloin, yuppie MBAs in the Marina, elderly Russians in the Richmond, working-class Latino families in the Mission) to the city's progressive free spirit (we voted to ban handguns; we embrace a photographer's project that involves naked people frolicking in trees on public land; our fortysomething mayor poses for GQ and hits the town with his actress wife . . .). Take all these things together and you'll begin to understand why, despite the dizzying cost of living here, many San Franciscans can't imagine calling anyplace else home.

San Francisco's charms are great and small. You wouldn't want to miss Golden Gate Park, the Palace of Fine Arts, the Golden Gate Bridge, or a cable-car ride over Nob Hill. Equally inspiring is a walk down the Filbert Steps or through Macondray Lane or an hour gazing at murals in the Mission or the thundering Pacific from the cliffs of Lincoln Park.

UNION SQUARE & CHINATOWN

Union Square bristles with big-city bravado, and just a stone's throw away is a place that feels like a city unto itself, Chinatown. Both have a strong commercial streak: crowds zigzag among upscale international brands in Union Square, while a few blocks north in Chinatown people dash between small neighborhood stores, arms draped with grocery- and souvenir-filled pink-plastic totes.

TOP 5 UNION SQUARE & CHINATOWN

1

Ross Alley, Chinatown: Breathe deeply as you watch the nimble hands at Golden Gate Fortune Cookie Factory, then cross the alley and duck into Sam Bo, purveyor of religious goods, and pick up $1 million worth of hell money—for about a buck.

Westin St. Francis Elevator, Union Square: Ride a glass elevator to the sky (or the 32nd floor) for a gorgeous view of the cityscape, especially in the evening when the lights come up.

Tin How Temple, Chinatown: Climb the narrow stairway to this space hung with hundreds of red lanterns, then step onto the tiny balcony and take in the alley scene below.

Cable Cars, Union Square: Join the crowd watching drivers and grips turn cable cars around at Powell and Market, then take a seat up the street in Union Square and listen to the clang of the bells and the humming of the cable as the cars rattle by.

Kid-friendly Shopping, Chinatown: Soak up the neighborhood's unique flavor at Chinatown Kites (717 Grant Ave.), which has been selling wafting Jolly Rogers and butterflies for decades; the live markets along Stockton, where chickens cluck, sharks swim, and frogs hop in (and sometimes out of) buckets; and China Gate Gifts (531 Grant Ave.), which will satisfy all your samurai sword and ninja knife needs. Be sure to be on the lookout for the candlelit, citrus-laden Buddhist altars that are in the rear of many stores.

In Union Square the city's finest department stores and exclusive emporiums put on their best faces. Older kids may enjoy browsing the tony shops and giant Niketown, Apple Store, and Virgin Megastore outposts, but this area can be challenging for tiny tots.

A favorite with kids and adults alike, dense and insular Chinatown is a full-sensory experience. Good-luck banners of crimson and gold hang beside dragon-entwined lampposts and pagoda roofs, the scent of vanilla and cigarette smoke fills the air, and honking cars chime in with shoppers bargaining loudly in Cantonese or Mandarin.

Both neighborhoods roll up the sidewalks when the shops drop their shutters, so visit between 10 AM and 6 PM to get the best feel; weekdays bring a welcome thinning of the crowds.

WHAT TO SEE IN UNION SQUARE

CABLE CAR TERMINUS. Two of the three cable car lines begin and end their runs at Powell and Market streets, a couple of blocks south of Union Square. These two lines are the most scenic, and both pass near Fisherman's Wharf, so they're usually clogged with first-time sightseers. The wait to board a cable car at this intersection is longer than at any other stop in the system. If you'd rather avoid the mob, board the less-touristy California line at the bottom of Market Street, at Drumm Street.

Lotta's Fountain. Saucy gold rush–era actress, singer, and dancer Lotta Crabtree so aroused the city's miners that they were known to shower her with gold nuggets and silver dollars after her performances. The peculiar, rather clunky fountain was her way of saying thanks to her fans. Given to the city in 1875, the fountain became a meeting place for survivors after the 1906 earthquake. Each April 18, the anniversary of the quake, San Franciscans—including an ever-dwindling handful of survivors—gather at this quirky monument. You can see an image of Lotta herself in one of the Anton Refregier murals in Rincon Center. Kids like to touch the lions' heads, which, alas, no longer spit water. ✉ *Traffic triangle at intersection of 3rd, Market, Kearny, and Geary Sts., Union Square.* 5+up

Maiden Lane. Known as Morton Street in the raffish Barbary Coast era, this former red-light district reported at least one murder a week during the late 19th century. Things cooled down after the 1906 fire destroyed the brothels, and these days Maiden Lane is a chic, boutique-lined pedestrian mall stretching two blocks between Stockton and Kearny streets. Wrought-iron gates close the street to traffic most days between 11 AM and 5 PM, when the lane becomes a patchwork of umbrella-shaded tables. The alfresco dining here is pleasant, but the rather extravagant nature of the lane's stores can make a meal here with little ones less relaxing.

At **140 Maiden Lane** you can see the only Frank Lloyd Wright building in San Francisco. Walking through the brick archway and recessed entry feels a bit like entering a glowing cave. The interior's graceful, curving ramp and skylights are said to have been his model for the Guggenheim Museum in New York. Xanadu Tribal Arts, a gallery showcasing Baltic, Latin American, and African folk art, now occupies the space. ✉ *Between Stockton and Kearny Sts., Union Square.* 9+up

Union Square & Chinatown

Pacific Ave.

Jackson Square Historic District

Beckett St.

St. Louis Pl.

Jackson St.

Gibb St.

Ils La.

Hotaling St.

Balance Al.

Custom House Pl.

Cable Car

Stone St.

Stockton St.

Washington St.

Golden Gate Fortune Cookie Factory

Old Chinese Telephone Exchange

Chinese Culture Center

Merchant St.

CHINATOWN

Spofford St.

Waverly Pl.

M. Twain Pl.

Clay St.

Parkhurst Al.

Kong Chow Temple

Portsmouth Square

Clay St.

Tin How Temple

Commercial St.

Chinese Historical Society of America-Museum and Learning Center

Chinese Six Companies

Sacramento St.

Spring St.

Leidesdorff St.

NOB HILL

Cable Car

Pratt Pl.

Joice St.

Tunnel

Old St. Mary's Cathedral

California St.

Vinton Ct.

Quincy St.

St. Mary's Sq.

Kearny St.

Pine St.

Hooker Al.

Powell St.

Bush St.

Emma St.

Grant Ave.

St. George Al.

La. Mark La.

Claude

Beiden St.

Chinatown Gate

Trinity St.

Anson Pl.

Harlan Pl.

Hardie Pl.

Hallidie Building

Delta Pl.

Sutter St.

Campton Pl.

Lick Pl.

San Francisco Museum of Craft + Design

MONTGOMERY ST. **b**ā

New Montgomery St.

Post St.

Union Square

Maiden Ln.

Lotta's Fountain

Annie St.

A. Bierce St.

Westin St. Francis Hotel

Maiden Lane

Market St.

Security Pacific Pl.

3rd St.

Geary St.

UNION SQUARE

Pacific Telephone Bldg.

American Conservatory Theater

O'Farrell St.

Mason St.

Ellis St.

Market St.

4th St.

Jessie St.

Mission St.

Pioneer Pl.

San Francisco Visitor Information Center

bā

POWELL ST.

Yerba Buena Gardens

Moscone Convention Center

Eddy St.

Market St.

5th St.

Mission St.

Holland Ct.

Stevenson St.

Old U.S. Mint

KEY

bā *Bart Stop*

.... *Cable Car*

WHERE CAN I FIND . . . IN UNION SQUARE & CHINATOWN?

Quick Meals	Location	Description
Sears Fine Food	439 Powell St., Union Square	Old-time San Francisco eatery famous for its pancakes; also serves gigantic lunches.
Eastern Bakery	720 Grant Ave., Chinatown	Good steamed pork buns to go for about $1; famous moon pies for dessert.

Good Coffee		
Citizen Cupcake	2 Stockton St., 3rd Floor (in Virgin Megastore), Union Square	Great big-city views and beautiful cupcakes with your high-quality joe.
Peet's coffee cart	120 Stockton St., outside Macy's Men's Store, Union Square	Great location: strong coffee where you need it.

Fun Stores		
Kar'ikter	418 Sutter St., Union Square	Chic and stylish spot for cool toys and doodads featuring friends from Wallace and Gromit to Babar.
Canton Bazaar	616 Grant Ave., Chinatown	Huge, Chinese Kmart of a place.

Playgrounds		
St. Mary's Square	Grant Ave. and California St., across from Old St. Mary's Church, Chinatown	Small, tidy green space for the younger set; giant statue of Sun Yat-sen adds historical interest

Public Bathrooms		
St. Mary's Square	Grant Ave. and California St., across from Old St. Mary's Church, Chinatown	Green booth with automated locking and cleaning.
Nordstrom	865 Market St., Union Square	Fit for princes and princesses: huge and clean, with fancy lounges.
Neiman Marcus	150 Stockton St., Union Square	Spotless and directly on the square.

San Francisco Museum of Craft + Design. You could be forgiven for walking by this museum, thinking that it's a private office or boutique. No one expects a front garden—a garden!—in this pack-in-every-square-foot neighborhood. It's a serene welcome to this stark three-room space, which opened in 2004. Quarterly exhibits focus on modern design of all sorts, from fanciful furniture to designer toys to wine labels. Whether you should visit depends entirely on the exhibit: if the theme grabs you, it's well worth coming by. Even younger children are drawn to the museum's sculptural, bright, often whimsical displays, but it is an inside-voice, walk-don't-run kind of place. Occasional children's programs introduce kids to various media based on the current exhibit, including a discussion of the artist's work and a chance to create their own. Call ahead or check online for dates. ⊠*550 Sutter St., Union Square* ☎*415/773–0303* ⊕*www.sfmcd.com* ⊠*$3 suggested donation*; children under 18 free ⊗*Tues., Wed., Fri., and Sat. 10–5, Thurs. 10–7, Sun. noon–5.* 5+up

GRAB A CITYPASS. **If you're planning to ride the cable cars and hit the big-ticket stops like the California Academy of Sciences, the Exploratorium, and SFMOMA, the CityPass ($59, $44 kids 5–17), good for nine days including seven days of transit, will save you about 50%. You can purchase it at the San Francisco Visitor Information Center (** ☎*888/330–5008* ⊕*www.citypass.com***) or at any of the attractions it covers.**

San Francisco Visitor Information Center. A multilingual staff operates this facility below the cable-car terminus. Staffers answer questions and provide maps and pamphlets. You can also pick up discount coupons—the savings can be significant, especially for families—and hotel brochures here. ⊠*Hallidie Plaza, lower level, Powell and Market Sts., Union Square* ☎*415/391–2000 or 415/283–0177* ⊕*www.onlyinsanfrancisco.com* ⊗*Weekdays 9–5, Sat. 9–3; also Sun. 9–3 in May–Oct.* All ages

Union Square. The heart of San Francisco's downtown since 1850, a 2½-acre square surrounded by department stores and the Westin St. Francis hotel, is about the only place you can sit for free in this part of town. With its pretty landscaping and the addition of a café, it's an improvement over the concrete wasteland it was until a 2002 redesign, but no one's beating a path downtown to hang out here. Today the square is a good place to take a break from shopping, watch street performers, and let the kids chase pigeons.

The square takes its name from the violent pro-union demonstrations staged here before the Civil War. At center stage, Robert Ingersoll Aitken's *Victory Monument* commemorates Commodore George Dewey's victory over the Spanish fleet at Manila in 1898. The 97-foot column was dedicated by Theodore Roosevelt in 1903 and withstood the 1906 earthquake.

On the eastern edge of Union Square, **TIX Bay Area** (☎*415/433–7827 info only* ⊕*www.theatrebayarea.org*) provides half-price day-of-performance tickets (cash or traveler's checks only) to performing-arts events. Union Square covers a convenient underground garage. Kids are especially drawn to the square during winter holidays, when a giant Christmas tree presides over the western end and enormous decorations bedeck Macy's across the street, both inside and out. ✉*Bordered by Powell, Stockton, Post, and Geary Sts., Union Square.* All ages

Westin St. Francis. The second-oldest hotel in the city, established in 1904, was conceived by railroad baron and financier Charles Crocker and his associates as a hostelry for their millionaire friends. Swift service and sumptuous surroundings have always been hallmarks of the property. After the hotel was ravaged by the 1906 fire, a larger, more luxurious Italian Renaissance–style residence was opened in 1907 to attract loyal clients from among the world's rich and powerful. The hotel's checkered past includes Al Jolson's death and Sara Jane Moore's 1975 attempt to shoot then-president Gerald Ford. As might be imagined, no plaques in the lobby commemorate these events. ■TIP➔**One of the best views in the city is from the glass elevators here—and best of all, it's free. Zip up to the 32nd floor for a bird's-eye view; the lights of the nighttime cityscape are particularly lovely.** Don't be shy if you're not a guest: some visitors make this a stop every time they're in town. Local families make an annual Christmastime pilgrimage here to view the lobby's fantastical and colossal gingerbread house; the well heeled plan a weekend visit to indulge in elegant holiday high tea. ✉*335 Powell St., at Geary St., Union Square* ☎*415/397–7000* ⊕*www.westinstfrancis.com.* 5+up

WHAT TO SEE IN CHINATOWN

Chinatown Gate. This is the official entrance to Chinatown. Stone lions flank the base of the pagoda-topped gate; the lions, dragons, and fish up top symbolize wealth, prosperity, and other good things. The four Chinese characters immediately beneath the pagoda represent the philosophy of Sun Yat-sen (1866–1925), the leader who unified China in the early 20th century. Sun Yat-sen, who lived in exile in San Francisco for a few years, promoted the notion of friendship and peace among all nations based on equality, justice, and goodwill. The vertical characters under the left pagoda read "peace" and "trust," the ones under the right pagoda "respect" and "love." The whole shebang usually telegraphs the internationally understood message of "photo op." ⊠*Grant Ave. at Bush St., Chinatown*. All ages

LOOK UP! When wandering around Chinatown, don't forget to look up! Above the chintziest souvenir shop might loom an ornate balcony or a curly pagoda roof. The best examples are on the 900 block of Grant Avenue (at Washington Street) and at Waverly Place.

Chinese Historical Society of America–Museum & Learning Center. This airy, light-filled gallery has displays about the Chinese-American experience from 19th-century agriculture to 21st-century food and fashion trends, including a poignant collection of racist games and toys. A separate room hosts rotating exhibits by contemporary Chinese-American artists. If you only bring your family to one Chinese exhibit space, make it this one. You won't find any children's programs here, but the exhibits are large scale and quick to view (though they reward deeper examination by older kids, too). ⊠*965 Clay St., Chinatown* ☎415/391–1188 ⊕*www.chsa.org* ⊠*$3, free 1st Thurs. of month*; $1 kids 6–17 ☉*Tues.–Fri. noon–5, Sat. 11–4.* 7+up

Golden Gate Fortune Cookie Factory. Follow your nose down Ross Alley to this tiny cookie factory. Workers sit at circular motorized griddles and wait for dollops of batter to drop onto a tiny metal plate, which rotates into an oven. A few moments later out comes a cookie that's pliable and ready for folding. It's easy to peek in for a moment, and hard to leave without a few free samples. A bagful of cookies—with mildly racy "adult" fortunes or more-benign ones—costs about $3. You can also purchase the cookies "fortuneless" in their waferlike unfolded state, which makes snacking that much more efficient. Being allowed to photograph the cookie makers at work will set you back 50¢. ⊠*56 Ross Alley, west of and parallel to Grant Ave. between Washington and Jackson Sts., Chinatown* ☎*415/781–3956* ⧉*Free* ⊙*Daily 9–8.* All ages

Kong Chow Temple. This ornate temple sets a somber, spiritual tone right away with a sign warning visitors not to touch *anything*. The god to whom the members of this temple pray represents honesty and trust. Chinese stores and restaurants often display his image because he's thought to bring good luck in business. Chinese immigrants established the temple in 1851; its congregation moved to this building in 1977. Take the elevator up to the fourth floor, where incense fills the air. You can show respect by placing a dollar or two in the donation box and by leaving your camera in its case. Amid the statuary, flowers, and richly colored altars (red wards off evil spirits and signifies virility, green symbolizes longevity, and gold connotes majesty), a couple of plaques announce that MRS. HARRY S. TRUMAN CAME TO THIS TEMPLE IN JUNE 1948 FOR A PREDICTION ON THE OUTCOME OF THE ELECTION . . . THIS FORTUNE CAME TRUE. The temple's balcony has a good view of Chinatown. ⊠*855 Stockton St., Chinatown* ☎*No phone* ⧉*Free* ⊙*Mon.–Sat. 9–4.* 7+up

Portsmouth Square. Chinatown's living room buzzes with activity. The square, with its pagoda-shaped structures, is a favorite spot for morning tai chi; by noon dozens of men huddle around Chinese chess tables, engaged in not-always-legal competition. Kids scamper about the square's two grungy playgrounds (warning: the bathrooms are sketchy). Back in the late 19th century this land was near the waterfront and Robert Louis Stevenson, the author of *Treasure Island*, often dropped by, chatting up the sailors who hung out here. Some of the information he gleaned about life at sea found its way into his fiction. A bronze galleon sculpture, a tribute to Stevenson, is anchored in a corner of the square. ⊠*Bordered by Walter Lum Pl. and Kearny, Washington, and Clay Sts., Chinatown.* 3+up

Tin How Temple. Duck into the inconspicuous doorway, climb three flights of stairs—on the second floor is a mah-jong parlor whose patrons hope the spirits above will favor them—and be assaulted by the aroma of incense in this tiny, altar-filled room. Day Ju, one of the first three Chinese to arrive in San Francisco, dedicated this temple to the Queen of the Heavens and the Goddess of the Seven Seas in 1852. In the temple's entryway, elderly ladies can often be seen preparing "money" to be burned as offerings to various Buddhist gods or as funds for ancestors to use in the afterlife. Hundreds of red-and-gold lanterns cover the ceiling; the larger the lamp, the larger its donor's contribution to the temple. Gifts of oranges, dim sum, and money left by the faithful, who kneel mumbling prayers, rest on altars to various gods. Tin How presides over the middle back of the temple, flanked by one red and one green lesser god. Take a good look around, since taking photographs is not allowed. ⊠*125 Waverly Pl., Chinatown* ☎*No phone* ⊠*Free, donations accepted* ⊙*Daily 9–4.* 7+up

SOMA & CIVIC CENTER

To a newcomer, SoMa (short for "south of Market") and Civic Center may look like cheek-by-jowl neighbors—they're divided by Market Street. To locals, though, these areas are firmly separate entities, especially since Market Street itself is considered such a strong demarcation line. Both neighborhoods have a core of cultural sights but more than their share of sketchy blocks, and both are designed decisively on a grown-up scale.

SoMa is less a neighborhood than it is a sprawling area of wide, traffic-heavy boulevards lined with office high-rises and pricey live-work lofts. In terms of sightseeing, SoMa's few points of interest cluster conveniently together just south of Market Street. Among these is Yerba Buena Gardens, an open, welcoming green space that's a godsend for lively kids and perfectly situated for burning off energy between SoMa's blockbuster sights.

Civic Center is an in-and-out kind of neighborhood. Casual wandering here is unrewarding; not even City Hall's central playground invites lingering. Two major draws make a detour here worthwhile: the wonderful Asian Art Museum and the city's premier performing arts venues. If those don't appeal to your family, catch a glimpse of City Hall's impressive gold dome on a drive-by and then check Civic Center off your list.

HAYES VALLEY. **Right next door to the Civic Center, Hayes Valley is an offbeat neighborhood with terrific eateries, cool watering holes, and great browsing in its funky clothing and home decor boutiques. Swing down main drag Hayes Street, between Frank-**

TOP 5 SOMA & CIVIC CENTER

Asian Art Museum, Civic Center: Stand face-to-face with a massive gold Buddha in one of the world's largest collections of Asian art.

Yerba Buena Gardens, SoMa: From running under waterfalls to racing down the giant metal tube slide, downtown's green oasis is a boon for the young set. Kids like to shake hands with the Shaking Man statue—a cool earthquake reminder minus the scary.

SFMOMA, SoMa: Cross the Turret Bridge suspended below the ceiling and experience an element of adventure unexpected in a museum visit.

Cartoon Art Museum, SoMa: Familiar faces greet kids at this small museum, a fun quick stop among SoMa's cultural heavy-hitters.

Zeum, SoMa: Mid-kids and teens can be rock stars by grabbing a mic and learning to make their own music videos at Zeum—just as much fun as Guitar Hero and more educational.

lin and Laguna, and you can hit the highlights, including two very popular restaurants, Absinthe and Suppenküche. Comfy Place Pigalle (at Hayes and Octavia streets) is also a favorite for its living-room atmosphere, wines, and microbrews. Locals love this quarter, but without any big-name draws, it remains off the radar for most visitors.

WHAT TO SEE IN SOMA

Cartoon Art Museum. Krazy Kat, Zippy the Pinhead, Batman, and other colorful cartoon icons greet you at the Cartoon Art Museum, established with an endowment from cartoonist-icon Charles M. Schulz. The museum's strength is its changing exhibits, which explore such topics as America from the perspective of international political cartoons, and the output of women and African-American cartoonists. Serious fans of cartoons—especially those on the quirky underground side—will likely enjoy the exhibits; those with a casual interest may be disappointed. The museum store carries lots of cool books. If your child aspires to be a cartoon artist, check out the Saturday cartooning classes; these meet once a month or so and are designed for kids 8–14 years old. ✉655 Mission St., SoMa ☎415/227–8666 ⊕www.cartoonart.org ⊠$6, pay what you wish 1st Tues. of month; students 13–17 $4; students 2–12 $2; children 5 and under free ⊙Tues.–Sun. 11–5. 7+up

Contemporary Jewish Museum. Stand on the Mission Street border of Yerba Buena Gardens and look across the way—next to St. Patrick's is the new home of the latest major museum to land in this neighborhood. "Starchitect" Daniel Libeskind's state-of-the-art building opened in June 2008, joining a 1906 power station with giant, blocky shapes sheathed in bright blue steel panels, a striking combination that makes it one of the most eye-catching in the neighborhood. The museum shows a series of temporary exhibits that often focus on political themes. These can be controversial but offer insight to anyone interested in contemporary Jewish life. The CJM is one museum at which kids aren't an afterthought. The ArtPack (free with admission) was designed to help families explore the space together to drop-in programs every Sunday, including tours for older kids and art projects for smaller ones. Free admission for kids; good, reasonably priced food at the attractive Café on the Square; and museum's innovative space make this a great family stop in SoMa. ✉ *736 Mission St., between 3rd and 4th Sts., SoMa* ☎ *415/655–7800* ⊕ *www.thecjm.org* ✑ *$10; $5 Thurs. after 5; kids 18 and under free* ⊘ *Thurs. 1–8:30, Fri. –Tues. 11–5:30.* All ages

Metreon. Child's play meets the 21st century at this high-tech mall, adored by gearheads and teenage boys obsessed with tabletop games. The complex houses the high-tech interactive arcade Tilt, a 15-screen multiplex and IMAX theater, retail shops such as PlayStation and Sony Style, and outposts of some of the city's favorite restaurants are all part of the complex. It's a good place to pick up lunch for a picnic in the Yerba Buena Gardens, right outside; if you forgot your blanket, head to the patio tables outside Metreon's second floor. ✉ *101 4th St., between Mission and Howard Sts., SoMa* ☎ *800/638–7366* ⊕ *http://westfield. com/metreon.* 7+up

Museum of the African Diaspora (MoAD). Dedicated to the influence that people of African descent have had all over the world, MoAD provokes discussion from the git-go with the question, "When did you discover you are African?" painted on the wall at the entrance. With no permanent collection, the museum is light on displays and heavy on interactive exhibits. For instance, you can sit in a darkened theater and listen to the moving life stories of slaves; hear snippets of music that helped create genres from gospel to hip-hop; and see videos about the civil rights movement or the Haitian Revolution. Some grumble that sweeping gener-

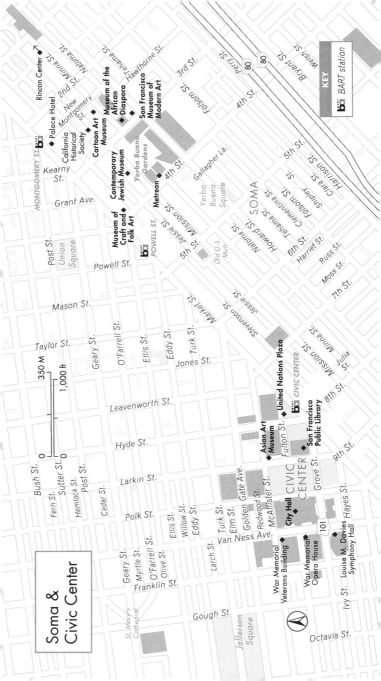

Soma & Civic Center

KEY

b *BART station*

Rincon Center

2nd St.

Minna St.

Natoma St.

New Montgomery St.

Palace Hotel **b**

California Historical Society

Cartoon Art Museum

Museum of the African Diaspora

Tehama St.

Hawthorne St.

3rd St.

San Francisco Museum of Modern Art

4th St.

Folsom St.

Perry St.

80

80

Bryant St.

Weiss St.

Kearny St.

Grant Ave.

MONTGOMERY ST.

Contemporary Jewish Museum

Yerba Buena Gardens

Metreon

Mission St.

4th St.

Gallagher La.

Yerba Buena Square

SOMA

5th St.

Clara St.

Shipley St.

Clementina St.

Tehama St.

Folsom St.

Harrison St.

Museum of Craft and Folk Art

POWELL ST.

b

Jessie St.

Mission St.

5th St.

Natoma St.

Howard St.

Tehama St.

Old U.S. Mint

6th St.

Harriet St.

Russ St.

Post St.

Union Square

Powell St.

Moss St.

7th St.

Mason St.

Market St.

Stevenson St.

Jessie St.

Taylor St.

Geary St.

O'Farrell St.

Ellis St.

Eddy St.

Turk St.

Jones St.

Leavenworth St.

United Nations Plaza

CIVIC CENTER

b

8th St.

Mission St.

Minna St.

Julia St.

350 M

1,000 ft

Hyde St.

Asian Art Museum

San Francisco Public Library

Fulton St.

9th St.

Bush St.

Fern St.

Sutter St.

Hemlock St.

Post St.

Cedar St.

Larkin St.

Polk St.

Turk St.

Golden Gate Ave.

Redwood St.

McAllister St.

Elm St.

Eddy St.

City Hall

CIVIC CENTER

Grove St.

9th St.

Geary St.

Myrtle St.

O'Farrell St.

Olive St.

Ellis St.

Willow St.

Eddy St.

Larch St.

Van Ness Ave.

101

Hayes St.

Louise M. Davies Symphony Hall

Franklin St.

War Memorial Veterans Building

War Memorial Opera House

Ivy St.

St. Mary's Cathedral

Gough St.

Jefferson Square

Octavia St.

alities replace specific information, but almost everyone can appreciate the museum's most striking exhibit, in the front window. The three-story mosaic, made from thousands of photographs, forms the image of a little girl's face. Walk up the stairs inside the museum and view the photographs up close—Malcolm X is there, Muhammad Ali, too, along with everyday folks—but the best view is from across the street. Family days (generally one Sunday per month) offer kids the opportunity to experiment with the medium featured in the museum's current exhibit. Any day of the week, though, the large-scale and often interactive exhibits here appeal to most kids and make for a pretty quick visit. ⊠ *685 Mission St., SoMa* ☎ *415/358–7200* ⊕ *www. moadsf.org* ⚑ *$10;* students 13–17 $5; kids 12 and under free ☉ *Wed.–Sat. 11–6, Sun. noon–5.* 7+up

Museum of Craft and Folk Art. If you're in the area, this one-room museum is a great way to spend a half hour. This bright space hosts five rotating exhibits per year showcasing American folk art, tribal art, and contemporary crafts. One exhibit saw the museum transformed into a forest of paper, all created by hand from plants, trees, and river water by an artisan in Japan. Another was devoted entirely to the art of the ukulele. Its tiny front space houses a shop with high-end, sometimes whimsical crafts from around the world. Depending on the exhibit, this can be a fantastic stop with kids—and if it turns out it's not, well, you've only lost about 10 minutes. ⊠ *51 Yerba Buena La., SoMa* ☎ *415/227–4888* ⊕ *www.mocfa.org* ⚑ *$5; free 1st Tues. of month;* kids 18 and under free ☉ *Mon., Tues., Thurs., Fri. 11–6; weekends 11–5.* 5+up

★ Fodor'sChoice **San Francisco Museum of Modern Art** *(SFMOMA).* With its brick facade and a striped central tower lopped at a lipsticklike angle, architect Mario Botta's SFMOMA building fairly screams "modern-art museum." Taking in all of SFMOMA's four exhibit floors can be overwhelming, so having a plan is helpful. ■TIP→ **With young children, head straight to the fourth and fifth floors for temporary exhibits— many of which are large scale and striking—and work your way back down.** The museum's heavy hitters are on the second (big-name traveling exhibits and collection highlights) and third floors (photography). If it's on display, don't miss sculptor Jeff Koons' memorably creepy, life-size gilded porcelain *Michael Jackson and Bubbles,* on the fifth floor at the end of the Turret Bridge, a vertiginous catwalk dangling under the central tower that's itself a kid highlight.

A fifth-floor, garage-top sculpture garden is to open in spring 2009.

Caffè Museo, accessible from the street, provides a refuge for quite good, reasonably priced drinks and light meals. It's easy to drop a fortune at the museum's large store, chockablock with fun gadgets, artsy doodads of all kinds, and possibly the best selection of kids' books in town. The museum's occasional family days include family tours and art-making for the kids (and free admission for the whole family). Any day, though, you have two options for taking a break from the galleries with antsy kids: visit the Koret Education Center and settle into a comfy chair with a mellow art-related activity, or take advantage of the museum's in-and-out privileges and head right across the street to the Yerba Buena Gardens for a running and shouting break without the withering stares. ✉*151 3rd St., SoMa* ☎*415/357–4000* ⊕*www.sfmoma.org* ✆*$12.50,* students 13–17 $7, kids 12 and under free; *free 1st Tues. of month, ½ price Thurs. 6–9;* ⊗*Labor Day–Memorial Day, Fri.–Tues. 11–5:45, Thurs. 11–8:45; Memorial Day–Labor Day, Fri.–Tues. 10–5:45, Thurs. 10–8:45.* 3+up

★ **Yerba Buena Gardens.** There's not much South of Market that encourages lingering outdoors, or indeed walking at all, with this notable exception. These two blocks encompass the **Center for the Arts, Metreon, Moscone Convention Center,** and the convention center's rooftop **Zeum,** but the gardens themselves are the everyday draw. Office workers escape to the green swath of the East Garden. The memorial to Martin Luther King Jr. is the focal point here. Powerful streams of water surge over large, jagged stone columns, mirroring the enduring force of King's words that are carved on the stone walls and on glass blocks behind the waterfall. Moscone North is behind the memorial, and an overhead walkway leads to Moscone South and its rooftop attractions. ■TIP→**The gardens are liveliest during the week and especially during the Yerba Buena Gardens Festival (May through October, www.ybgf.org), when free performances run from Latin music to Balinese dance.**

Atop the Moscone Convention Center perch a few lures for kids. The historic **Looff carousel** ($3 for two rides) twirls daily 11–6. South of the carousel is **Zeum** (☎*415/820–3320* ⊕*www. zeum.org*), a high-tech, interactive arts-and-technology center ($8, 3–18 $6) geared to children ages eight and over. Kids can make Claymation videos, work in a computer lab, and view exhibits and performances. Zeum is open 1–5 Wednesday through Friday and 11–5 weekends during the school year and Tuesday through Sunday when school's out.Also part of the rooftop complex are gardens, an ice-skating rink, a bowling alley, and a very popular, very long tube slide. ✉*Bordered by 3rd, 4th, Mission, and Folsom Sts., SoMa* ☎*No phone* ⊕*www.yerbabuenagardens.com* ⊡*Free* ☉*Daily sunrise–10* PM. All ages

WHAT TO SEE IN CIVIC CENTER

★ **Asian Art Museum.** Expecting a building full of Buddhas and jade? Well, yeah, you can find plenty of those here. Happily, though, you don't have to be a connoisseur of Asian art to appreciate a visit to this splendidly renovated museum, whose monumental exterior conceals a light, open, and welcoming space. The fraction of the museum's items on display (about 2,500 pieces from a 15,000-plus-piece collection) is laid out thematically and by region, making it easy to follow developments.

Begin on the third floor, where highlights of Buddhist art in Southeast Asia and early China include a large, jewel-encrusted, exquisitely painted 19th-century Burmese Buddha and clothed rod puppets from Java. On the second floor you can find later Chinese works, as well as pieces from Korea and Japan. Look for a cobalt tiger jauntily smoking a pipe on a whimsical Korean jar and delicate Japanese tea implements. The ground floor displays rotating exhibits, including contemporary and traveling shows. ■TIP➔**If you'd like to attend one of the occasional tea ceremonies and tastings at the Japanese Teahouse, call ahead, since preregistration is required.** Kids' programs abound at the Asian Art Museum, clustering on weekends and especially Sundays, which bring storytelling; kids' yoga classes and art-making opportunities round out the calendar. Be sure to ask about the family activity kit that accompanies most major exhibits. ✉*200 Larkin St., between McAllister and Fulton Sts., Civic Center* ☎*415/581–3500* ⊕*www.asianart.org* ⊡*$12, free 1st Sun. of month; $5 Thurs. 5–9*; students 13–17 $7; 12 and under free; *tea ceremony $20, includes museum* ☉ *Tues., Wed., and Fri.–Sun. 10–5, Thurs. 10–9.* 5+up

City Hall. This imposing 1915 structure with its massive gold-leaf dome—higher than the U.S. Capitol's—is about as close to a palace as you're going to get in San Francisco. (The metal detectors take something away from the grandeur, though.) Modeled after St. Peter's cathedral in Rome, it has impressive grand columns and a sweeping central staircase.

Some of the noteworthy events that have taken place here include the marriage of Marilyn Monroe and Joe DiMaggio (1954); the hosing—down the central staircase—of civil-rights and freedom-of-speech protesters (1960); and the murders of Mayor George Moscone and openly gay supervisor Harvey Milk (1978). In February 2004—the "Winter of Love"—thousands of gay and lesbian couples were married here before the state Supreme Court stepped in. Free tours are offered weekdays at 10, noon, and 2.

The South Light Court houses a modest display from the collection of the **Museum of the City of San Francisco** (⊕*www.sfmuseum.org*), including the enormous, 700-pound iron head that crowned the statue atop City Hall during the 1906 earthquake.

Across Polk Street in **Civic Center Plaza** you'll find a playground, an underground parking garage, and a large part of the city's homeless population. The city's Web site has a downloadable activity book for school-age kids that can make a visit more interesting for little ones. ✉*Bordered by Van Ness Ave. and Polk, Grove, and McAllister Sts., Civic Center* ☎*415/554–6023* ⊕*www.sfgov.org/site/cityhall* ☎*Free* ☉*Weekdays 8–8.* 7+up

NEED A BREAK? Once exclusively a bakery and sandwich joint, star pastry chef Elizabeth Falkner's **Citizen Cake** (✉*399 Grove St., Civic Center* ☎*415/861–2228*) is now a full-fledged restaurant, but it's still a very worthwhile detour. Choose a sweet—cookies, pastries, chocolates, even house-made ice cream—to go from the patisserie case, or stake out a table in the urban-industrial space.

San Francisco Public Library. Topped with a swirl like an art deco nautilus, the library's seven-level glass atrium fills the building with light. Opened in 1996, the New Main (as Herb Caen dubbed it) is a modernized version of the old Beaux-Arts-style library. Local researchers take advantage of centers dedicated to gay-and-lesbian, African-American, Chinese, and Filipino history, and everyone appreciates the basement-level café, Wi-Fi, and 15-minute Internet terminal access. On the sixth floor, an exhibit inside the San Francisco History Center includes doodads from the 1894 Mid-

Winter Fair and the 1915 Pan-Pacific Exhibition, as well as the "valuable emeralds" philanthropist Helene Strybing left to the city—alas, green glass. ■ TIP→ **Noir fans should head to the back of the center; you can see a** *Maltese Falcon* **statue in the Flood Building but this is the only place to see novelist Dashiell Hammett's typewriter.** Free tours of the library are conducted the second Wednesday of the month at 2:30. At the Fisher Children's Center, on the second floor, librarians expect kids to be noisy; the atmosphere is anything but stuffy. Here you'll find the Electronic Discovery Center, loaded with computers where kids can read stories and play video games. Story time for families of preschoolers is at 11 on Saturday, and lasts about half an hour (story times also take place some weekdays at 10:30). Outside the Children's Center, entertaining exhibits often grab kids' attention even before they step inside. Some of these, such as an elaborate Thomas the Tank Engine Christmas train, are worth a visit on their own. Teenagers should check out the third-floor Teen Center. Downstairs the small, pleasant Library Café has sandwiches and soups at reasonable prices. ✉ *100 Larkin St., at Grove St., Civic Center* ☎ *415/557–4400* ⊕ *sfpl.lib.ca.us* ⊗ *Mon. and Sat. 10–6, Tues.–Thurs. 9–8, Fri. noon–6, Sun. noon–5.* All ages

United Nations Plaza. Locals know this plaza for two things: its Wednesday and Sunday farmers' market—cheap and earthy to the Ferry Building's pricey and beautiful—and its homeless population, which seems to return no matter how many times the city tries to shunt them aside. Brick pillars listing various nations and the dates of their admittance into the United Nations line the plaza, and its floor is inscribed with the goals and philosophy of the United Nations charter, which was signed at the War Memorial Opera House in 1945. Older kids may be interested in the historical aspect of the square; otherwise this is strictly a cut-through—and not a particularly pleasant one at that. ✉ *Fulton St. between Hyde and Market Sts., Civic Center.* All ages

NORTH BEACH

San Francisco novelist Herbert Gold calls North Beach "the longest-running, most glorious American bohemian operetta outside Greenwich Village." Indeed, to anyone who's spent some time in its eccentric old bars and cafés, North Beach evokes everything from the Barbary Coast days to the no-less-rowdy beatnik era. With its outdoor café tables, human-scale architecture full of quirky storefronts, daytime buzz, and central green space for running, North Beach is a kid-friendly, browsable neighborhood.

The neighborhood truly was a beach at the time of the gold rush—the bay extended into the hollow between Telegraph and Russian hills. Once almost exclusively Italian-American, today North Beach is a mixture of Italian, Chinese, and San Francisco yuppie. But walk down narrow Romolo Place (off Broadway east of Columbus) or Genoa Place (off Union west of Kearny) and you can feel the immigrant Italian roots of this neighborhood. Locals know that most of the city's finest Italian restaurants are elsewhere, but North Beach puts folks in mind of Italian food, and there are many decent options to choose from. Bakeries sell focaccia fresh from the oven, and the aroma of coffee beans, deli meats and cheeses, Italian pastries, and—always—pungent garlic fill the air.

WHAT TO SEE IN NORTH BEACH

Beat Museum. It's hard to tell whether the folks who opened this small museum in 2006 are serious—what would the counterculture say about the $18 "Beat beret"? But if you're truly Beat-curious, stop by. Check out the "Beat pad," a mockup of one of the cheap, tiny North Beach apartments the writers and artists populated in the 1950s, complete with bongos and bottle-as-candleholder. Memorabilia includes the shirt Neal Cassady wore while driving Ken Kesey's Merry Prankster bus, *Further.* An early photo of the legendary bus is juxtaposed with a more current picture showing it covered with moss and overgrowth, labeled NOTHING LASTS. Indeed. There are also manuscripts, letters, and early editions by Jack Kerouac, Allen Ginsberg, and Lawrence Ferlinghetti. The gift store has a good selection of Beat philosophy, though it's nothing you won't find across the street at City Lights. On one hand, the kids will have to know something about the Beats to get much out of this museum; on the other hand, it's a very quick stop. The owner may warn you that some of the exhibits may include nudity. ✉*540 Broadway, North Beach* ☎*415/399–9626* ⊕*www.thebeatmuseum.org* ✄*$5;* students 13–17 $4; kids 12 and under free ☉*Tues.–Thurs. noon–10, Fri.–Sun. 10–10.* 12+up

TOP 5 NORTH BEACH

Filbert Steps: Walk down this dizzying stairway from Telegraph Hill's Coit Tower, past lush private gardens and jaw-dropping bay views—and listen for the hill's famous screeching parrots.

Chocolate on Columbus: Visit two of the best chocolatiers in the city—XOX Truffles (754 Columbus Ave.) and Z Cioccolato (474 Columbus Ave.)—three blocks apart, and conduct your own taste test. (Better go back and forth a couple times just to be sure.)

Grant Avenue: Check out vanguard boutiques and rambling antiques shops, all chockablock on narrow Grant Avenue. You'll stop dead in your tracks in front of I Dream of Cake (1351 Grant Ave.), displaying the most impressive cakes in the universe.

Pastries Everywhere: Sacripantina from Stella Pastry or a cream puff from Victoria Pastry or tiramisu at Caffè Greco? North Beach is all about espresso, but we dare you to have a treat every time you pass an inviting bakery.

Washington Square Park: Grab some lunch and join the locals of all ages who congregate on the grass here to soak up the neighborhood vibe and enjoy great people- (and dog-) watching under the spires of Saints Peter and Paul.

WORD OF MOUTH. **"One strong point is that [North Beach] is often sunny and warm when other parts of SF are cold and/or foggy. It is low-keyed and casual. Well, maybe not low-key on weekend nights, but it is fun." —LoveItaly**

★ **Coit Tower.** Whether you think it resembles a fire hose or something more, ahem, adult, this 210-foot tower is among San Francisco's most distinctive skyline sights. Although the monument wasn't intended as a tribute to firemen, it's often considered as such because of the donor's special attachment to the local fire company. As the story goes, a young gold rush–era girl, Lillie Hitchcock Coit (known as Miss Lil), was a fervent admirer of her local fire company—so much so that she once deserted a wedding party and chased down the street after her favorite engine, Knickerbocker No. 5, while clad in her bridesmaid finery. She became the Knickerbocker Company's mascot and always signed her name "Lillie Coit 5." When Lillie died in 1929 she left the city $125,000 to "expend in an appropriate manner . . . to the beauty of San Francisco."

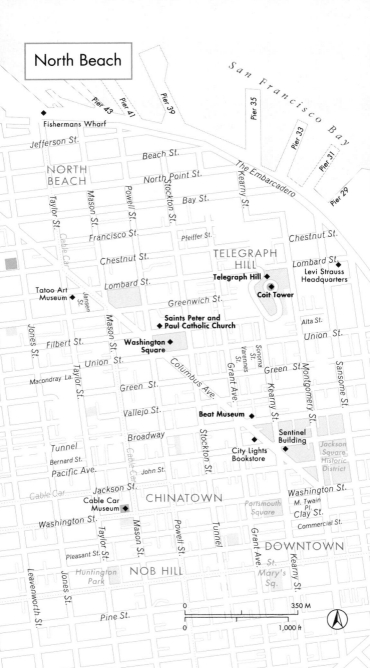

North Beach

San Francisco Bay

Pier 43
Pier 41
Pier 39
Pier 35
Pier 33
Pier 31
Pier 29

Fishermans Wharf

Jefferson St.

NORTH BEACH

Beach St.

North Point St.

The Embarcadero

Taylor St.

Mason St.

Powell St.

Stockton St.

Kearny St.

Bay St.

Francisco St.

Pfeiffer St.

Chestnut St.

Chestnut St.

TELEGRAPH HILL

Telegraph Hill ◆

Lombard St.

Levi Strauss Headquarters

Tatoo Art Museum ◆

Jansen St.

Lombard St.

Coit Tower ◆

Greenwich St.

Alta St.

Saints Peter and Paul Catholic Church ◆

Union St.

Jones St.

Filbert St.

Mason St.

Washington Square ◆

Sonoma St.

Varennes St.

Green St.

Sansome St.

Taylor St.

Union St.

Columbus Ave.

Grant Ave.

Kearny St.

Montgomery St.

Macondray La.

Green St.

Vallejo St.

Beat Museum ◆

Tunnel

Broadway

Stockton St.

Sentinel Building ◆

Bernard St.

Cable Car

City Lights Bookstore ◆

Jackson Square Historic District

Pacific Ave.

John St.

Cable Car

Jackson St.

CHINATOWN

Washington St.

M. Twain Pl.

Cable Car Museum ◆

Washington St.

Portsmouth Square

Clay St.

Commercial St.

Taylor St.

Mason St.

Powell St.

Tunnel

Grant Ave.

Kearny St.

Pleasant St.

DOWNTOWN

Leavenworth St.

Jones St.

Huntington Park

NOB HILL

St. Mary's Sq.

Pine St.

0   350 M
0   1,000 ft

You can ride the elevator to the top of the tower—the only thing you have to pay for here—to enjoy the view of the Bay Bridge and the Golden Gate Bridge; due north is Alcatraz Island. ■TIP→ **The views from the base of the tower are expansive—and free. Parking at Coit Tower is limited; in fact, you may have to wait (and wait) for a space. Save yourself some frustration and take the 39 bus which goes all the way up to the tower's base or, if you're in good shape, hike up.**

Inside the tower, 19 Depression-era murals depict California's economic and political life. The federal government commissioned the paintings from 25 local artists, and ended up funding quite a controversy. The radical Mexican painter Diego Rivera inspired the murals' socialist-realist style, with its biting cultural commentary, particularly about the exploitation of workers. At the time the murals were painted, clashes between management and labor along the waterfront and elsewhere in San Francisco were widespread. Kids get a kick out of the stories the mural tells; see how many San Francisco landmarks they can find and whether they can spot the holdup in progress. On the way down the hill, be sure to keep your eyes—and ears—peeled for the Telegraph Hill parrots that roost here. ⊠*Telegraph Hill Blvd. at Greenwich St. or Lombard St., North Beach* ☎*415/362–0808* ⌦*Free; elevator to top $5,* kids 12–17 $3, kids 5–11 $1.50, kids 4 and under free ⊙*Daily 10–6.* All ages

Saints Peter and Paul Catholic Church. Camera-toting visitors focus their lenses on the Romanesque splendor of what's often called the Italian Cathedral. Completed in 1924, the church has Disneyesque stone-white towers that are local landmarks. Mass reflects the neighborhood; it's given in English, Italian, and Chinese. Following their 1954 City Hall wedding, Marilyn Monroe and Joe DiMaggio had their wedding photos snapped here. ■TIP→ **On the first Sunday of October a mass followed by a parade to Fisherman's Wharf celebrates the Blessing of the Fleet. Another popular event is the Columbus Day pageant in North Beach, with a parade that ends at the church.** For kids the best thing about the cathedral by far is its location just across from Washington Square Park, a perfect place to let off some steam before visiting these hallowed halls. ⊠*666 Filbert St., at Washington Sq., North Beach* ☎*415/421–0809* ⊕*www.stspeterpaul.san-francisco.ca.us/church.* 7+up

★ Fodor's Choice **Telegraph Hill.** Hill residents have some of the best views in the city, as well as the most difficult ascents

The Birds

While on Telegraph Hill, you might be startled by a chorus of piercing squawks and a rushing sound of wings. No, you're not about to have a Hitchcock bird-attack moment. These small, vivid green parrots with cherry-red heads number in the hundreds; they're descendants of former pets that escaped or were released by their former owners. (The birds dislike cages and they bite if bothered…must've been some disillusioned owners along the way.)

The parrots like to roost high in the aging cypress trees on the hill, chattering and fluttering, sometimes taking wing en masse. They're not popular with most residents, but they did find a champion in local bohemian Mark Bittner, a former street musician. Bittner began chronicling their habits, publishing a book and battling the home owners who wanted to cut down the cypresses. A documentary, *The Wild Parrots of Telegraph Hill*, made the issue a cause célèbre. In 2007, City Hall, which recognizes a golden goose when it sees one, stepped in and brokered a solution to keep the celebrity birds in town. The city will cover the homeowners' insurance worries and plant new trees for the next generation of wild parrots.

—Denise M. Leto

to their aeries. The hill rises from the east end of Lombard Street to a height of 284 feet and is capped by Coit Tower (*see above*). Imagine lugging your groceries up that! If you brave the slope, though, you can be rewarded with a "secret treasure" San Francisco moment. Filbert Street starts up the hill then becomes the Filbert Steps when the going gets too steep. You can cut between the Filbert Steps and another flight, the Greenwich Steps, on up to the hilltop. As you climb, you can pass some of the city's oldest houses and be surrounded by beautiful, flowering private gardens. In some places the trees grow over the stairs so they feel like a green tunnel; elsewhere, you'll have wide-open views of the bay. And the telegraphic name? It comes from the hill's status as the first Morse code–signal station back in 1853. With kids, the best way to take in the steps is from the top: start at Coit Tower and work your way down. Be aware that there's no way to schlep a stroller down the steps, and even energetic kids may run out of steam. If you're lucky, the wild parrots will entertain your group. ✉*Bordered by Lombard, Filbert, Kearny, and Sansome Sts., North Beach.* 5+up

Washington Square. Once the daytime social heart of Little Italy, this grassy patch has changed character numerous times over the years. The Beats hung out in the 1950s, hippies camped out in the 1960s and early '70s, and nowadays you're just as likely to see kids of Southeast Asian descent tossing a Frisbee as Italian men or women chatting about their children and the old country. In the morning elderly Asians perform the motions of tai chi, but by mid-morning groups of conservatively dressed Italian men in their 70s and 80s begin to arrive. Any time of day, the park may attract a number of homeless people, who stretch out to rest on the benches and grass, and young locals sunbathing or running their dogs. Lillie Hitchcock Coit, in yet another show of affection for San Francisco's firefighters, donated the statue of two firemen with a child they rescued. ■TIP→**The North Beach Festival, the city's oldest street fair, celebrates the area's Italian culture here each June.** This is the best picnicking spot in town, so bring provisions. The streets surrounding the square offer some great dessert opportunities, like Italian ice cream at Gelato Classico on Union. After lunch the kids may want to check out the small playground in the corner near the firefighter statues. ✉*Bordered by Columbus Ave. and Stockton, Filbert, and Union Sts., North Beach.* All ages

NOB HILL & RUSSIAN HILL

In place of the quirky charm and cultural diversity that mark other San Francisco neighborhoods, Nob Hill exudes history and good breeding. Topped with some of the city's most elegant hotels, Gothic Grace Cathedral, and private blue-blood clubs, it's the pinnacle of privilege. One hill over, across Pacific Avenue, is another old-family bastion, Russian Hill. It may not be quite as wealthy as Nob Hill, but it's no slouch—and it's known for its jaw-dropping views.

Nob Hill was officially dubbed during the 1870s when "the Big Four"—Charles Crocker, Leland Stanford, Mark Hopkins, and Collis Huntington, who were involved in the construction of the transcontinental railroad—built their hilltop estates. By 1882 so many estates had sprung up on Nob Hill that Robert Louis Stevenson called it "the hill of palaces." But the 1906 earthquake and fire destroyed all the palatial mansions, except for portions of the Flood brownstone. There's not much here of interest to children except a

CLOSE UP

3 Reasons to Love the Espresso in North Beach

Cafés are a way of life in North Beach, and if you're as serious about your coffee as the average San Franciscan or Fodor's editor, you might want to stop in at all three of these spots.

The Giotta family celebrates the art of a good espresso as well as a good tune at **Caffe Trieste** (⊠ *601 Vallejo St., at Grant Ave., North Beach* ☎ *415/392–6739*). Every Saturday (as they have since 1971) from noon to 2 PM, the family presents a weekly musical. Arrive early to secure seats. The program ranges from Italian pop and folk music to operas—patrons are encouraged to participate. If you're one of the few people in creation who haven't gotten started on a screenplay, you may take inspiration from the fact that Francis Ford Coppola reportedly wrote the screenplay for *The Godfather* here.

Intimate, triangular **Mario's Bohemian Cigar Store** (⊠ *566 Columbus Ave., North Beach* ☎ *415/362–0536*) serves up great hot focaccia sandwiches and North Beach–

worthy espresso at its few tables and beautiful antique oak bar under old-time posters. On sunny days, take your order across the street to Washington Square for a classic San Francisco picnic.

A glance at the menu board—"Espresso: $1.80, Espresso with lemon: $10"—will clue you in that **Caffé Roma** (⊠ *526 Columbus Ave., North Beach* ☎ *415/296–7942*) takes its coffee a lot more seriously than it takes itself. And if you've got a problem with that, owner Tony Azzollini will convince you, from his refusal to make your coffee extra hot to his insistence that you drink your espresso the moment it's brewed. Airy and decidedly undistracting—black and white marble is the predominant theme—Roma is a no-nonsense coffee drinker's pit stop for a hot cup as well as coffee drinks, pastries, and wine. Spot the massive red roaster in the window and you'll know you're there. And if you insist on the lemon twist, you deserve to pay.

small park and playground atop the hill; for most visitors, a casual glimpse from a cable car will be enough.

Essentially a tony residential neighborhood, Russian Hill has outdoor sights with plenty of room for kids to romp while parents take in the sweeping bay views. Here you'll find some of the city's loveliest stairway walks, hidden garden ways, and steepest streets—get ready for shrieks from the backseat—not to mention those bay views. Several stories explain the origin of Russian Hill's name. One legend has it that Russian farmers raised vegetables here for Farallon Islands seal hunters; another attributes the name to a Russian sailor of prodigious drinking habits who drowned when he fell into a well on the hill. A plaque at the top of the Vallejo Steps gives credence to the version that says sailors of the Russian-American company were buried here in the 1840s. Be sure to visit the sign for yourself—its location offers perhaps the finest vantage point on the hill.

WHAT TO SEE IN NOB HILL

Cable Car Museum. This is one of the city's best offerings, and an absolute must for kids. (You can even ride a cable car there, since all three lines stop between Russian Hill and Nob Hill.) The museum, which is inside the city's last cable car barn, takes the top off the system to let you see how it all works. Eternally humming and squealing, the massive powerhouse cable wheels steal the show. You can also climb aboard a vintage car and take the grip, let the kids ring a cable-car bell (briefly), and check out vintage gear dating from 1873. Transportation nerds will happily sit through the museum's 16-minute film detailing cable car history and mechanics. Also be sure to allow time for kids to browse the museum's small gift shop; the cable car souvenirs here far outshine those found elsewhere in town. If you're in town in June, take the kids down to Union Square to see serious bell ringers in action at the annual bell-ringing competition. ⊠ *1201 Mason St., at Washington St., Nob Hill* ☎ *415/474–1887* ⊕ *www.cablecarmuseum.org* ☞ *Free* ⊙ *Oct.–Mar., daily 10–5; Apr.–Sept., daily 10–6.* 3+up

Grace Cathedral. Not many churches can boast a Keith Haring sculpture and not one but two labyrinths. The seat of the Episcopal Church in San Francisco, this soaring Gothic-style structure, erected on the site of Charles Crocker's mansion, took 53 years to build, wrapping up in 1964. The gilded bronze doors at the east entrance were taken from casts of Lorenzo Ghiberti's incredible *Gates of Paradise,* which are on the baptistery in Florence, Italy. A black-and-bronze stone sculpture of *St. Francis* by Beniamino Bufano greets you as you enter.

The 35-foot-wide labyrinth, a large, purplish rug, is a replica of the 13th-century stone maze on the floor of the

TOP 5 NOB HILL & RUSSIAN HILL

Cable Car Museum, Nob Hill: Ride a cable car all the way back to the barn, hanging on tight as it clack-clack-clacks its way up Nob Hill, then go behind the scenes at the museum.

Play "Bullitt" on the Steepest Streets, Russian Hill: For the ride of your life, take a drive up and down the city's steepest streets on Russian Hill. A trip over the precipice of Filbert or Jones will make you feel like you're falling off the edge of the world.

Cable Car Signal Box, Nob Hill: Watch the signalman in the city's last remaining signal box directing cable cars at Powell and California streets, where the tracks cross. These streets are so steep cable car drivers can't see one another approaching.

Lombard Street, Russian Hill: Even local kids adore the ride down the "crookedest street in the world," especially if the driver pretends to have trouble negotiating the switchbacks.

San Francisco Art Institute, Russian Hill: Contemplate a Diego Rivera mural and stop at the café for cheap organic coffee and a priceless view of the city and the bay. It may be the best way to spend an hour for a buck in town.

Chartres Cathedral. All are encouraged to walk the ¼-mi-long labyrinth, a ritual based on the tradition of meditative walking. There's also a terrazzo outdoor labyrinth on the church's north side. The AIDS Interfaith Chapel, to the right as you enter Grace, contains a metal triptych sculpture by the late artist Keith Haring and panels from the AIDS Memorial Quilt. ■TIP→**Especially dramatic times to view the cathedral are during Thursday-night evensong (5:15) and during special holiday programs.** The folks at Grace are well used to visitors of all ages and heartily welcome children. If yours are smaller, do steer them toward the outside labyrinth and remind them that there's "no passing!" Huntington Park across the street is perfect for more energetic playing. ✉*1100 California St., at Taylor St., Nob Hill* ☎*415/749–6300* ⊕*www.gracecathedral.org* ⊙*Weekdays 7–6, Sat. 8–6, Sun. 7–7.* 5+up

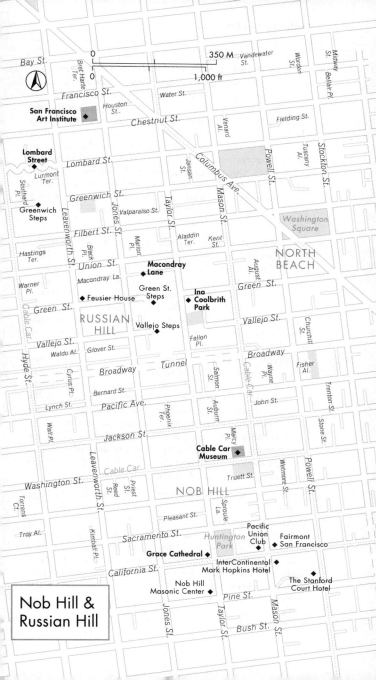

Bay St.

Francisco St.

Water St.

Vandewater St.

Worden St.

Midway St.

Belair Pl.

Bret Harte Ter.

0   350 M

0   1,000 ft

Houston St.

Chestnut St.

Fielding St.

San Francisco Art Institute

Lombard St.

Venard Al.

Columbus Ave.

Powell St.

Stockton St.

Tuscany Al.

Lombard Street

Lurmont Ter.

Southard Pl.

Greenwich St.

Jones St.

Valparaiso St.

Taylor St.

Mason St.

Jansen St.

Greenwich Steps

Leavenworth St.

Filbert St.

Black Pl.

Marion Pl.

Aladdin Ter.

Kent St.

NORTH BEACH

Hastings Ter.

Union St.

Macondray Lane

Green St.

August Al.

Washington Square

Warner Pl.

Macondray La.

Green St. Steps

Ina Coolbrith Park

RUSSIAN HILL

♦ Feusier House

Green St.

Green St.

Cable Car

Vallejo St.

Waldo Al.

Vallejo Steps

Vallejo St.

Churchill St.

Hyde St.

Glover St.

Fallon Pl.

Broadway

Fisher Al.

Cyrus Pl.

Broadway

Tunnel

Salmon St.

Wayne Pl.

Lynch St.

Bernard St.

Pacific Ave.

Phoenix Ter.

Auburn St.

John St.

Trenton St.

Wall Pl.

Jackson St.

Marcy Pl.

Stone St.

Cable Car Museum

Washington St.

Leavenworth St.

Cable Car

Reed St.

Priest St.

Truett St.

Wetmore St.

Powell St.

Torrens Ct.

NOB HILL

Sproule La.

Troy Al.

Pleasant St.

Sacramento St.

Kimball Pl.

Huntington Park

Pacific Union Club

Fairmont San Francisco

Grace Cathedral ♦

InterContinental Mark Hopkins Hotel

California St.

Nob Hill Masonic Center ♦

The Stanford Court Hotel

Pine St.

Jones St.

Taylor St.

Mason St.

Bush St.

Nob Hill & Russian Hill

WHAT TO SEE IN RUSSIAN HILL

★ **Ina Coolbrith Park.** If you make it all the way up here, you may have the place all to yourself, or at least feel like you do. The park's terraces are carved from a hill so steep that it's difficult to see if anyone else is there or not. Locals love this park because it feels like a secret no one else knows about—one of the city's magic hidden gardens, with a meditative setting and spectacular views of the bay peeking out from among the trees. A poet, Oakland librarian, and niece of Mormon prophet Joseph Smith, Ina Coolbrith (1842–1928) entertained literary greats in her Macondray Lane home near the park. In 1915 she was named poet laureate of California. ⊠ *Vallejo St. between Mason and Taylor Sts., Russian Hill.* All ages

Lombard Street. The block-long "Crookedest Street in the World" makes eight switchbacks down the east face of Russian Hill between Hyde and Leavenworth streets. Residents bemoan the traffic jam outside their front doors, and occasionally the city attempts to discourage drivers by posting a traffic cop near the top of the hill, but the determined can find a way around. If no one is standing guard, join the line of cars waiting to drive down the steep hill, or avoid the whole mess and walk down the steps on either side of Lombard. You take in super views of North Beach and Coit Tower whether you walk or drive—though if you're the one behind the wheel, you'd better keep your eye on the road lest you become yet another of the many folks who ram the garden barriers. ■TIP→**Can't stand the throngs? Thrill seekers of a different stripe may want to head two blocks south of Lombard to Filbert Street. At a gradient of 31.5%, the hair-raising descent between Hyde and Leavenworth streets is the city's steepest. Go slowly!** ⊠ *Lombard St. between Hyde and Leavenworth Sts., Russian Hill.* 3+up

★ Fodor's Choice **Macondray Lane.** San Francisco has no shortage of impressive, grand homes, but it's the tiny fairy-tale lanes that make most folks want to move here, and Macondray Lane is the quintessential hidden garden. Enter under a lovely wooden trellis and proceed down a quiet, cobbled pedestrian lane lined with Edwardian cottages and flowering plants and trees. ■TIP→**Watch your step—the cobblestones are quite uneven in spots.** A flight of steep wooden stairs at the end of the lane leads to Taylor Street—on the way down you can't miss the bay views. If you've read any of Armistead Maupin's *Tales of the City* books, you may find the lane vaguely familiar. It's the thinly disguised setting for part of the series' action. Residents of Macondray Lane knew what they were getting into when they bought these cute homes; looky-loos come with the territory. It's a good idea to remind little ones that the lane isn't a park, though, and that they are, indeed, in someone's front yard. ⊠*Between Jones and Taylor Sts., and Union and Green Sts., Russian Hill.* 7+up

★ **San Francisco Art Institute.** A Moorish-tile fountain in a tree-shaded courtyard draws the eye as soon as you enter the institute. The number-one reason for a visit is Mexican master Diego Rivera's *Making of a Fresco Showing the Building of a City* (1931), in the student gallery to your immediate left inside the entrance. Rivera himself is in the fresco—his broad behind is to the viewer—and he's surrounded by his assistants. They in turn are surrounded by a construction scene, laborers, and city notables such as sculptor Robert Stackpole and architect Timothy Pfleuger. *The Making of a Fresco* is one of three San Francisco murals painted by Rivera. The number-two reason to come here is the café, or more precisely the eye-popping, panoramic view from the café, which serves surprisingly decent food for a song.

The older portions of the Art Institute, including the lovely Mission-style bell tower, were erected in 1926. To this day, otherwise pragmatic people claim that ghostly footsteps can be heard in the tower at night. Kids seem compelled to scramble on various structures at the institute, such as inverted cement cones and glass pyramids looking down into studios. The littlest guests may not get past the koi in the fountain at the entrance. ⊠*800 Chestnut St., North Beach* ☎*415/771–7020* ⊕*www.sfai.edu* ⊠*Free* ⊗*Student gallery daily 8:30–8:30.* All ages

ON THE WATERFRONT

San Francisco's waterfront neighborhoods have fabulous views and utterly different personalities. Kitschy, overpriced Fisherman's Wharf struggles to maintain the last shreds of its existence as a working wharf, whereas Pier 39 is a full-fledged consumer circus, the closest thing in town to an amusement park. Both these areas are on the don't-miss list for kids . . . but plan carefully or resign yourself to dropping a pretty penny here. The Ferry Building draws well-heeled locals with its culinary pleasures, firmly reconnecting

TOP 5 WATERFRONT

Ferry Building: San Francisco's foodie paradise shows off caviar, oysters, and great bay views; kids will appreciate the perfect pastries, chocolate, and gelato.

Hyde Street Pier: Feel the rocking of the waves aboard the gorgeously restored 19th-century *Balclutha*, where park rangers teach visitors to sing sea chanteys and raise the sails.

Alcatraz: Go from a scenic bay tour to "the hole"—solitary confinement in absolute darkness—while inmates and guards tell you stories about what life was really like on the Rock.

F-line: Grab a polished wooden seat aboard one of the city's lovingly restored vintage streetcars and clatter down the tracks toward the Ferry Building's spire.

Musée Mécanique: Take a pocketful of quarters and step through the gaping mouth of Laffing Sal to this arcade of vintage machines.

the Embarcadero to downtown. Between the Ferry Building and Pier 39, a former maritime no-man's land is filling in a bit—especially near Pier 33, where the perpetually booked Alcatraz cruises depart—with a waterfront restaurant here and a restored pedestrian-friendly pier there.

Today's shoreline was once Yerba Buena Cove, filled in during the latter half of the 19th century when San Francisco was a brawling, extravagant gold-rush town. Jackson Square, now a genteel and upscale corner of the inland Financial District, was the heart of the Barbary Coast, bordering some of the roughest wharves in the world. Below Montgomery Street (in today's Financial District), between California Street and Broadway, lies a remnant of these wild days: more than 100 ships abandoned by frantic crews and passengers caught up in gold fever lie under the foundations of buildings here.

WHAT TO SEE ON THE WATERFRONT

★ Fodor'sChoice **Alcatraz.** The boat ride to the island is brief (15 minutes) but affords beautiful views of the city, Marin County, and the East Bay. The audio tour, highly recommended, includes observations by guards and prisoners about life in one of America's most notorious penal colonies. Plan your schedule to allow at least three hours for the visit and boat rides combined. Buying your tickets in advance, even in the off-season, is strongly recommended. ⊠*Pier 33, Fisherman's Wharf* ☎*415/981–7625* ⊕*www. nps.gov/alca, www.parkconservancy.org/visit/alcatraz, www.alcatrazcruises.com* ☜*$26, including audio tour; kids 5–11 $16. $33 evening tour, including audio; kids 5–11 $19.50* ☉*Ferry departs every 30–45 mins Sept.–late May, daily 9:30–2:15, 4:20 for evening tour Thurs.–Mon. only; late May–Aug., daily 9–4, 6:10 and 6:50 for evening tour.* **5+up**

Angel Island. For an outdoorsy adventure, consider a day at this island northwest of Alcatraz. Discovered by Spaniards in 1775 and declared a U.S. military reserve 75 years later, the island was used as a screening ground for Asian immigrants—who were often held for months, even years, before being granted entry—from 1910 until 1940. Starting in 2009, you can visit the restored Immigration Station; from the dock where detainees landed to the barracks you can see the poems in Japanese script they etched onto the walls. In 1963 the government designated Angel Island a state park. Today people come for picnics, hikes along the scenic 5-mi path that winds around the island's perimeter, and tram tours that explain the park's history. Twenty-five bicycles are permitted on the ferry on a first-come, first-served basis, and you can rent mountain bikes for $10 an hour or $35 a day at the landing (daily April to October; call during other times). There are also nine primitive, public campsites. Blue and Gold Fleet is the only Angel Island ferry service with departures from San Francisco. On weekdays boats leave the Ferry Building (9:20 AM) and Pier 41 (9:45 AM and 1:05 AM) and return at 10:10 AM, 2 PM, and 3:25 PM; on weekends they sail from the Ferry Building (9:20 AM and 11:20 AM) and Pier 41 (9:40 AM, 11:45 AM, and 1:50 PM) and return at 10:15 AM, 12:15 PM, 2:55 PM, and 4:15 PM. During the summer you can combine a trip here with a visit to Alcatraz through Alcatraz Cruises (although this can make for a very long day for young children.) Especially during summer, the events calendar at Angel Island is packed with special offerings that appeal to kids, from Civil War days and guided bike tours to Victorian Days, when costumed soldiers from the Spanish-American and Indian wars fire cannons and give weapons demonstrations. ⊠*Pier 41, Fisherman's Wharf* ☎*415/435–1915 park information and ferry schedules, 415/705–5555, 800/426–8687 tickets* ⊕*www.angelisland.org* ☜*$15; kids 5–11 $9, kids 4 and under free* ☉*Open daily 8 AM to sunset.* **5+up**

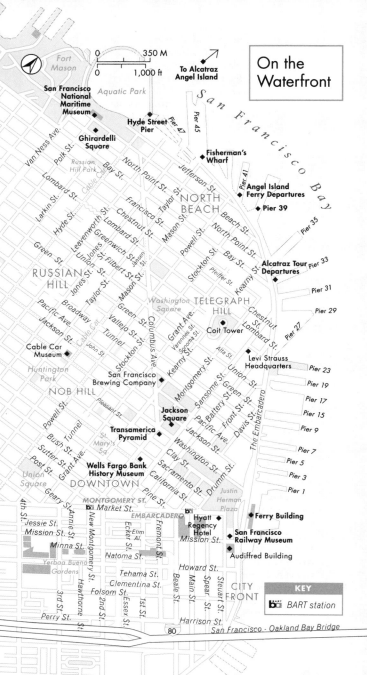

On the Waterfront

Fort Mason

San Francisco National Maritime Museum

Aquatic Park

To Alcatraz Angel Island

San Francisco Bay

Ghirardelli Square

Hyde Street Pier

Pier 47

Pier 45

Fisherman's Wharf

Pier 41

Angel Island Ferry Departures

Van Ness Ave.

Polk St.

Russian Hill Park

Bay St.

North Point St.

Jefferson St.

Pier 39

Lombard St.

Larkin St.

Francisco St.

Taylor St.

Mason St.

NORTH BEACH

Beach St.

Pier 35

Hyde St.

Chestnut St.

Powell St.

North Point St.

Green St.

Leavenworth St.

Lombard St.

Greenwich St.

Jones St.

Filbert St.

Jansen St.

Bay St.

Stockton St.

Pfeiffer St.

Kearny St.

Alcatraz Tour Departures

Pier 33

RUSSIAN HILL

Union St.

Taylor St.

Mason St.

Washington Square

TELEGRAPH HILL

Pier 31

Jones St.

Green St.

Columbus Ave.

Grant Ave.

Varennes St.

Sonoma St.

Coit Tower

Chestnut St.

Pier 29

Broadway

Vallejo St.

Green St.

Kearny St.

Alta St.

Lombard St.

Pier 27

Pacific Ave.

Jackson Ave.

Cable Car

Tunnel

John St.

Stockton St.

Levi Strauss Headquarters

Pier 23

Cable Car Museum

Montgomery St.

Sansome St.

Union St.

Pier 19

Huntington Park

San Francisco Brewing Company

Kearny St.

Green St.

Battery St.

Front St.

Pier 17

NOB HILL

Pleasant St.

Pacific Ave.

Davis St.

Pier 15

Powell St.

Jackson Square

Jackson St.

Pier 9

Bush St.

Tunnel

Mary's Sq.

Transamerica Pyramid

Washington St.

The Embarcadero

Pier 7

Sutter St.

Grant Ave.

Clay St.

Pier 5

Post St.

Wells Fargo Bank History Museum

Sacramento St.

California St.

Pier 3

Union Square

DOWNTOWN

Pine St.

Justin Herman Plaza

Pier 1

Geary St.

Annie St.

MONTGOMERY ST.

Market St.

New Montgomery St.

EMBARCADERO

Ferry Building

4th St.

Jessie St.

Mission St.

Ecker St.

Elim Al.

Fremont St.

Hyatt Regency Hotel

San Francisco Railway Museum

Minna St.

Hawthorne St.

Natoma St.

Mission St.

Audiffred Building

Yerba Buena Gardens

Tehama St.

Clementina St.

Beale St.

Main St.

Spear St.

Steuart St.

3rd St.

Folsom St.

2nd St.

Essex St.

1st St.

Howard St.

CITY FRONT

Perry St.

Harrison St.

80

San Francisco - Oakland Bay Bridge

0   350 M

0   1,000 ft

KEY	
🚇	BART station

F-LINE TROLLEYS

The F-line, the city's system of vintage electric trolleys, gives the cable cars a run for their money as San Francisco's best-loved mode of transportation. These beautifully restored streetcars—some dating from the 19th century—run from the Castro all the way down Market Street to the Embarcadero, then north to Fisherman's Wharf. Each car is unique, restored to the colors of its city of origin, from New Orleans and Philadelphia to Moscow and Milan. The line is so popular that there's talk of extending it to Fort Mason. Purchase tickets on board; exact change is required. ⊕*www.streetcar.org* ✉*$1.50*, kids 5–17 50¢, kids 4 and under free.

NEED A BREAK? Even locals love the cheery **Buena Vista Café** (⊠*2765 Hyde St., Fisherman's Wharf*☎*415/474–5044*), which claims to be the first place in the United States to have served Irish coffee. The café opens at 9 AM weekdays (8 AM weekends), and dishes up a great breakfast. They serve about 2,000 Irish coffees a day, so it's always crowded; try for a table overlooking nostalgic Victorian Park and its cable-car turntable.

★ Fodor'sChoice **Ferry Building.** Renovated in 2003, the Ferry Building is the jewel of the Embarcadero. The beacon of the port area, erected in 1896, has a 230-foot clock tower modeled after the campanile of the cathedral in Seville, Spain. On the morning of April 18, 1906, the tower's four clock faces, powered by the swinging of a 14-foot pendulum, stopped at 5:17—the moment the great earthquake struck—and stayed still for 12 months.

Today San Franciscans flock to the street-level Market Hall, stocking up on supplies from local favorites such as Acme Bread, Scharffen Berger Chocolate, and Cowgirl Creamery. Lucky diners claim a coveted table at Slanted Door, the city's beloved high-end Vietnamese restaurant. The seafood bars at Hog Island Oyster Company and Ferry Plaza Seafood have fantastic city panoramas. With kids you may choose to take your purchases around to the building's bay side, where benches face views of the Bay Bridge. Saturday mornings, the plaza in front of the building buzzes with an upscale, celebrity-chef-studded farmers' market. Extending from the piers on the north side of the building south to the Bay Bridge, the waterfront promenade is a favorite among joggers and picnickers, with a front-row view of the sailboats slipping by. The Ferry Building also serves actual ferries: from behind the building they sail to Sausalito, Larkspur, Tiburon, and the East Bay. The Ferry Building itself is a pretty grownup place, and though you won't see many children here (especially during the week), the promise of pigeon-chasing, boat-watching, and a sweet treat is often enough to gain foodie parents an hour or two here. 5+up ⊠*Embarcadero at foot of Market St., Embarcadero* ⊕*www.ferrybuildingmarketplace.com.*

Fisherman's Wharf. It may be one of the city's best-known attractions, but the wharf is a no-go zone for most locals, who shy away from the difficult parking, overpriced food, and cheesy shops at third-rate shopping centers like the Cannery at Del Monte Square. For kids, though, Fisherman's Wharf is on the must-see list. Come early to avoid the crowds and get a sense of the wharf's functional role—it's not just an amusement park replica.

Most of the entertainment at the wharf is schlocky and overpriced, with one notable exception: the splendid **Musée Mécanique** (☎*415/346–2000* ⊙*Weekdays 10–7, weekends 10–8*), a time-warped arcade with antique mechanical contrivances, including peep shows and nickelodeons. Some favorites are the giant and rather creepy "Laffing Sal" (you enter the museum through his gaping mouth), an arm-wrestling machine, the world's only steam-powered motorcycle, and mechanical fortune-telling figures that speak from their curtained boxes. Keep your eyes open for depictions of race that betray the prejudices of the time: stoned Chinese figures in the "Opium-Den" and clown-faced African-Americans eating watermelon in the "Mechanical Farm." Admission is free, but you'll need quarters to bring the machines to life.

Among the two floors of exhibits at **Ripley's Believe It or Not! Museum** (⊠*175 Jefferson St., Fisherman's Wharf* ☎*415/771–6188* ⊕*www.ripleysf.com*) is an 8-foot-long scale model of a cable car, made entirely of matchsticks. Admission to Ripley's, open Sunday through Thursday 10–10 and Friday and Saturday 10 AM–midnight, is $14.99 (kids 5–12 $8.99). Notables from local boy Robin Williams to Jesus await at the **Wax Museum** (⊠*145 Jefferson St., Fisherman's Wharf* ☎*415/439–4305* ⊕*www.waxmuseum.com*), open weekdays 10–9, weekends 9 AM–11 PM. Admission is $12.95 (kids 12–17 $9.95, kids 6–11 $6.95).

WHERE CAN I FIND . . . ON THE WATERFRONT?

Quick Meals	Location	Description
Taylor's Automatic Refresher	Ferry Building, Embarcadero	Juicy burgers, creamy shakes, and great patio seating for sunny days.
Boudin Sourdough Bakery & Café	160 Jefferson St., Fisherman's Wharf	Classic San Francisco sourdough, available in sandwich or soup bowl form.
Grocery Stores		
Ferry Building	Ferry Building, Embarcadero	The entire place is filled with food shops selling prepared foods and organic produce, artisanal cheeses, and fresh bread...all at gourmet prices.
Trader Joe's	401 Bay St., at Mason St., Fisherman's Wharf	A real grocery store with grocery store prices.
Good Coffee		
Blue Bottle	Ferry Building, Embarcadero	Fresh roasted and brewed to order, it's all the rage.
Peet's Coffee & Tea	Ferry Building, Embarcadero	Dependable, strong coffee, and faster than Blue Bottle.
Fun Stores		
Marine Mammal Center Store	Pier 39	Sale of the high-quality toys and books here benefit the eponymous Sausalito center for injured marine mammals.
Playgrounds		
Aquatic Park	Beach and Polk Sts., Fisherman's Wharf	There's no play equipment here, but the small, sandy beach provides a welcome natural break
Public Bathrooms		
San Francisco Maritime National Historic Park Visitor Center	499 Jefferson St., at Hyde St., Fisherman's Wharf	Super-convenient location, clean, rarely a wait.
Pier 39	Upstairs and downstairs, Pier 39	Tidy though well used; head upstairs to the less busy facilities.

The **USS _Pampanito_** (⊠*Pier 45, Fisherman's Wharf* ☎*415/ 775-1943* ⊙*Oct.–Memorial Day, Sun.–Thurs. 9–6, Fri. and Sat. 9–8; Memorial Day–Sept., Thurs.–Tues. 9–8, Wed. 9–6*) provides an intriguing if mildly claustrophobic glimpse into life on a submarine during World War II. The sub sank six Japanese warships and damaged four others. Admission is $9 (kids 6–12 $4, kids 5 and under free); the family pass is a great deal at $20 for two adults and up to four kids. One of the most pleasant times to visit the wharf is in the evening during the Christmas holidays, when many fishing boats twinkle with lights; look across the bay from here to see the lighted cross atop the peak of Angel Island. Also, be aware that although there are public parking lots near the wharf, you'll pay dearly for them (check for validation options). It's probably cheaper (and more fun) to take a cable car or trolley. ⊠*Jefferson St. between Leavenworth St. and Pier 39, Fisherman's Wharf.* 3+up

Ghirardelli Square. Most of the redbrick buildings in this early-20th-century complex were once part of the Ghirardelli factory. Tourists come here to pick up the famous chocolate, but you can purchase it all over town and save yourself a trip to what is essentially a mall. (If you're a shopaholic, though, it definitely beats the Cannery.) There are no less than three Ghirardelli stores here, as well as gift shops and a couple of restaurants—including Ana Mandara—that even locals love. Placards throughout the square describe the factory's history. For kids, chocolate is *the* reason to come here, and it's fun to watch the giant gears of the original chocolate maker swirling inside the Ghirardelli Ice Cream and Chocolate Shop. ⊠*900 N. Point St., Fisherman's Wharf* ☎*415/775–5500* ⊕*www. ghirardellisq.com.* 5+up

☖ **Hyde Street Pier.** Cotton candy and souvenirs are all well and
★ good, but if you want to get to the heart of the Wharf—boats—there's no better place to do it than this pier, by far one of the Wharf area's best bargains. Depending on the time of day, you might see boatbuilders at work or children pretending to man an early-1900s ship (your own might even get the chance to join in).

Don't pass up the centerpiece collection of historic vessels, part of the **San Francisco Maritime National Historic Park,** almost all of which can be boarded. The *Balclutha,* an 1886 full-rigged three-masted sailing vessel that's more than 250 feet long, sailed around Cape Horn 17 times; kids especially love the *Eureka,* a side-wheel passenger and car ferry, for her onboard collection of vintage cars; the *Hercules* is a steam-powered tugboat. The *C. A. Thayer,* a three-masted schooner, recently underwent a painstaking restoration and is back on display. Across the street from the pier and almost a museum in itself is the San Francisco Maritime National Historic Park's **Visitor Center** (✉ *499 Jefferson St., at Hyde St., Fisherman's Wharf* ☎ *415/447–5000* ⊙ *Memorial Day–Sept., daily 9:30–7; Oct.–Memorial Day, daily 9:30–5*), happily free of mind-numbing, text-heavy displays. Instead, fun, large-scale exhibits, such as a huge First Order Fresnel lighthouse lens and a shipwrecked boat, make this an engaging and relatively quick stop. The calendar here is packed, especially on summer weekends, with activities that appeal to all kinds of kids, from sea chantey sing-alongs to model shipbuilding activities. Swing by the activity board in the morning to see what would most appeal to your family. ✉ *Hyde and Jefferson Sts., Fisherman's Wharf* ☎ *415/561–7100* ⊕ *www.nps.gov/safr* ✍ *Ships $5*, kids 15 and under free ⊙ *Memorial Day–Sept., daily 9:30–5:30; Oct.–Memorial Day, daily 9:30–5*. 5+up

OFF THE BEATEN PATH. S.S. *Jeremiah O'Brien.* **A participant in the D-day landing in Normandy during World War II, this Liberty Ship freighter is one of two such vessels (out of 2,500 built) still in working order. To keep the 1943 ship in sailing shape, the steam engine—which appears in the film** *Titanic*—**is operated dockside seven times a year on special "steaming weekends." Cruises take place several times a year between May and October. Visiting with small children can be harrowing; the ship is positively full of things to trip over and run into, and places to duck into. If you do bring little ones aboard, hang onto them! Or better yet, save this visit until it's safe to take your eyes off them.** ✉ *Pier 45, Fisherman's Wharf* ☎ **415/544–0100** ⊕ **www.ssjeremiahobrien. org** ✍ **$8, kids 6–14 $4, kids 5 and under free; family pass for 2 adults and 2 children $20** ⊙ **Daily 9–4.** 5+up

Jackson Square. This was the heart of the Barbary Coast of the Gay '90s (the 1890s, that is). Although most of the red-light district was destroyed in the fire that followed the 1906 earthquake, old redbrick buildings and narrow alleys recall the romance and rowdiness of San Francisco's early days. The days of brothels and bar fights are long gone—now Jackson Square is a genteel, quiet corner of the Financial District. It's of interest to the historically inclined and antiques-shop browsers, but otherwise safely skipped.

Some of the city's first business buildings, survivors of the 1906 quake, still stand between Montgomery and Sansome streets. After a few decades of neglect, these old-timers were adopted by preservation-minded interior designers and wholesale-furniture dealers for use as showrooms. In 1972 the city officially designated the area—bordered by Columbus Avenue on the west, Broadway and Pacific Avenue on the north, Washington Street on the south, and Sansome Street on the east—San Francisco's first historic district. When property values soared, many of the fabric and furniture outlets fled to Potrero Hill. Advertising agencies, attorneys, and antiques dealers now occupy the Jackson Square–area structures.

Historically minded kids might be interested to stand at the western terminus of the Pony Express, about a block away on Clay near Montgomery (look for the plaques). On the same block near Sansome another plaque marks the resting spot of the *Niantic,* one of the ships abandoned at dock during the gold rush (and later turned into a hotel). ✉ *Jackson Sq. district bordered by Broadway and Washington, Kearny, and Sansome Sts., Financial District.* **7+up**

San Francisco National Maritime Museum. You'll feel as if you're out to sea when you step aboard, er, inside this sturdy, round, ship-shaped structure dubbed "the Bathhouse." Part of the **San Francisco Maritime National Historical Park,** the museum has three floors that exhibit intricate ship models, beautifully restored figureheads, photographs of life at sea, and other artifacts chronicling the maritime history of San Francisco and the West Coast. The views from the top floor are stunning, and be sure to step onto the first-floor balcony, which overlooks the beach, and check out the lovely WPA–era tile designs on your way to the steamships exhibit. At this writing the museum was closed, but it was expected to open in the second half of 2009 (call ahead to check before visiting). Any kid who's ever assembled a model will stand gape-mouthed before the re-creations of ships on display here. Little ones tend to like the large-format exhibits, such as the ship figureheads. ✉ *Aquatic Park foot of Polk St., Fisherman's Wharf* ☎ *415/561–7100* ⊕ *www.nps.gov/safr* ✉ *Donation suggested* ☉ *Daily 10–5.* **5+up**

Pier 39. The city's most popular waterfront attraction draws millions of visitors each year who come to browse through its vertiginous array of shops and concessions hawking every conceivable form of souvenir. The pier can be quite crowded, and the numerous street performers may leave you feeling more harassed than entertained. Arriving early in the morning ensures you a front-row view of the sea lions, but if you're here to shop—and make no mistake about it, Pier 39 wants your money—be aware that most stores don't open until 9:30 or 10 (later in winter).

Pick up a buckwheat hull–filled otter-neck wrap or a plush sea lion to snuggle at the **Marine Mammal Store** (☎415/289–7373), whose proceeds benefit Sausalito's respected wild-animal hospital, the Marine Mammal Center. Sales of the excellent books, maps, and collectibles—including a series of gorgeous, distinctive art deco posters for Alcatraz, the Presidio, Fort Point, and the other members of the Golden Gate National Recreation Area—at the **National Park Store** (☎415/433–7221)help to support the National Park Service. Brilliant colors enliven the double-decker **San Francisco Carousel** (☎$3 per ride), decorated with images of such city landmarks as the Golden Gate Bridge and Lombard Street.Follow the sound of barking to the northwest side of the pier to view the hundreds of sea lions that bask and play on the docks. At **Aquarium of the Bay** (☎415/623–5300 or 888/732–3483 ⊕www. aquariumofthebay.com ☎$14.95, kids 3–11 $8), moving walkways transport you through a space surrounded on three sides by water filled with indigenous San Francisco Bay marine life, from fish and plankton to sharks. Many find the aquarium overpriced; if you can, take advantage of the family rate—$37.95 for two adults and two kids under 12. (Better yet, skip the aquarium and put that money toward admission to the spectacular but pricey California Academy of Sciences.) The aquarium is open June through September daily 9–8; during the rest of the year it's open Monday through Thursday 10–6 and Friday through Sunday 10–7.

The **California Welcome Center** (☎415/981–1280 ⊙Daily 10–5 ⊕www.visitcwc.com), on Pier 39's second level, offers free Internet access. Expensive parking (free with validation from a Pier 39 restaurant) is at the Pier 39 Garage, off Powell Street at the Embarcadero. If the frenetic energy of Pier 39 isn't enough for your kids, whip out your wallet and amp up the excitement at the pier's big-money attractions: Frequent Flyers, where harnessed kids on a trampoline pretend they're circus acrobats, or TurboRide, a combination 3-D movie and rollercoaster adventure. Or toss them a few quarters and send them off to the Riptide

Arcade. ⊠*Beach St. at Embarcadero, Fisherman's Wharf* ⊕*www.pier39.com.* 3+up

San Francisco Railway Museum. A labor of love brought to you by the same vintage-transit enthusiasts responsible for the F-line's revival, this one-room museum and store celebrates the city's storied streetcars and cable cars with photographs, models, and artifacts. The permanent exhibit will eventually include the (replicated) end of a streetcar with a working cab for kids to explore. In the meantime, little ones will have to content themselves with operating the cool, antique Wiley birdcage traffic signal and viewing (but not touching) models and display cases. Right on the F-line track, just across from the Ferry Building, this is a quick stop. This is a great place to pick up books for your little transportation enthusiast; the vintage tales of San Francisco's cable cars and trolleys make wonderful city souvenirs. ⊠*77 Steuart St., in Hotel Vitale, Embarcadero* ☎*415/974–1948* ⊕*www.streetcar.org* ⊠*Free* ☉*Wed.–Sun. 10–6.* 3+up

Transamerica Pyramid. It's neither owned by Transamerica nor is it a pyramid, but this 853-foot-tall obelisk *is* the most photographed of the city's high-rises. Excoriated in the design stages as "the world's largest architectural folly," the icon was quickly hailed as a masterpiece when it opened in 1972. Today it's probably the city's most recognized structure after the Golden Gate Bridge. A fragrant redwood grove along the east side of the building, replete with benches and a cheerful fountain, is a placid patch in which to unwind. Bring small kids here to burn off some energy in this green patch, a welcome break in the Financial District. Bronze frogs on lily pads and the statue *Puddle Jumpers* contribute to the feeling that this is a kids' place among the skyscrapers. ⊠*600 Montgomery St., Financial District* ⊕*www.transamerica.com.* All ages

Wells Fargo Bank History Museum. There were no formal banks in San Francisco during the early years of the gold rush, and miners often entrusted their gold dust to saloon keepers. In 1852 Wells Fargo opened its first bank in the city, and the company soon established banking offices in mother-lode camps throughout California. Stagecoaches and pony-express riders connected points around the burgeoning state, where the population boomed from 15,000 to 200,000 between 1848 and 1852. The museum displays samples of nuggets and gold dust from mines, a mural-size

1

map of the mother lode, mementos of the poet bandit Black Bart (who signed his poems "Po8"), and an old telegraph machine on which you can practice sending codes. The showpiece is a red Concord stagecoach, the likes of which carried passengers from St. Joseph, Missouri, to San Francisco in just three weeks during the 1850s. ✉ *420 Montgomery St., Financial District* ☎ *415/396–2619* ⊕ *www. wellsfargohistory.com* 🎫 *Free* ⊙ *Weekdays 9–5.* 5+up

THE MARINA & THE PRESIDIO

Yachts bob at their moorings, satisfied-looking folks jog along the Marina Green, and multimillion-dollar homes overlook the bay in this picturesque neighborhood. Does it all seem a bit too perfect? Well, it got this way after the hard knock of Loma Prieta—the current pretty face was put on after hundreds of homes collapsed in the 1989 earthquake.

On weekends, the Marina crowd—a young, fairly homogeneous, well-to-do lot—floods the yuppie cafés and lively bars here. South of Lombard Street is the Marina's affluent neighbor, Cow Hollow, whose main drag, Union Street, has some of the city's best boutique shopping. Joggers and kite-flyers head to the Marina Green, the strip of lawn between the yacht club and the mansions of Marina Boulevard.

After you've seen the fun kid sights here (the Exploratorium chief among them), head straight for the natural beauty and wide open spaces of the Presidio. Once a military base, this sprawling, wooded park is mostly green space, with hills, woods, and the delightful shoreline paths, lawns, and beaches of Crissy Field. The Presidio has superb views and the best hiking and biking areas in San Francisco; a drive through the lush area is also a treat.

WHAT TO SEE IN THE MARINA

★ **Exploratorium.** Walking into this fascinating "museum of science, art, and human perception" is like visiting a mad scientist's laboratory. Most of the exhibits are super-size, and you can play with everything. You can feel like Alice in Wonderland in the distortion room, where you seem to shrink and grow as you walk across the slanted, checkered floor. In the shadow room, a powerful flash freezes an image of your shadow on the wall; jumping is a favorite pose. "Pushover" demonstrates cow-tipping, but for

TOP 5 MARINA & PRESIDIO

Golden Gate Bridge, Presidio: Get a good look at San Francisco's iconic span from the Presidio, then bundle up and walk over the water.

Exploratorium and the Palace of Fine Arts, Marina: The hands-on Exploratorium is a perennial kids' fave. Just outside is the stunning, Romanesque Palace of Fine Arts.

Crissy Field, Presidio: Try to spot egrets and herons from the bayside wooden boardwalk over this restored tidal marshland under the Golden Gate Bridge.

Wandering, Presidio: Lace up your walking shoes and follow one of the wooded trails, or hop the free PresidiGo shuttle around the park. The view from Inspiration Point lookout will take your breath away, and you'll pass by the pet cemetery, usually a hit with children.

Star Wars Sightings, Presidio: Swing by George Lucas's Letterman Digital Arts Center to see the Yoda Fountain. Also peek into the building behind Yoda; it's closed to the public, but you can't miss the life-size Boba Fett and Darth Vader standing guard inside.

people: stand on one foot and try to keep your balance while a friend swings a striped panel in front of you (trust us, you're going to fall).

More than 650 other exhibits focus on sea and insect life, computers, electricity, patterns and light, language, the weather, and much more. "Explainers"—usually high-school students on their days off—demonstrate cool scientific tools and procedures, like DNA sample-collection and analysis. One surefire hit is the pitch-black, touchy-feely Tactile Dome. In this geodesic dome strewn with textured objects, you crawl through a course of ladders, slides, and tunnels, relying solely on your sense of touch. ■TIP→**Reservations are required for the Tactile Dome and will get you 75 minutes of access. You have to be at least seven years old to go through the dome, and the space is not for the claustrophobic.** ✉*3601 Lyon St., at Marina Blvd., Marina* ☎*415/561–0360 general information, 415/561–0362 Tactile Dome reservations* ⊕*www.exploratorium.edu* ✉*$14;* students 13–17 $11, kids 4–12 $9, kids 3 and under free; *free 1st Wed. of month; Tactile Dome $3 extra;* ☉*Tues.–Sun. 10–5.* 3+up

OFF THE BEATEN PATH. **Wave Organ.** Conceived by environmental artist Peter Richards and fashioned by master stonecutter

George Gonzales, this unusual wave-activated acoustic sculpture gives off subtle harmonic sounds produced by seawater as it passes through 25 tubes. The sound is loudest at high tide. The granite and marble used for walkways, benches, and alcoves that are part of the piece were salvaged from a gold-rush-era cemetery. ⊠ *North of Marina Green at end of jetty by Yacht Rd., park in lot north of Marina Blvd. at Lyon St., Marina.* All ages

★ **Fodor's**Choice **Palace of Fine Arts.** At first glance this stunning, rosy rococo palace seems to be from another world, and indeed, it's the sole survivor of the many tinted-plaster structures (a temporary classical city of sorts) built for the 1915 Panama-Pacific International Exposition, the world's fair that celebrated San Francisco's recovery from the 1906 earthquake and fire. The expo buildings originally extended about a mile along the shore. Bernard Maybeck designed this faux Roman Classic beauty, which was reconstructed in concrete and reopened in 1967.

A victim of the elements, the palace is currently undergoing a piece-by-piece renovation; stand under the rotunda and look up to see the net that's protecting you from falling debris. The massive columns (each topped with four "weeping maidens"), great rotunda, and swan-filled lagoon have been used in countless fashion layouts, films, and wedding photo shoots. After admiring the lagoon, look across the street to the house at 3460 Baker Street. If the maidens out front look familiar, they should—they're original casts of the lovely "garland ladies" you can see in the Palace's colonnade. Kids may be more interested in the lagoon, where swans swim, fountains spray, and you can play spot the turtle. ⊠*Baker and Beach Sts., Marina* ☎*415/561–0364 palace history tours* ⊕*www.exploratorium.edu/palace* ⊠*Free* ⊙*Daily 24 hrs.* All ages

WHAT TO SEE IN THE PRESIDIO

Fort Point. Dwarfed today by the Golden Gate Bridge, this brick fortress constructed between 1853 and 1861 was designed to protect San Francisco from a Civil War sea attack that never materialized. It was also used as a coastal-defense-fortification post during World War II, when soldiers stood watch here. This National Historic Site is now a sprawling museum filled with military memorabilia, surrounding a lonely, windswept courtyard. The building has a gloomy air and is suitably atmospheric. (It's usually chilly

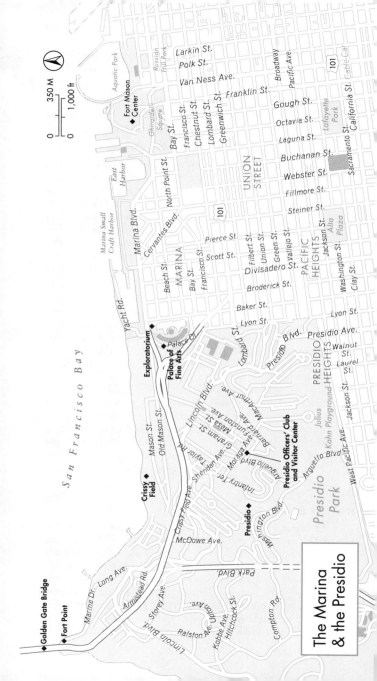

The Marina
& the Presidio

Golden Gate Bridge

Fort Point

San Francisco Bay

Marine Dr.

Long Ave.

Armistead Rd.

Lincoln Blvd.

Storey Ave.

Ralston Ave.

Kobbe Ave.

Upton Ave.

Hitchcock St.

Compton Rd.

Park Blvd.

McDowe Ave.

Presidio

Crissy Field

Mason St.

Old Mason St.

Yacht Rd.

Crissy Field Ave.

Lincoln Blvd.

Sheridan Ave.

Taylor Rd.

Infantry Ter.

Graham St.

Mesa St.

Funston Ave.

Barnard Ave.

Moraga Ave.

Wash'n Blvd.

McArthur Ave.

Presidio Officers' Club and Visitor Center

Washington Blvd.

Arguello Blvd.

Julius Kahn Playground

Presidio Park

West Pacific Ave.

Jackson St.

PRESIDIO HEIGHTS

Walnut St.

Laurel St.

Presidio Ave.

Lyon St.

Exploratorium

Palace of Fine Arts

Presidio Blvd.

Lombard St.

Presidio Blvd.

Lyon St.

Baker St.

Broderick St.

Divisadero St.

Scott St.

Pierce St.

Filbert St.

Union St.

Green St.

Vallejo St.

Steiner St.

Fillmore St.

Webster St.

Buchanan St.

Laguna St.

Octavia St.

Gough St.

Franklin St.

Van Ness Ave.

Polk St.

Larkin St.

Broadway

Pacific Ave.

California St. Cable Car

Sacramento St.

Clay St.

Washington St.

Jackson St.

Alta Plaza

Lafayette Park

PACIFIC HEIGHTS

MARINA

Beach St.

Bay St.

Francisco St.

Cervantes Blvd.

Marina Blvd.

North Point St.

Bay St.

Lombard St.

Chestnut St.

Francisco St.

Greenwich St.

Marina Small Craft Harbor

East Harbor

Ghirardelli Square

Aquatic Park

Fort Mason Center

UNION STREET

350 M

1,000 ft

San Francisco Bay

and windy, too, so bring a jacket.) On days when Fort Point is staffed, guided group tours and cannon drills take place. The top floor affords a unique angle on the bay. ■TIP→ **Take care when walking along the front side of the building, as it's slippery and the waves have a dizzying effect.** Call ahead for hours; during summer the fort may be open beyond weekends. Visitors rave about candlelight tours of the fort, offered by reservation Saturday evenings November through February; it's a trip back in time, recommended for kids 10 and over. Visiting the fort anytime can be vertigo-inducing, and the higher points can feel downright dangerous, especially on windy days. Hang on to little kids or forgo the sweeping views from the top level. ⊠*Marine Dr. off Lincoln Blvd., Presidio* ☎*415/556–1693* ⊕*www.nps.gov/fopo* ⊠*Free* ☙*Fri.–Sun. 10–5.* 5+up

WORD OF MOUTH. "I would highly recommend a bike ride over the Golden Gate Bridge and down into Sausalito. It is a tough ride in some spots but it was amazing. The view from the bridge was incredible! The hill down into Sausalito is steep and long but very fun!" —Kerry392

★ Fodor'sChoice **Golden Gate Bridge.** The suspension bridge that connects San Francisco with Marin County has long wowed sightseers with its simple but powerful art deco design. Completed in 1937 after four years of construction, the 2-mi span and its 750-foot towers were built to withstand winds of more than 100 MPH. It's also not a bad place to be in an earthquake: designed to sway up to 27.7 feet, the Golden Gate Bridge, unlike the Bay Bridge, was undamaged by the 1989 Loma Prieta quake. (If you're on the bridge when it's windy, stand still and you can feel it swaying a bit.) Though it's frequently gusty and misty—always bring a jacket, no matter what the weather's like—the bridge provides unparalleled views of the Bay Area. Muni buses 28 and 29 make stops at the Golden Gate Bridge toll plaza, on the San Francisco side. However, drive to fully appreciate the bridge from multiple vantage points in and around the Presidio; you'll be able to park at designated areas.

From the bridge's eastern-side walkway—the only side pedestrians are allowed on—you can take in the San Francisco skyline and the bay islands; look west for the wild hills of the Marin Headlands, the curving coast south to Lands End, and the Pacific Ocean. On sunny days, sailboats dot the water, and brave windsurfers test the often-treacherous tides beneath the bridge. ■ TIP→ **A vista point on the Marin side gives you a spectacular city panorama.**

If you have younger kids, a walk on the bridge can be harrowing; the railing is only four feet high (and climbable at that), and traffic whizzes by right next to the walkway. With kids under 10, walking a little ways out over the water and heading back to the vista point is plenty. You can easily combine visits to the bridge and Fort Point; add Crissy Field and you can make a day of it. ⌂*Lincoln Blvd. near Doyle Dr. and Fort Point, Presidio* ☎*415/921–5858* ⊕*www.goldengatebridge.org* ☉*Pedestrians Mar.–Oct., daily 5 AM–9 PM; Nov.–Feb., daily 5 AM–6 PM; hrs change with daylight saving time. Bicyclists daily 24 hrs.* 5+up

DON'T LOOK DOWN! Armed only with helmets, safety harnesses, and painting equipment, a full-time crew of 38 painters keeps the Golden Gate Bridge clad in International Orange. Contrary to a favorite bit of local lore, they don't actually sweep on an entire coat of paint from one end of the bridge to the other, but instead scrape, prime, and repaint small sections that have rusted from exposure to the elements.

★ **Presidio.** When San Franciscans want to spend a day in the woods, they head here. The Presidio has 1,400 acres of hills and majestic woods, two small beaches, and—the one thing Golden Gate Park doesn't have—stunning views. ■ TIP→ **The best lookout points lie along Washington Boulevard, which meanders through the park.**

Part of the **Golden Gate National Recreation Area,** the Presidio was a military post for more than 200 years. Today the area is being transformed into a self-sustaining national park; it's also home to Bay Area filmmaker George Lucas's **Letterman Digital Arts Center,** and a Walt Disney museum is on the way.

★ Especially popular is **Crissy Field,** a stretch of restored marshlands along the sand of the bay. Kids on bikes, folks walking dogs, and joggers share the paved path along the shore, often winding up at the Warming Hut for a hot chocolate in the shadow of the Golden Gate Bridge. Midway along the path is the Gulf of the Farallones National Marine Sanctuary Visitor Center, where kids can get a close-up view of small sea creatures and learn about the rich ecosystem offshore. Toward the promenade's eastern end, Crissy Field Center offers great children's programs and has cool science displays. ⊠*Between Marina and Lincoln Park, Presidio* ⊕*www.nps.gov/prsf and www.presidio.gov.* All ages

Presidio Officers' Club and Visitor Center. A remnant of the days when the Presidio was an army base, this Mission-style clubhouse now doubles as a temporary visitor center and exhibit space. Hit the visitor center for maps, schedules of the walking and biking tours, recaps of the Presidio's history, and a good selection of Bay Area books and souvenirs.

The club's temporary art exhibitions explore the unique cultural identity of the American West and the Pan-Pacific, such as Japanese wood-block prints. In one of the Presidio's most exciting projects, the parade-ground parking lot (on what's known as the Main Post) is slated to become a lodge—most likely a swank and green one—and a swath of restored habitat that will stretch all the way to Crissy Field. For kids this is a very quick stop, a good place to hop off the Presidigo shuttle and pick up maps and schedules then get back outside. ⊠*50 Moraga Ave., Presidio* ☎*Visitor center 415/561–4323, 415/561–5500 for exhibits* ⊕*www. presidiotrust.gov* ⊗*Visitor center daily 9–5; exhibit space Wed.–Sun. 11–5.* 5+up

GOLDEN GATE PARK & THE WESTERN SHORELINE

Whether you come to watch penguins waddle, have a sandwich in a sculpture garden, or walk among the kind of ferns that dinosaurs munched, Golden Gate Park is the perfect family playground. More than 1,000 acres, stretching from the Haight all the way to the windy Pacific coast, the park is a vast patchwork of woods, trails, lakes, lush gardens, sports facilities, museums—even a herd of buffalo. You can hit the highlights in a few hours, but it would literally take days to fully explore the entire park.

There's more natural beauty beyond the park's borders, along San Francisco's wild Western Shoreline. From Lands End in Lincoln Park you have some of the best views of the Golden Gate and the Marin Headlands. From the historic Cliff House south to the sprawling San Francisco Zoo, the Great Highway and Ocean Beach run along the western edge of the city. (If you're here in winter or spring, keep your eyes peeled for migrating gray whales.) The wind is often strong along the shoreline, summer fog can blanket

TOP 5 GG PARK & WESTERN SHORELINE

California Academy of Sciences, GG Park: See a rare albino alligator, watch penguins frolic, sail above the rain forest's tree canopy, marvel at the living roof...the spectacular new academy is the one absolute must for kids in the park.

Conservatory of Flowers, GG Park: The sheer beauty of the white wood-and-glass domed structure may not grab young imaginations—but the awesome carnivorous plant collection inside should do the trick.

de Young Museum and Japanese Tea Garden, GG Park: Watch the kids scramble over the steep humpback bridge in the perfectly groomed Japanese Tea Garden, then head to the observation floor at the copper-covered de Young and take in the sweeping view.

Lands End, Western Shoreline: Head down the freshly restored Coastal Trail near the Cliff House; you'll quickly find yourself in a forest with unparalleled views of the Golden Gate Bridge.

Botanical Garden at Strybing Arboretum, GG Park: Wander through a landscape of horsetails, gingko trees, and other dinosaur-era plants at the arboretum's Primitive Plant Garden, then stretch out on the grass and watch turtles sunning themselves at the pond.

the ocean beaches, and the water is cold and usually too rough for swimming. Don't forget your jacket!

WHAT TO SEE IN GOLDEN GATE PARK

Botanical Garden at Strybing Arboretum. One of the best picnic spots in a very picnic-friendly park, this 55-acre arboretum specializes in plants from areas with climates similar to that of the Bay Area. Walk the Eastern Australian garden to see tough, pokey shrubs and plants with cartoonlike names, such as the hilly-pilly tree. Kids gravitate toward the large shallow fountain and the pond with ducks, turtles, and egrets. Another favorite is an area devoted to aromatic plants; take a deep sniff of lemon verbena or lavender. The bookstore is also a great resource. Maps are available at the main and Eugene L. Friend entrances. Older children might enjoy one of the free daily walking tours of the gardens, and 4- to 8-year-olds will dig the Library of Horticulture's bimonthly Sunday story times, followed by kid-centric garden tours. And any day is a good time to browse the library's unusually large, nature-related kids' collection. For most kids, though, the best part about the gardens is the wide-open space. ⊠*Enter the park at 9th Ave. at Lincoln Way, Golden Gate Park* ☎*415/661–1316* ⊕*www.sfbotanicalgarden.org* ⊡*Free* ⊙*Weekdays 8–4:30, weekends 10–5.* All ages

California Academy of Sciences. Renzo Piano's audacious, prescient design for this natural history museum—which opened in September of 2008—is an eco-friendly, energy-efficient adventure in biodiversity and green architecture. That might impress parents, but the kids will be too busy climbing to the top of the domed rain forest, looking for piranhas as they walk through the Amazonian tank, and giggling at penguin antics to think much about this dazzling building. Everyone can appreciate the dramatic living roof, covered with native plants. At the Naturalist Center kids can get up close and personal with the academy's fantastic specimen collection, from human skulls to giant stuffed owls; it's a priceless resource for those interested in further exploration. Daily programs include the popular penguin feedings (10:30 and 3:30); coral reef dives, when divers hand-feed fish in the coral reef exhibit (11 and 2); and hourly planetarium shows. Those with deep pockets who want an extra special visit should consider an hour-long Deep Dive Tour ($75) or a 2½-hour Platinum Tour ($225), both of which offer budding scientists behind-the-scenes access.

Everyone agrees that the new academy is spectacular . . . and so are the prices. It may be tempting to take advantage of the monthly free day, but the overwhelming crowds can ruin a visit. Two tips: consider the San Francisco CityPass—which at just over twice the price of admission includes many other attractions and cable car tickets—and definitely bring your own food. ⊠*55 Music Concourse Dr., Golden Gate Park* ☎*415/379–8000* ⊕*www.calacademy. org* ⊡*$24.95,* kids 12–17 *$19.95,* kids 7–11 *$14.95,* kids 6 and under free; free 3rd Wed. of the month ⊙*Mon.–Sat. 9:30–5, Sun. 11–5.* 3+up

Conservatory of Flowers. Whatever you do, be sure to at least drive by the Conservatory of Flowers—it's just too darn pretty to miss. The gorgeous, white-framed 1878 glass structure is topped with a 14-ton glass dome. Stepping inside the giant greenhouse is like taking a quick trip to the rain forest; it's humid, warm, and smells earthy. The undeni-

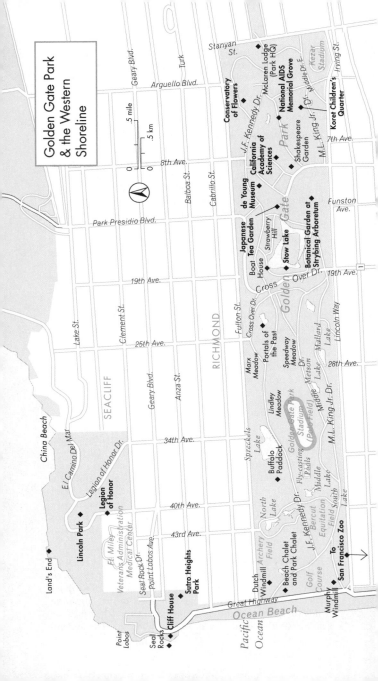

Golden Gate Park & the Western Shoreline

Stanyan St.

Geary Blvd.

Turk

Arguello Blvd.

McLaren Lodge (Park HQ)

Kezar Stadium

Irving St.

Conservatory of Flowers

National AIDS Memorial Grove

J.F. Kennedy Dr.

Middle Dr. E.

M.L. King Jr. Dr.

Koret Children's Quarter

8th Ave.

California Academy of Sciences

Shakespeare Garden

7th Ave.

Balboa St.

Cabrillo St.

de Young Museum

Golden Gate

Park Presidio Blvd.

Japanese Tea Garden

Strawberry Hill

Funston Ave.

Boat House

Stow Lake

Botanical Garden at Strybing Arboretum

19th Ave.

Cross Over Dr.

19th Ave.

Over Dr.

Lincoln Way

Lake St.

Clement St.

Fulton St.

RICHMOND

Cross Over Dr.

Portals of the Past

25th Ave.

Marx Meadow

Speedway Meadow

Mallard Lake

28th Ave.

China Beach

Geary Blvd.

Anza St.

Lindley Meadow

Metson Lake

M.L. King Jr. Dr.

SEACLIFF

34th Ave.

Golden Gate Park Stadium (Polo Field)

Lincoln Way

El Camino Del Mar

Legion of Honor Dr.

Lincoln Park

Legion of Honor

Spreckels Lake

Buffalo Paddock

Fly-casting Pools

40th Ave.

Ft. Miley Veterans Administration Medical Center

North Lake

Middle Lake

43rd Ave.

Seal Rock Dr.

Point Lobos Ave.

Sutro Heights Park

Dutch Windmill

Archery Field

Bercut Equitation

J.F. Kennedy Dr.

Golf Course

Middle Lake South Lake

To San Francisco Zoo

Land's End

Cliff House

Beach Chalet and Park Chalet

Murphy Windmill

Great Highway

Ocean Beach

Point Lobos

Seal Rocks

Pacific Ocean

.5 mile

.5 km

19th Ave.

able highlight is the Aquatic Plants section, where lily pads float and carnivorous plants dine on bugs to the sounds of rushing water. On the east side of the conservatory (to the right as you face the building), cypress, pine, and redwood trees surround the Dahlia Garden, which blooms in summer and fall. To the west is the Rhododendron Dell, which contains 850 varieties, more than any other garden in the country. It's a favorite local Mother's Day picnic spot. ✉*John F. Kennedy Dr. at Conservatory Dr., Golden Gate Park* 📞*415/666–7001* ⊕*www.conservatoryofflowers.org* 💲*$5, kids 12–17 $3, kids 5–11 $1.50, kids 4 and under free; free 1st Tues. of month* ⏱*Tues.–Sun. 9–5, last entry at 4:30.* 3+up

de Young Museum. It seems that everyone in town has a strong opinion about the new museum, unveiled in 2005. Some adore the striking copper facade, while others grimace and hope that the green patina of age will mellow the effect. Most maligned is the 144-foot tower, but the view from its ninth-story observation room, ringed by floor-to-ceiling windows, is fantastic (and gloriously free). The building almost overshadows the de Young's respected collection of American, African, and Oceanic art. Works by Wayne Thiebaud, John Singer Sargent, Winslow Homer, and Richard Diebenkorn are the painting collection's highlights. Your ticket here is also good for same-day admission to the Legion of Honor. The King Tut exhibit, scheduled to run here from June 2009 to March 2010, is certain to bring spectacle, crowds . . . and a hefty additional admission price. Saturday at the deYoung, designed for kids 4–12, includes a guided gallery walk-through followed by art projects. Also for kids 4–12, the weekend program Doing & Viewing Art focuses on one piece of the museum's collection. ✉*50 Hagiwara Tea Garden Dr., Golden Gate Park* 📞*415/863–3330* ⊕*www.deyoungmuseum.org* 💲*$10, kids 13–17 $6, kids 12 and under free; free 1st Tues. of month* ⏱*Tues.–Sun. 9:30–5:15, Fri. 9:30–8:45.* 5+up

Koret Children's Quarter. The country's first public children's playground reopened in 2007 after a spectacular renovation, with wave-shaped climbing walls, old-fashioned cement slides, and a 20-plus-foot rope-climbing structure that kids love and parents fear. Thankfully, the one holdover is the beautiful, handcrafted 1912 Herschell-Spillman Carousel. Most kids 12 and under will find enough to do here to fill half a day. Be aware that the playground isn't enclosed and sightlines can be obstructed; keep an eye on the littlest players. Park in the free lot near the playground just off Bowling Green Drive and you'll avoid the unpleasant pedestrian tunnel between the park and the Haight. ✉*Bowling Green Dr., off Martin Luther King Jr. Dr., Golden Gate Park* ☎*415/831–2700* ✆*Playground free; carousel $1.50, kids 6 and up 50¢, kids 5 and under free* ☉*Playground daily dawn–dusk; carousel Memorial Day–Labor Day, daily 10–4:30, Labor Day–Memorial Day, Fri.–Sun. 10–4:30.* All ages

Japanese Tea Garden. As you amble through the manicured landscape, past Japanese sculptures and perfect miniature pagodas, over ponds of carp that have been here since before the 1906 quake, you may be transported to a more peaceful plane. Or maybe the shrieks of kids clambering over the almost vertical "humpback" bridges will keep you firmly in the here and now. Either way, this garden is one of those tourist spots that's truly worth a stop (a half-hour will do). At five acres, it's large enough that you'll always be able to find a bit of serenity, even when the tour buses drop by. The garden is especially lovely in April, when the cherry blossoms are in bloom. Keep an eye on smaller children, especially near the railless bridges; yours wouldn't be the first to take an unexpected plunge. ✉*Hagiwara Tea Garden Dr., off John F. Kennedy Dr., Golden Gate Park* ✆*$5, kids 12–17 $3, kids 5–11 $1.50, kids 4 and under free; free Mon., Wed., and Fri. 9 AM–10 AM* ☉ *Mar.–Sept., daily 9–6; Oct.–Feb., daily 9–4:45.* All ages

National AIDS Memorial Grove. This lush, serene 7-acre grove, started in the early 1990s by people with AIDS and their families and friends, was conceived as a living memorial to the disease's victims. Coast live oaks, Monterey pines, coast redwoods, and other trees flank the grove. There are also two stone circles, one recording the names of the dead and their loved ones, the other engraved with a poem. Free 20-minute tours are available from the Main Portal some Saturdays, though a walk on your own might be preferable. This is possibly the one place in Golden Gate Park that calls more for quiet contemplation vs. all-out romping. ✉*Middle Dr. E, west of tennis courts, Golden Gate Park* ☎*415/765–0497* ⊕*www.aidsmemorial.org.* 9+up

WHERE CAN I FIND . . . IN GOLDEN GATE PARK & THE WESTERN SHORELINE?

Quick Meals	Location	Description
Arizmendi	1331 9th Ave., south of the park, the Sunset	Fantastic vegetarian pizza and (limited) outdoor seating just south of the park.
de Young Café	50 Hagiwara Tea Garden Dr., Golden Gate Park	The museum's restaurant (open to the public) has a good seasonal menu created from local ingredients; enjoy your snack inside or outdoors in the sculpture garden.
Grocery Stores		
Arguello Super Market	782 Arguello Blvd., north of the park, the Richmond	Well-stocked deli and produce section, at prices between supermarket and highway robbery; just north of the park.
Good Coffee		
Lava Java	852 Stanyan St., southeast corner of Golden Gate Park	Good, reasonably priced coffee just across the street from the park (and a few minutes' walk from the children's playground).
Java Beach Café	1396 La Playa St., at Judah St., Outer Sunset	Strong, organic coffee and outdoor tables just across the street from Ocean Beach.
Playgrounds		
Koret Children's Quarter	Golden Gate Park	Huge climbing pyramid, old-fashioned cement slides, and a vintage carousel make this park beloved by local kids
Public Bathrooms		
Botanical Garden at Strybing Arboretum	Golden Gate Park	Clean, up-to-date, and plentiful in the gardens.
Koret Children's Quarter	Golden Gate Park	Ancient, large facilities that'll do the trick if you're at the playground.

Stow Lake. One of the most photogenic spots in Golden Gate Park, this placid body of water surrounds Strawberry Hill. Cross one of the bridges—the 19th-century stone bridge on the southwest side is lovely—and ascend the hill, topped with a waterfall. An elaborate Chinese Pavilion, a gift from the city of Taipei, stands guard directly on the water. At the boathouse, you can rent a boat, surrey, or bicycle. For the youngest tots, watching the turtles that sun themselves on logs near the boathouse is a treat; the 5-and-up crowd love to power those pedal boats around the lake. ✉*Off John F. Kennedy Dr., Golden Gate Park* ☎*Boat rental 415/752–0347; surrey and bicycle rental 415/668–6699* ☉*Boat rentals daily 10–4, surrey and bicycle rentals daily 9–dusk.* All ages

BATHROOM BREAKS. **In Golden Gate Park, free public restrooms are fairly common and mostly clean, especially around the eastern end's attractions. The Botanical Garden at Strybing Arboretum has numerous facilities, including inside each gate. Enter the de Young Museum at the sculpture garden and café patio and you can use the public restrooms there. Farther west, behind Stow Lake's boathouse and near the Koret Children's Quarter are facilities. Near the ocean, there are public restrooms at the Beach Chalet–Park Chalet. And you can always duck into the bar at the Cliff House (immediate left inside the door) and enjoy historic black-and-white photos on the way to the snazzy bathrooms there.**

WHAT TO SEE ON THE WESTERN SHORELINE

Cliff House. A meal at the Cliff House isn't about the food— the spectacular ocean view is what brings folks here. The vistas, which include offshore Seal Rock (the barking marine mammals who reside there are actually sea lions), can be 30 mi or more on a clear day.

Three buildings have occupied this site since 1863. The current building dates from 1909; a 2004 renovation has left a strikingly attractive restaurant and a squat concrete viewing platform out back.

Sitting on the observation deck is the 1940s **Giant Camera,** a cute yellow-painted wooden model of an old-fashioned camera with its lens pointing skyward. Step into the dark, tiny room inside (for a rather steep $5 fee); a fascinating 360-degree image of the surrounding area—which rotates as the "lens" on the roof rotates—is projected on a large, circular table. ■TIP➔ **In winter and spring, you may also glimpse migrating gray whales from the observation deck.**

Sure-footed kids will enjoy climbing around the ruins of the Sutro Baths, just below the Cliff House, with cement walkways over water-filled tanks and a creepy tunnel toward the ocean. This is also a favorite birding spot, so keep your eyes peeled for egrets, herons, and ospreys. ✉*1090 Point Lobos Ave., Outer Richmond* ☎*415/386-3330* ⊕*www. cliffhouse.com* ⊠*Free* ⊙*Weekdays 9* AM*–9:30* PM*, weekends 9* AM*–10* PM. 5+up

Legion of Honor. The dramatic location—situated on cliffs overlooking the ocean, the Golden Gate Bridge, and the Marin Headlands—is what makes a visit to this museum of European art worthwhile. A pyramidal glass skylight in the entrance court illuminates the lower-level galleries, and an original cast of Rodin's *The Thinker* welcomes you as you walk through the courtyard. The **Legion Café,** on the lower level, serves tasty light meals (soup, sandwiches, grilled chicken). ■TIP→**Admission to the Legion also counts as same-day admission to the de Young Museum.**

Of all San Francisco's museums, this is perhaps the one most geared toward adults: no family programs are regularly offered, and the hushed galleries feel awfully serious. On the upside, the stunning Lincoln Park setting means you can enjoy sweeping views of the Golden Gate while the kids run around—away from disapproving eyes. ✉*34th Ave. at Clement St., Outer Richmond* ☎*415/750-3600* ⊕*www. thinker.org* ⊠*$10, kids 13–17 $6, kids 12 and under free; $2 off with Muni transfer, free 1st Tues. of month* ⊙*Tues.– Sun. 9:30–5:15. 9+up

★ **Lincoln Park.** Although many of the city's green spaces are gentle and welcoming, Lincoln Park is a wild 275-acre park with windswept cliffs and sweeping views. The newly renovated Coastal Trail, the park's most dramatic, leads out to **Lands End;** pick it up west of the Legion of Honor (at the end of El Camino del Mar) or from the parking lot at Point Lobos and El Camino del Mar. Time your hike to hit Mile Rock at low tide, and you might catch a glimpse of two wrecked ships peeking up from their watery graves. ⚠ **Do be careful if you hike here; landslides are frequent, and many people have fallen into the sea by standing too close to the edge of a crumbling bluff top.**

Near the beginning of the Coastal Trail stands a memorial to the USS *San Francisco,* a battleship damaged in World War II at the Battle of Guadalcanal. Seeing the actual damaged bridge up close impresses most kids, especially transportation fans. ✉*Entrance at 34th Ave. at Clement St., Outer Richmond. 3+up

Get Outta Town

MARIN COUNTY

Marin County beckons from the other side of the Golden Gate Bridge—the ultimate playground for families who like being outdoors. Your kids will stand in awe beneath the huge redwoods in Muir Woods National Monument, and the views of the Bay Area from Mt. Tamalpais are amazing. Scenery buffs can also head to the Marin Headlands, Stinson Beach, and the Point Reyes National Seashore to gaze at the vast Pacific. Over 40% of Marin County is parkland, so there are plenty of places to hike and reconnect with nature.

The towns in Marin are small and low-key, with varying degrees of chic. Two easy-to-reach choices are Sausalito, with its yachts and boutiques, and Tiburon, with its gallery-lined Main Street. You can reach both from San Francisco via ferry, which just adds to the fun.

BERKELEY

Berkeley is defined by its University of California (often referred to as "Cal") campus and its liberal-to-radical politics. Ever since the Free Speech Movement ignited at the Cal campus in the 1960s, Berkeley has been *the* place for renegade spirits, bursting bookstores, and caffeine-fueled debates. If your kids liked seeing weird stuff in San Francisco, they're gonna love seeing the counterculture on Berkeley's Telegraph Avenue.

Berkeley is also a great place to eat; there are countless tasty treasures to be sampled in the Gourmet Ghetto, home to the famous Chez Panisse restaurant. Or you can shop for indie tracks at Amoeba Music and obscure tomes at Cody's Books. Another great option for families is to take a tour of the beautiful Cal campus—it's never too early to get the kids excited about college.

Ocean Beach. Stretching 3 mi along the western side of the city from the Richmond to the Sunset, this sandy swath of the Pacific coast is good for jogging or walking the dog—but not for swimming. The water is so cold that surfers wear wet suits year-round, and riptides are strong. As for sunbathing, it's rarely warm enough here; think meditative walking instead of sun worshipping.

Paths on both sides of the Great Highway lead from Lincoln Way to Sloat Boulevard (near the zoo); the beachside path winds through landscaped sand dunes, and the paved path across the highway is good for biking and in-line skating. (Though you have to rent bikes elsewhere.) The

Beach Chalet restaurant and brewpub is across the Great Highway from Ocean Beach, about five blocks south of the Cliff House. On the southern end of Ocean Beach, Fort Funston is one of the most popular hang-gliding spots in the Bay Area; watching gliders drift off the coast is the perfect meditative activity for this windswept edge of the city. If you prefer restaurants and shops to solitude, raise your umbrella near Judah Street on the northern end, Noriega Street in the middle, or Taraval Street along the southern stretch. Be aware, though, that crossing the Great Highway is a lot like crossing a highway. ⊠*Along Great Hwy. from Cliff House to Sloat Blvd. and beyond.* All ages

San Francisco Zoo. Awash in bad press since one of its tigers escaped its enclosure and killed a visitor on Christmas day 2007, the city's zoo is struggling to polish its image, update its habitats, restore its reputation with animal welfare organizations, and avoid the direct oversight of the city's Board of Supervisors. Nestled onto prime oceanfront property, the zoo—which some have accused of caring more about human entertainment than the welfare of its wards—is touting its metamorphosis into the "New Zoo," a wildlife-focused recreation center that inspires visitors to become conservationists. Integrated exhibits group different species of animals from the same geographic areas together in enclosures that don't look like cages. More than 250 species reside here, including endangered species such as the Sumatran tiger and grizzly bear.

The zoo's superstar exhibit is **Grizzly Gulch,** where orphaned sisters Kachina and Kiona enchant visitors with their frolicking and swimming. When the bears are in the water, the only thing between you and them is (thankfully thick) glass. Grizzly feedings are 10:30 AM daily.

The **Lemur Forest** has five varieties of the bug-eyed, long-tailed primates from Madagascar. You can help hoist food into the lemurs' feeding towers and watch the fuzzy creatures climb up to chow down. African Kikuyu grass carpets the circular outer area of **Gorilla Preserve,** one of the largest and most natural gorilla habitats of any zoo in the world. Trees and shrubs create communal play areas.

Ten species of rare monkeys—including colobus monkeys, white ruffed lemurs, and macaques—live and play at the two-tier **Primate Discovery Center,** which contains 23 interactive learning exhibits on the ground level.

Magellanic penguins waddle about the rather sad **Penguin Island,** splashing and frolicking in its 200-foot pool. Feeding time is 2:30 PM. Koalas peer out from among the trees in **Koala Crossing,** and kangaroos and wallabies headline the **Australian Walkabout** exhibit. The 7-acre **Puente al Sur** (Bridge to the South) re-creates habitats in South America, replete with giant anteaters and capybaras.

An **African Savanna** exhibit mixes giraffe, zebra, kudu, ostrich, and many other species, all living together in a 3-acre section with a central viewing spot, accessed by a covered passageway.

The 7-acre **Children's Zoo** has about 300 mammals, birds, and reptiles, plus an insect zoo, a meerkat and prairie-dog exhibit, a nature trail, a nature theater, a restored 1921 Dentzel carousel, and a mini–steam train. A ride on the train costs $4, and you can hop astride one of the carousel's 52 hand-carved menagerie animals for $2. ⊠*Sloat Blvd. and 47th Ave., Sunset* ✛ *Muni L–Taraval streetcar from downtown* ☎*415/753–7080* ⊕*www.sfzoo.org* ☕*$15*, kids 4–14 $9, kids 3 and under free; *$1 off with Muni transfer* ⊙*Daily 10–5. Children's zoo 10–4:30.* All ages

Sutro Heights Park. Crows and other large birds battle the heady breezes at this cliff-top park on what were once the grounds of the home of Adolph Sutro, an eccentric mining engineer and former San Francisco mayor. An extremely wealthy man, Sutro may have owned about 10% of San Francisco at one point, but he couldn't buy good taste: a few remnants of his gaudy, faux-classical statue collection still stand (including the lions at what was the main gate). Monterey cypresses and Canary Island palms dot the park, and photos on placards depict what things looked like before the house burned down in 1896, from the greenhouse to the ornate carpet-bed designs.

All that remains of the main house is its foundation. Climb up for a sweeping view of the Pacific Ocean and the Cliff House below (which Sutro owned), and try to imagine what the perspective might have been like from one of the upper floors. San Francisco City Guides (☎415/557–4266) runs a free Saturday tour of the park that starts at 2 (meet at the lion statue at 48th and Point Lobos avenues). Unless you have historically minded kids specifically interested in seeing the site of Sutro's home, Lincoln Park is a better all-around choice in this part of town: the views there are more spectacular and there's more room to run around. ⊠*Point Lobos and 48th Aves., Outer Richmond.* All ages

THE HAIGHT, THE CASTRO & NOE VALLEY

Once you've seen the blockbuster sights and you're getting curious about the neighborhoods where the city's heart beats, come out to these three, eminently strollable areas. The hippie haven that was 1960s Haight-Ashbury is today a politically engaged area of terrific second-hand and music shops, beautifully restored Victorians, and aggressive panhandling. Teens gravitate toward the Haight and tend to find it fascinating, though to some people it's scummy and intimidating. The brash and sassy Castro District—the social, political, and cultural center of San Francisco's thriving gay (and, to a lesser extent, lesbian) community, is one of the city's liveliest, especially on weekends. Brightly painted, intricately restored Victorians line the streets here, making the Castro another good place to view striking examples of the architecture San Francisco is famous for. (But be aware that explicit window displays along Castro Street can be a bit, um, confusing for children.) Noe Valley, the little kid-friendliest of these hoods, is still farther south. Also known as "Stroller Valley" for its relatively high concentration of little ones, this upscale but relaxed enclave is home to laid-back cafés, kid-friendly restaurants, and comfortable, old-time shops.

WHAT TO SEE IN THE HAIGHT

Buena Vista Park. If you can manage the steep climb, this eucalyptus-filled park has great city views. Be sure to scan the stone rain gutters lining many of the park's walkways for inscribed names and dates; these are the remains of gravestones left unclaimed when the city closed the Laurel Hill cemetery around 1940. You might also come across used needles and condoms; definitely avoid the park after dark, when these items are left behind. The small playground here has the usual slides and sand, and it's a fine stop if your little kids are itching to play. (But be prepared to practice some urban parenting: street people need a place to relax, too.) ⊠*Haight St. between Lyon St. and Buena Vista Ave. W, Haight.* All ages

TOP 5 HAIGHT, CASTRO & NOE VALLEY

Vintage Shopping, Haight: Fashion-conscious teens can find the perfect chiffon dress at La Rosa, a pristine faux-leopard coat at Held Over, or the motorcycle jacket of their dreams at Buffalo Exchange, then wade through the CDs at giant Amoeba.

24th Street Stroll, Noe: Take a leisurely ramble down love-able Noe Valley's main drag, past a plethora of toy and cute kid clothing shops.

Look an Owl in the Eye, Castro: When you bring your kids to the Randall Museum, be sure to watch their faces so you experience the exact moment they realize the uncaged raptors here are alive.

Dig into a Late Breakfast, Haight: Stroll Haight Street late in the morning and treat the kids to large portions of breakfast favs in a space loud enough that they (and you) won't have to worry about inside voices.

Trolley Watching, Noe: Pay homage to Noe Valley's golden fire hydrant, at the edge of Dolores Park, then stick around to watch Muni's geometrical streetcars clatter by and into the tunnel.

Grateful Dead house. On the outside, this is just one more well-kept Victorian on a street that's full of them—but true fans of the Dead may find some inspiration at this legendary structure. The three-story house (closed to the public) is tastefully painted in sedate mauves, tans, and teals (no bright tie-dye colors here). ⊠*710 Ashbury St., just past Waller St., Haight.* 13+up

Haight-Ashbury intersection. On October 6, 1967, hippies took over the intersection of Haight and Ashbury streets to proclaim the "Death of Hip." If they thought hip was dead then, they'd find absolute confirmation of it today, what with the only tie-dye in sight on the Ben & Jerry's storefront on the famed corner.

Everyone knows the Summer of Love had something to do with free love and LSD, but the drugs and other excesses of that period have tended to obscure the residents' serious attempts to create an America that was more spiritually oriented, more environmentally aware, and less caught up in commercialism. The Diggers, a radical group of actors and populist agitators, for example, operated a shop where everything was free (and coined immortal phrases like "Do your own thing").

The Haight,
the Castro &
Noe Valley

Among the folks who hung out in or near the Haight during the late 1960s were writers Allen Ginsberg, Ken Kesey, and Gary Snyder; anarchist Abbie Hoffman; rock performers Jerry Garcia, Janis Joplin, and Grace Slick; and LSD champion Timothy Leary. If you're keen to feel something resembling the hippie spirit these days, there's always Hippie Hill, just inside the Haight Street entrance of Golden Gate Park. Think drum circles, guitar players, and whiffs of pot smoke. All ages

WHAT TO SEE IN THE CASTRO

★ **Castro Theatre.** There are worse ways to while away an afternoon than catching a flick at this gorgeous, 1,500-seat art deco theater; opened in 1922, it's the grandest of San Francisco's few remaining movie palaces. The neon marquee, which stands at the top of the Castro strip, is the neighborhood's great landmark. The Castro's elaborate Spanish baroque interior is fairly well preserved. Before many shows the theater's pipe organ rises from the orchestra pit and an organist plays pop and movie tunes, usually ending with the Jeanette McDonald standard "San Francisco" (go ahead, sing along). The crowd can be enthusiastic and vocal, talking back to the screen as loudly as it talks to them. Classics such as *Who's Afraid of Virginia Woolf?* take on a whole new life, with the assembled beating the actors to the punch and fashioning even snappier comebacks for Elizabeth Taylor. Head here to catch classics, a Fellini film retrospective, or the latest take on same-sex love. Watch for occasional mostly-for-kids events, like the *Little Mermaid* sing-along. Definitely check the calendar before you go; some of the programming is for adults only. ⊠ *429 Castro St., Castro* ☎ *415/621–6120.* 13+up

Harvey Milk Plaza. An 18-foot-long rainbow flag, a gay icon, flies above this plaza named for the man who electrified the city in 1977 by being elected to its Board of Supervisors as an openly gay candidate. In the early 1970s, Milk had opened a camera store on the block of Castro Street between 18th and 19th streets. The store became the center for his campaign to gain thorough inclusion for gays in the city's social and political life.

The liberal Milk hadn't served a full year of his term before he and Mayor George Moscone, also a liberal, were shot in November 1978 at City Hall. The murderer was a conservative ex-supervisor named Dan White, who had recently

PINK TRIANGLE PARK

On a median near the Castro's huge rainbow flag stands this memorial to the gays, lesbians, and bisexual and transgender people whom the Nazis forced to wear pink triangles. Fifteen triangular granite columns, one for every 1,000 gays, lesbians, bisexual, and transgender people estimated to have been killed during and after the Holocaust, stand at the tip of a pink-rock-filled triangle—a reminder of the gay community's past and ongoing struggle for civil rights. While some memorial spaces are scenic or even suitable for frolicking, this one, surrounded by the street, is somber, small, and best appreciated by middle-school kids. ⊠*Corner of Market, Castro, and 17th Sts., Castro.* 13+up

resigned his post and then became enraged when Moscone wouldn't reinstate him. Milk and White had often been at odds on the board, and White thought Milk had been part of a cabal to keep him from returning to his post. Milk's assassination shocked the gay community, which became infuriated when the infamous "Twinkie defense"—that junk food had led to diminished mental capacity—resulted in a manslaughter verdict for White. During the so-called White Night Riot of May 21, 1979, gays and their sympathizers stormed City Hall, torching its lobby and several police cars.

Milk, who had feared assassination, left behind a tape recording in which he urged the community to continue the work he had begun. His legacy is the high visibility of gay people throughout city government. A plaque at the base of the flagpole lists the names of past and present openly gay and lesbian state and local officials. With Sean Penn's portrayal of Milk in the eponymous film, older kids will likely gain a new appreciation for his historical significance—while the younger set will probably just be impressed by the huge rainbow flag. ⊠*Southwest corner of Castro and Market Sts., Castro.* 13+up

Randall Museum. The best thing about visiting this free nature museum for kids may be its tremendous views of San Francisco. Younger kids who are still excited about petting a rabbit, touching a snakeskin, or seeing a live hawk will enjoy a trip here. (Many of the creatures here can't be released into the wild due to injury or other problems.) The museum sits beneath a hill variously known as Red Rock, Museum Hill, and, correctly, Corona Heights; hike up the steep but short trail for great, unobstructed city views. ■TIP→It's a great resource for local families, but if you're going to take the kids to just one museum in town, make it the Exploratorium. During the week the museum is uncrowded, and you might have a naturalist all to yourself. Saturdays are lively, with drop-in family ceramics at 10:15, "meet the animals" presentations at 11:15, and hands-on science and art workshops from 1 to 4; some programs have small fees ($3–$5). If you visit on Saturday, be sure to check out the Golden Gate Model Railroad Club's elaborate model train layout, with hundreds of feet of track, in the museum's basement. ✉*199 Museum Way, off Roosevelt Way, Castro* ☎*415/554–9600* ⊕*www.randallmuseum.org* ✉*Free* ☉*Tues.–Sat. 10–5.* All ages

WHAT TO SEE IN NOE VALLEY

Golden fire hydrant. When all the other fire hydrants went dry during the fire that followed the 1906 earthquake, this one kept pumping. Noe Valley and the Mission District were thus spared the devastation wrought elsewhere in the city, which explains the large number of prequake homes here. Every year on April 18 (the anniversary of the quake), the famous hydrant gets a fresh coat of gold paint. ✉*Church and 20th Sts., southeast corner, across from Dolores Park, Noe Valley.* 5+up

TWIN PEAKS. Windswept and desolate Twin Peaks yields sweeping vistas of San Francisco and the neighboring east and north bay counties. You can get a real feel for the city's layout here; arrive before the late-afternoon fog turns the view into pea soup during the summer. To drive here, head west from Castro Street up Market Street, which eventually becomes Portola Drive. Turn right (north) on Twin Peaks Boulevard and follow the signs to the top. Muni Bus 37–Corbett heads west to Twin Peaks from Market Street. Catch this bus above the Castro Street Muni light-rail station on the island west of Castro at Market Street.

Noe Valley/Sally Brunn Branch Library. In the early 20th century, philanthropist Andrew Carnegie told Americans he would build them elegant libraries if they would fill them with books. A community garden flanks part of the yellow-brick library Carnegie financed (completely renovated and reopened in 2008), and there's a deck (accessed through the children's book room) with picnic tables where you can relax and admire Carnegie's inspired structure. ⊠451 Jersey St.,Noe Valley ☎415/355–5707 ⊘Tues. 10–9, Wed. 1–9, Thurs. and Sat. 10–6, Fri. 1–6. All ages

THE MISSION

The Mission has a number of distinct personalities: it's the Latino neighborhood, where working-class folks raise their families and where gangs occasionally clash; it's the hipster hood, where tattooed and pierced twenty- and thirtysomethings hold court in the coolest cafés and bars in town; it's a culinary epicenter of destination restaurants and affordable ethnic cuisine; and it's the artists' quarter, where murals adorn literally blocks of walls. It's also the city's equivalent of the Sunshine State—this neighborhood's always the last to succumb to fog.

Valencia Street between 16th and 24th streets typifies the neighborhood's diversity. Businesses here include the Bombay Ice Creamery (try a scoop of the zesty cardamom ice cream) and adjacent Indian grocery and sundries store, a tattoo parlor, the yuppie-chic Blondie's bar, a handful of funky home decor stores, a taquería, a Turkish restaurant, and a sushi bar. Mission Street itself, three blocks east, is mostly a down-in-the-mouth row of check-cashing places, dollar stores, and residential hotels—but there are more than a few great taquerías. ■TIP➔ **Bring the kids to the Mission to enjoy a sunny day taking in the history of Mission Dolores, lively Dolores Park, the neighborhood's treasure of murals, and some of the best food in town.**

WHAT TO SEE IN THE MISSION

Balmy Alley. Mission District artists have transformed the walls of their neighborhood with paintings, and Balmy Alley is one of the best-executed examples. Murals fill the one-block alley, with newer ones continually filling in the blank spaces. Local children working with adults started the project in 1971. Since then dozens of artists have steadily added to it, with the aim of promoting peace in Central America, as well as community spirit and AIDS awareness. ⚠ **Be alert here: the 25th Street end of the alley adjoins a somewhat dangerous area.** Younger kids may enjoy checking out the murals—"spot the corn husk" or "spot the parrot"

TOP 5 MISSION

Ice Cream Taste-Off: Compare ice cream from three very different, much-loved shops: Indian scoops at Bombay Ice Creamery, fru-fru and scrumptious at Bi-Rite Creamery, and creamy, old-time style Mitchell's. Bonus: a banana split at the vintage St. Francisco Fountain.

Vivid Murals: Check out dozens of energetic, colorful public artworks in alleyways and on building exteriors.

Fantastical Shopping: Barter for buried treasure at 826 Valencia and its Pirate Supply Store, then hop next door and say hello to the giraffe's head at the mad taxidermy-cum-garden store hodgepodge that is Paxton Gate.

Hang Out in Dolores Park: Join Mission locals and their dogs on this hilly expanse of green with—wait for it—a glorious view of downtown and, if you're lucky, the Bay Bridge.

Chow Down on Phenomenal, Cheap Ethnic Food: Keen appetites and thin wallets will meet their match here. Just try to decide between deliciously fresh burritos, garlicky falafel, thin-crust pizza, savory crepes, and more.

can be fun—but older kids can really get into the stories conveyed. Either plan to take a guided tour through the Precita Eyes Mural Center or at least pick up some of their brochures, and you'll all get more out of your stroll. ⊠*24th St. between and parallel to Harrison and Treat Sts., alley runs south to 25th St., Mission.* 5+up

Creativity Explored. Joyous, if chaotic, creativity pervades the workshops of this art-education center and gallery for developmentally disabled adults. Several dozen adults work at the center each day—guided by a staff of working artists—painting, working in the darkroom, producing videos, and crafting prints, textiles, and ceramics. On weekdays you can drop by and see the artists at work. The art produced here is striking, and some of it is for sale; this is a great place to find a unique San Francisco masterpiece to take home. Since the kids can watch art being created—but can't get their own hands dirty—this may be a quick stop; plan to swing through on your way to Mission Dolores, a block away. ⊠*3245 16th St., Mission* ☎*415/863–2108* ⊕*www.creativityexplored.org* ☎*Free* ☉*Mon.–Wed. and Fri. 10–3, Thurs. 10–7, Sat. 1–6.* 7+up

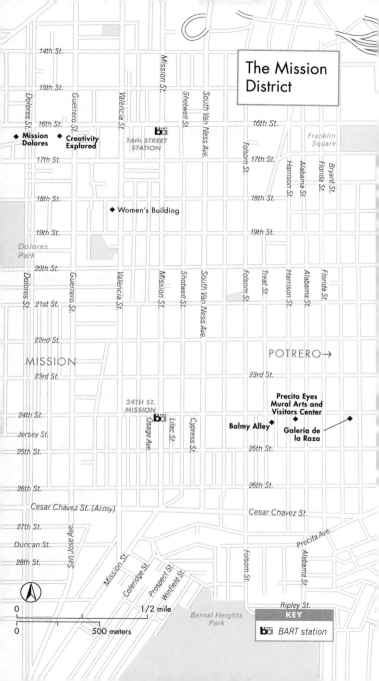

The Mission District

14th St.

15th St.

16th St.

◆ **Mission Dolores**   ◆ **Creativity Explored**

17th St.

18th St.

◆ **Women's Building**

19th St.

Dolores Park

20th St.

21st St.

22nd St.

MISSION

23rd St.

24TH ST. MISSION

24th St.

Jersey St.

25th St.

26th St.

Cesar Chavez St. (Army)

27th St.

Duncan St.

28th St.

Mission St.

14th St.
15th St.
Guerrero St.
Valencia St.
Mission St.
Shotwell St.
South Van Ness Ave.
16th St.
Folsom St.
17th St.
18th St.
19th St.

Dolores St.

Guerrero St.
Valencia St.
Mission St.
Shotwell St.
South Van Ness Ave.
Folsom St.
Treat St.
Harrison St.
Alabama St.
Florida St.

Franklin Square

Harrison St.
Alabama St.
Bryant St.
Florida St.

16th 5TREET STATION

POTRERO→

23rd St.

Precita Eyes Mural Arts and Visitors Center ◆

Balmy Alley ◆   **Galería de la Raza** ◆   ◆

25th St.

26th St.

Cesar Chavez St.

Osage Ave.
Lilac St.
Cypress St.

San Jose Ave.
Mission St.
Coleridge St.
Prospect St.
Winfield St.

Folsom St.

Alabama St.

Precita Ave.

Bernal Heights Park

Ripley St.

0 ——————— 1/2 mile

0 ——————— 500 meters

KEY

🚇 *BART station*

Galería de la Raza. San Francisco's premier showcase for contemporary Latino art, the gallery exhibits the works of mostly local artists. Events include readings and spoken word by local poets and writers, screening of Latin American and Spanish films, and theater works by local minority theater troupes. Just across the street amazing art festoons the 24th Street/York Street Mini Park, a tiny urban playground. A mosaic-covered Quetzalcoatl serpent plunges into the ground and rises, creating hills for little ones to clamber over, and mural-covered walls surround the space. Most events here take place in the evenings, so the kids will likely only get to see the visual arts exhibits and the small shop. The calendar is spotty, so be sure to call ahead. ✉*2857 24th St., at Bryant St., Mission* ☎*415/826–8009* ⊕*www.galeriadelaraza.org* ⊙*Gallery Tues. 1–7, Wed.–Sat. noon–6.* 7+up

★ **Mission Dolores.** Two churches stand side-by-side at this mission, including the small adobe **Mission San Francisco de Asís,** the oldest standing structure in San Francisco. Completed in 1791, it's the sixth of the 21 California missions founded by Father Junípero Serra in the 18th and early 19th centuries. Its ceiling depicts original Ohlone Indian basket designs, executed in vegetable dyes. The tiny chapel includes frescoes and a hand-painted wooden altar. There's a hidden treasure here, too. In 2004, an archaeologist and an artist crawling along the ceiling's rafters opened a trap door behind the altar and rediscovered the mission's original mural, painted with natural dyes by Native Americans in 1791. The centuries have taken their toll, so the team photographed the 20-by-22-foot mural and began digitally restoring the photographic version. Among the images is a dagger-pierced Sacred Heart of Jesus.

There's a small museum covering the mission's founding and history, and the pretty little mission cemetery (made famous by a scene in Alfred Hitchcock's *Vertigo*) maintains the graves of mid-19th-century European immigrants. (The remains of an estimated 5,000 Native Americans lie in unmarked graves.) Services are held in both the Mission San Francisco de Asís and next door in the handsome multidomed basilica. ✉*Dolores and 16th Sts., Mission* ☎*415/621–8203* ⊕*www.missiondolores.org* ⊟*$5 donation, audio tour $7* ⊙*Nov.–Apr., daily 9–4; May–Oct., daily 9–4:30.* All ages

CLOSE UP

Murals with a Mission

1

San Francisco fairly teems with murals. Since the 1970s, groups of artists have worked to transform the city's walls into canvases, art accessible to everyone. Muralists here fall into two loose categories: those in the Latin American tradition of addressing political- and social justice issues through art, and everyone else (those who simply paint on a large scale and like lots of people to see it).

Rediscovering the work of Mexican liberal artist and muralist Diego Rivera in the 1960s, Latino muralists began to address public issues on the community's walls. Heavily Latino since the 1970s, the Mission District became the collective canvas for these artists.

Here are the best and brightest of the Mission District:

■ **Balmy Alley.** The most famous of the Mission's murals—a vivid sweep from end to end. This group series began in 1971 and still gets new additions.

■ **Clarion Alley.** A new generation of muralists is creating a fresh alley-cum-gallery here, between Valencia and Mission streets by 17th and 18th streets. The loosely connected artists of the Clarion Alley Mural Project (CAMP) represent a broad range of style and imagery. Carpet-draped Indonesian elephants plod calmly

down the block; kung fu movie-style headlines shout slogans. The works here offer a dense glimpse at the Mission's contemporary art scene.

■ **24th Street.** Several murals on the buildings along 24th Street, including St. Peter's (at Alabama Street) and even McDonald's (at Mission Street).

■ **Women's Building.** *Maestrapeace—the impressive, towering mural that seems to enclose this building—* celebrates women around the world who work for peace.

■ **826 Valencia.** Fans of graphic novelist Chris Ware will want to take a good look at the facade here. Ware designed the intricate mural for the storefront, a meditation on the evolution of human communication.

■ **Shotwell Street Grocery.** A bit off the beaten path but well worth the detour is Brian Barneclo's gigantic *Food Chain.* This adorns the grocery store on Shotwell Street between 14th and 15th streets. It's a retro, 1950s-style celebration of the city's many neighborhoods (and the food chain), complete with an ant birthday party and worms finishing off a human skull. But in a cute way. Barneclo fans can see more of his work at cool watering hole Rye and hipster restaurant Nopa.

—Denise M. Leto

SAFETY IN THE MISSION. **The Mission is a vibrant area but it does have dodgy zones. The safest area is bordered by Mission, Dolores, 16th, and 20th streets—where everything is happening anyway. Plenty of homeless people crash in doorways, and robberies and assaults are not uncommon. After dark, the areas east of Mission Street and south of 24th Street can feel unsafe, with empty stretches or groups of loitering toughs. If you're in this area after dark, stick to main drags like Mission and 24th streets. If you keep your wits about you and stick to well-lighted areas, you're unlikely to run into trouble.**

Precita Eyes Mural Arts and Visitors Center. Founded by muralists, this nonprofit arts organization designs and creates murals. The artists themselves lead informative guided walks of murals in the area. Most tours start with a 45-minute slide presentation. The bike and walking trips, which take between one and three hours, pass several dozen murals. May is Mural Awareness Month, with visits to murals-in-progress and presentations by artists. You can pick up a map of 24th Street's murals at the center and buy art supplies, T-shirts, postcards, and other mural-related items. Bike tours are available by appointment; Saturday's 11 AM walking tour meets at Cafe Venice, at 24th and Mission streets. (All other tours meet at the center.) Younger kids will start to squirm long before the slide presentation is over; consider grabbing a guide to the murals and striking out at your own pace with little ones. Drop-in art classes for toddlers to teens take place at the center most weekdays; kids work in a variety of media. Call ahead for the schedule and prices. ⊠*2981 24th St., Mission* ☎*415/285–2287* ⊕*www.precitaeyes.org* ⊠*Center free; tours $10–$12,* students 12–17 $5, kids 11 and under $2 ⊙*Center weekdays 10–5, Sat. 10–4, Sun. noon–4; walks weekends at 11 and 1:30 or by appointment.* Tour 7+up

PACIFIC HEIGHTS & JAPANTOWN

Pacific Heights and Japantown are something of an odd couple: privileged, old-school San Francisco and the workaday commercial center of Japanese-American life in the city, stacked virtually on top of each other. Nancy Pelosi and Dianne Feinstein, Larry Ellison and Gordon Getty all own impressive homes in Pacific Heights, which defines San Francisco's most expensive and dramatic real estate and gives way to the more modest Victorians and unas-

TOP 5 PACIFIC HEIGHTS & JAPANTOWN

Kid Shopping, Japantown: Grownups may gravitate toward superfine Pacific Heights shopping, but kids prefer the anime action figures, tiny school supplies, and manga of Japantown.

View from a Bridge, Japantown: Watch your little ones delight in the sight of double-long buses and semitrucks passing directly beneath them on the Japan Center's Webster Street Bridge.

Picnic with a View at Alta Plaza Park, Pacific Heights: Gather supplies along Fillmore Street, hike up to the top of this park, and take in sweeping views of the city while the kids frolic at the terrific big-kid/little-kid playground.

Asian food Galore, Japantown: Graze your way through Japan Center, from sushi boat offerings at Isobune to quick bean-paste snacks at May's Coffee Stand, decked out like an open-air Japanese restaurant.

Pedigree-Spotting at Lafayette Park, Pacific Heights: Dog-loving kids ogle the pedigreed canines at this lovely park—far more interesting than the tiny playground.

suming housing tracts of Japantown. Pacific Heights' cool boutiques and cafés line northern Fillmore Street, while the most interesting shops and restaurants in Japantown huddle in the Japan Center, the neighborhood's two-block centerpiece, and along Post Street. ■TIP→**Japantown is a relatively safe area, but the Western Addition, south of Geary Boulevard, can be dangerous even during the daytime.**

For most kids, Pacific Heights is a quick stop (if it's a stop at all); architecture-loving parents can stretch out time here with a strategically purchased pastry and a romp at one of the neighborhood's lovely parks. Japantown's fun shops appeal to mid-kids and teens, and its noodle shops please even the youngest palates.

WHAT TO SEE IN PACIFIC HEIGHTS

Alta Plaza Park. Golden Gate Park's fierce longtime superintendent, John McLaren, designed Alta Plaza in 1910, modeling its terracing on the Grand Casino in Monte Carlo, Monaco. From the top you can see Marin to the north, downtown to the east, Twin Peaks to the south, and Golden Gate Park to the west. Kids love the many play structures at the large, enclosed playground at the top; everywhere else is dog territory. ⊠*Bordered by Clay, Steiner, Jackson, and Scott Sts., Pacific Heights.* All ages

Lafayette Park. Clusters of trees dot this four-block-square oasis for sunbathers and dog-and-Frisbee teams. During the 1860s a tenacious squatter, Sam Holladay, built himself a big wooden house in the center of the park. Holladay even instructed city gardeners as if the land were his own and defied all orders to leave. The house was finally torn down in 1936. On the south side of the park, squat but elegant **2151 Sacramento,** a private condominium, is the site of a home occupied by Sir Arthur Conan Doyle in the late 19th century. Coats of arms blaze in the front stained-glass windows. The park itself is a lovely neighborhood space, where Pacific Heights residents laze in the sun or exercise their pedigreed canines while gazing at downtown's skyline in the distance. ⊠*Bordered by Laguna, Gough, Sacramento, and Washington Sts., Pacific Heights.* All ages

Octagon House. This eight-sided home sits across the street from its original site on Gough Street; it's one of two remaining octagonal houses in the city (the other is on Russian Hill), and the only one open to the public. Inside, it's full of antique American furniture, decorative arts (paintings, silver, rugs), and documents from the 18th and 19th centuries. Not many kids will be excited by this rather low-key museum, but if your gang will get a kick out of seeing the actual John Hancocks of most of the signers of the Declaration of Independence, plan your visit ahead of the time. The hours are so few and far between that you're unlikely to stumble upon the place when it's open. ⊠*2645 Gough St., Pacific Heights* ☎*415/441–7512* ⊠*Free, donations encouraged* ☉*Feb.–Dec., 2nd Sun. and 2nd and 4th Thurs. of month noon–3; group tours weekdays by appointment.* 9+up

WHAT TO SEE IN JAPANTOWN

Japan Center. The noted American architect Minoru Yamasaki created this 5-acre complex, which opened in 1968. Architecturally the development hasn't aged well, and its Peace Plaza, where seasonal festivals are held, is an unwelcoming sea of cement. The Japan Center includes the shop- and restaurant-filled Kintetsu and Kinokuniya buildings; the excellent Kabuki Springs & Spa; the Hotel Kabuki; and the Sundance Kabuki, Robert Redford's fancy, reserved-seating cinema/restaurant complex.

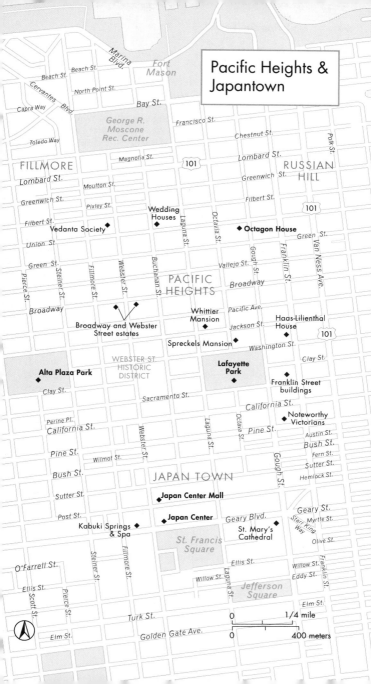

Pacific Heights & Japantown

Marina Blvd.

Fort Mason

Beach St.

Beach St.

Cervantes Blvd.

North Point St.

Capra Way

Toledo Way

Bay St.

Francisco St.

George R. Moscone Rec. Center

Polk St.

Chestnut St.

FILLMORE

Magnolia St.

101

Lombard St.

RUSSIAN HILL

Lombard St.

Moulton St.

Greenwich St.

Greenwich St.

Pixley St.

Filbert St.

Filbert St.

101

Wedding Houses

Filbert St.

Vedanta Society ◆

◆ Octagon House

Green St.

Union St.

Laguna St.

Octavia St.

Gough St.

Franklin St.

Van Ness Ave.

Green St.

Vallejo St.

Steiner St.

Webster St.

Buchanan St.

PACIFIC HEIGHTS

Broadway

Pierce St.

Fillmore St.

Broadway

Broadway and Webster Street estates

Whittier Mansion ◆

Pacific Ave.

Haas-Lilienthal House ◆

Jackson St.

101

Spreckels Mansion ◆

Washington St.

Clay St.

WEBSTER ST. HISTORIC DISTRICT

Lafayette Park ◆

Alta Plaza Park

Franklin Street buildings ◆

Clay St.

Sacramento St.

California St.

Perine Pl.

California St.

Laguna St.

Octavia St.

Pine St.

Noteworthy Victorians ◆

Austin St.

Bush St.

Pine St.

Wilmot St.

Webster St.

Fern St.

Bush St.

Gough St.

Sutter St.

JAPAN TOWN

Hemlock St.

Sutter St.

Japan Center Mall ◆

Geary St.

Star King Way

Myrtle St.

Post St.

◆ Japan Center

Geary Blvd.

Kabuki Springs & Spa ◆

St. Mary's Cathedral

Olive St.

St. Francis Square

O'Farrell St.

Steiner St.

Fillmore St.

Ellis St.

Willow St.

Laguna St.

Willow St.

Eddy St.

Franklin St.

Ellis St.

Scott St.

Pierce St.

Jefferson Square

Elm St.

Turk St.

0   1/4 mile

Elm St.

Golden Gate Ave.

0   400 meters

The Kinokuniya Bookstores, in the Kinokuniya Building, has an extensive selection of Japanese-language books, *manga* (graphic novels), books on design, and English-language translations and books on Japanese topics. On the bridge connecting the center's two buildings, check out Shige Antiques for *yukata* (lightweight cotton kimonos) for kids and lovely silk kimonos, and Asakichi and its tiny incense shop for tinkling wind chimes and display-worthy tea kettles. Continue into the Kintetsu Building for a selection of Japanese restaurants.

Between the Miyako Mall and Kintetsu Building are the five-tier, 100-foot-tall **Peace Pagoda** and the Peace Plaza. Continue into the Miyako Mall to Ichiban Kan, a Japanese dollar store where you can pick up fun Japanese kitchenware, tote bags decorated with hedgehogs, and erasers shaped like food. Kids who are into anime will be in heaven digging through the overloaded shelves of models, figures, and doodads at Japantown Collectibles, tucked away in a corner of the mall. ✉ *Bordered by Geary Blvd. and Fillmore, Post, and Laguna Sts., Japantown* ☎ *No phone.* 7+up

Japan Center Mall. The buildings lining this open-air mall are of the shoji school of architecture. The mall's many good restaurants draw a lively crowd of nearby workers for lunch, but the atmosphere remains weirdly hushed. The shops are geared more toward locals—travel agencies, electronics shops—but there are some fun Japanese goods stores. Arrive early in the day and you may score some fabulous *mochi* (a soft, sweet Japanese rice treat) at **Benkyodo** (✉ *1747 Buchanan St., Japantown* ☎ *415/922–1244*). It's easy to spend hours among the fabulous origami and craft papers at **Paper Tree** (✉ *1743 Buchanan St., Japantown* ☎ *415/921–7100*), open since the 1960s. Be sure to swing around the corner, just off the mall, to **Super 7** (✉ *1628 Post St., Japantown* ☎ *415/409–4700*), home of many large plastic Godzillas, glow-in-the-dark robots, and cool graphic tees. You can have a seat on local artist Ruth Asawa's twin origami-style fountains, which sit in the middle of the mall; they're squat circular structures made of fieldstone, with three levels for sitting and a brick floor. ✉ *Buchanan St. between Post and Sutter Sts., Japantown* ☎ *No phone.* 5+up

Where to Eat

WORD OF MOUTH

"re: dim sum, we like Ton Kiang on Geary, between 22 Ave. and 23 Ave. Excellent dim sum and we always see kids there. It's not too far from Golden Gate Park, so might be good to go to on a day you're exploring the park or on that side of town. They usually serve dim sum every day till 3:00 PM or so (they serve 'regular' Chinese food for dinner) and later on weekends."

—NorCalif

www.fodors.com/forums

Updated
by Denise
M. Leto

SAN FRANCISCO IS A FOODIE town. Locals know food and will engage in passionate discussion about everything from the city's best chefs to the tastiest taco-truck fare. You'll find a huge variety of cuisines here—everything from Afghan to Vietnamese. And you don't just go out for Chinese here: regional offerings range from the classic Cantonese to the obscure Hakka cuisine of southern China. And although locals have long headed to the Mission District for Latin food, Chinatown for Asian food, and North Beach for Italian food, they also know that every part of the city offers dining experiences beyond the neighborhood tradition.

The last decade has seen a noticeable uptick in the number of families dining out together at previously adults-only restaurants. Local parents are raising cuisine-savvy children, dining with their kids at some of the city's best tables—and you may be surprised to find that some top spots also have kids' menus. Some favorite neighborhood joints have gone a step farther, offering "family nights," when parents don't have to dine in constant fear that their child will cry or leave the table.

That said, in general San Francisco restaurants don't love your kids. The restaurant staff will usually be gracious, but fellow diners may not be. Rely on the usual secrets to successful dining out with children: bring distractions, bring hungry but not starving kids, don't let the kids run around, and be prepared to leave before you'd like to. And if you're unsure about your restaurant choice, call and ask whether children are frequent guests (and if they're welcome).

HOURS

Unless otherwise noted, the restaurants listed in this guide are open daily for lunch and dinner. Prime time for dinner is around 7:30 or 8 PM, and although places for night owls to fuel up are plentiful, most restaurants stop serving around 10 PM. Restaurants, along with bars and clubs, may serve alcohol between the hours of 6 AM and 2 AM. The legal age to buy alcoholic beverages in California is 21 years old.

WHAT TO WEAR

In general, San Franciscans are neat but casual dressers; only at the top-notch dining rooms do you see a more formal style. But the way you look can influence how you're treated—and where you're seated. Generally speaking, jeans will suffice at most table-service restaurants in the $ to $$ range. Moving up from there, many pricier restaurants require jackets, and some insist on ties. In reviews,

TOP 5 FAMILY RESTAURANTS

Capp's Corner, North Beach: Dig into huge portions of Italian food served up family-style at this friendly, hopping eatery.

Foreign Cinema, Mission: Pull up a high chair at one of the Mission's hippest eateries—part foodie temple and part movie theater—and dig into terrific Sunday brunch, including a three-course meal just for kids.

Park Chow, Inner Sunset: After a long day in Golden Gate Park, snuggle up to the fire place and tuck in to deli-cious comfort food at casual Park Chow, a perennial favorite with local parents.

Ti Couz, Mission: What kid doesn't love dinner slathered in whipped cream? Sweet and savory crepes delight kids and adults alike at this lively, enduring Breton eatery.

Tommaso's, North Beach: Generations of San Francisco kids have grown up on Tommaso's brick-oven pizza and homemade ravioli, served up in a cozy dining room off the main drag.

we mention dress only when men are required to wear a jacket or a jacket and tie. Note that shorts, sweatpants, and sports jerseys are rarely appropriate. When in doubt, call the restaurant and ask.

RESERVATIONS

Plan ahead if you're determined to snag a sought-after reservation. Some renowned restaurants are booked weeks or even months in advance. But you can get lucky at the last minute if you're flexible—and friendly. Most restaurants keep a few tables open for walk-ins and VIPs. Show up for dinner early (5:30 PM) or late (after 9 PM) and politely inquire about any last-minute vacancies or cancellations. If you're calling a few days ahead of time, ask if you can be put on a waiting list. Occasionally, an eatery may ask you to call the day before your scheduled meal to reconfirm: don't forget or you could lose out.

WINE

Some of the city's top restaurants still automatically stock historic French vintages, but most wine lists respect the origin of the cuisine being served, with Italian restaurants primarily pouring Italian labels, Spanish restaurants pouring Spanish, and so on. Of course, California wines are commonly in the mix, too, with those from limited-production, lesser-known wineries on the better lists. Some restaurants even deliberately keep their wine lists small, so they can change them frequently to match the season and the menu. Half bottles are becoming more prevalent, and good wines by the glass are everywhere. Don't hesitate to ask for recommendations. Even restaurants without a sommelier on staff will appoint knowledgeable servers to lend a hand with wine selections.

TIPPING & TAXES

In most restaurants, tip the waiter 16%–20%. (To figure the amount quickly, just double the tax noted on the check—it's 8.5% of your bill—and add a bit more if the service merited it.) Bills for parties of six or more sometimes include the tip. Tip at least $1 per drink at the bar. Tipping the maître d' is not necessary unless you're trying to pave your way to being a regular. Also be aware that many restaurants, now required to fund the city's new universal health care ordinance, are passing these costs along to their customers—usually in the form of a 3%–4% surcharge or a $1–$1.50-per-head charge.

PARKING

Most upper-end restaurants offer valet parking—worth considering in crowded neighborhoods such as North Beach, Union Square, Civic Center, and the Mission. There's often a nominal charge and a time restriction on validated parking.

PRICES

If you're watching your budget, be sure to ask the price of daily specials recited by the waiter or captain. The charge for these dishes can sometimes be out of line with the other prices on the menu. And always review your bill. If you eat early or late you may be able to take advantage of a prix-fixe deal not offered at peak hours. Many upscale restaurants offer lunch deals with special menus at bargain prices. Credit cards are widely accepted, but some restaurants (particularly smaller ones) accept only cash. If you plan to use a credit card, it's a good idea to double-check its acceptability when making reservations or before sitting down to eat. Some restaurants are marked with a price range ($$–$$$, for example). This indicates one of two things: either the average cost straddles two categories, or if you order strategically, you can get out for less than most diners spend.

WHAT IT COSTS AT DINNER				
¢	$	$$	$$$	$$$$
under $10	$10–$14	$15–$22	$23–$30	over $30

Prices are per person for a typical main course or equivalent combination of smaller dishes. Note: if a restaurant offers only prix-fixe (set-price) meals, it has been given the price category that reflects the full prix-fixe price.

RESTAURANT REVIEWS

UNION SQUARE

$$–$$$ ✕**Canteen.** *American*. Blink and you'll miss this place. Chef-owner Dennis Leary has transformed this narrow coffee shop into one of the most sought-after dinner reservations in town. The homey place has just 20 counter seats and a quartet of wooden booths. But that's all Leary, with a modest open kitchen and a single assistant, can handle. The dinner menu, which changes often, offers only four first courses, four mains, and three desserts. A typical meal might start with a delicious celery root soup with salt cod and bacon, followed by spice-crusted venison or pan-roasted rockfish with pumpkin seeds, and then a dreamy lemon or vanilla soufflé. On Tuesday night, a three-course prix-fixe menu is in force (no choices within each course) for $38. Because this is a one-man band, your food arrives at a leisurely pace. If a dinner reservation is elusive, try for lunch on weekdays or weekend brunch. **Family Matters:** While menu options are usually limited and sophisticated, brunch is a great time to bring the kids (they'll have to struggle to choose what to order). ✉*Commodore Hotel, 817 Sutter St., Union Sq.* ☎*415/928–8870* ⌂*Reservations essential* ▤*AE, MC, V* ✸*Closed Mon. No lunch Tues. or weekends.*

$$$ ✕**Restaurant Jeanne D'Arc.** *French*. When San Franciscans want a big, bourgeois French dinner, but their wallets hold only enough for a top-end main course, they head to Restaurant Jeanne D'Arc, quietly tucked into the lower level of the charming Cornell Hotel de France. Surrounded by faux 15th-century tapestries and fresh flowers is the largest collection of Joan of Arc memorabilia in the United States, so says the management. Dig into a four-course supper for $38, with a dozen main course options, like rabbit in white wine, duck confit, or filet mignon with mushroom sauce ($4 extra). For dessert there's apple tart or Grand Marnier soufflé, capping off a meal that you might find in a small town in Provence. **Family Matters:** The tight quarters make this an option only with kids small enough to be held or old enough to stay put through all four courses. ✉*Cornell Hotel de France, 715 Bush St., Union Sq.* ☎*415/421–3154* 🖃*AE, D, DC, MC, V* ⊙*Closed Sun. No lunch.*

$$$ ✕**Scala's Bistro.** *Italian.* Smart leather-and-wood booths, a pressed-tin ceiling, a menu of Italian (and a few French) dishes, a steady hum of activity—it's hard not to like the big-city feel of this hotel dining room at breakfast, lunch, and dinner. *Fritto misto* of shrimp, squid, and fennel, rigatoni with duck Bolognese sauce, and salmon with buttermilk mashed potatoes are among the evening choices. The room is open late, making it a welcome dessert destination—with sweet successes like burnt caramel *panna cotta* and chocolate IV (mousse, pecan crust, gelato, sauce)—after the theater. **Family Matters:** Weary from a morning of shopping the square with your kids? It's delightful to sink into Scala's—it's elegant and inviting with gracious service for young diners. ✉*Sir Francis Drake Hotel, 432 Powell St., Union Sq.* ☎*415/395–8555* 🖃*AE, D, DC, MC, V.*

CHINATOWN

$–$$$ ✕**Great Eastern.** *Chinese.* Don't be tempted to order a Szechuan or Beijing dish here or you'll leave unhappy. This is a Cantonese restaurant, and that means fresh, simply prepared seafood, quickly cooked vegetables and meats, clear soups, and no fiery chiles. Tanks filled with crabs, black bass, catfish, shrimp, and other freshwater and saltwater creatures occupy a corner of the street-level main dining room. Look to them for your meal, but check prices, as swimming seafood isn't cheap. **Family Matters:** Kids will find their Chinese-restaurant favorites here: stir-fried noodles, cashew chicken, fried rice. Avoid the basement dining room, which is brightly lighted but also claustrophobic. Toward midnight, Chinese night owls drop in for a plate of noodles or a bowl of *congee* (rice porridge). ✉*649 Jackson St., Chinatown* ☎*415/986–2550* 🖃*AE, MC, V.*

$–$$$ ✕**R&G Lounge.** *Chinese.* The name conjures up an image of a dark, smoky bar with a piano player, but this Cantonese restaurant is actually as bright as a new penny. On the lower level (entrance on Kearny Street) is a no-tablecloth dining room that's packed at lunch and dinner. The classy upstairs space (entrance on Commercial Street) is a favorite stop for Chinese businessmen on expense accounts and special-occasion banquets. The street-level room on Kearny is a comfortable spot to wait for a table to open. A menu with photographs helps you pick from the many wonderful, sometimes pricey, always authentic dishes, such as salt-and-pepper Dungeness crab, roast squab, and shrimp-stuffed tofu. You can sip a lychee or watermelon martini while waiting for your table. **Family Matters:** The R&G is a good choice for families who want the familiarity of Chinese food without the fast-food feel of many Chinatown restaurants. ⊠*631 Kearny St., Chinatown* ☎*415/982–7877 or 415/982–3811* ▱*AE, D, DC, MC, V.*

SOMA

$$$–$$$$ ✕**Acme Chophouse.** *Steak house.* Dine here and you'll agree that cows shouldn't eat corn. Grass-fed beef, served up as a filet mignon and tartare, is the specialty at this old-style chophouse next door to the Giants baseball park. The kitchen stocks only naturally raised local meats and poultry, including a 22-ounce rib eye that's sized to satisfy a sumo wrestler and priced for an emperor. All the familiar chophouse sides—creamed spinach, onion rings, scalloped potatoes—will keep traditionalists smiling. The setting is suitably casual, with lots of wood; TV monitors in the bar area mean no inning is missed. The lunch menu is more casual, with burgers, a crab and shrimp salad, pastrami on rye, and a flatiron steak that won't break the bank. **Family Matters:** Though the Chophouse doesn't have a kids' menu, they do have mac and cheese (which will tempt even the grownups). The restaurant's location at the ballpark means they see plenty of kid traffic. ⊠*24 Willie Mays Plaza, SoMa* ☎*415/644–0240* ▱*AE, DC, MC, V* ⊗*Closed Sun. and Mon. No lunch Sat.*

¢–$ ✕**Chaat Café.** *Indian.* This no-frills spot (part of a small chain) trades in cheap and tasty Indian snacks called *chaat.* Standout dishes include *pani puri* (small, hollow bread puffs you fill with seasoned potatoes and chickpeas) and chicken and fish *pakora* fritters. Chewy naan is served alongside simple fish, lamb, chicken, and vegetable curries. The flatbread is also used for wraps, including one filled with tandoori chicken, onions, and cilantro. *Lassi* (a yogurt drink) lovers can satisfy their cravings with salty, sweet, and mango versions. At lunchtime, order at the counter;

Acme Chophouse, **3**	Chow, **67**	Home, **68**
Angkor Borei, **55**	Dosa, **58**	Indian Oven, **64**
B44, **14**	Dragonfly, **69**	Katia's, **46**
Bar Jules, **49**	El Raigón, **23**	La Ciccia, **63**
Bocadillos, **17**	Florio, **39**	La Santaneca
Bodega Bistro, **36**	Fog City Diner, **22**	de la Mission, **60**
Burger Joint, **56**	Foreign Cinema, **59**	Limón, **52**
Café Claude, **15**	Great Eastern, **20**	Los Jarritos, **54**
Canteen, **33**	Greens Restaurant, **29**	L'Osteria del Forno, **26**
Capp's Corner, **27**	Hayes Street Grill, **51**	Lulu, **1**
Chaat Café, **2**	Helmand Palace, **31**	Luna Park, **61**
Charanga, **57**	Hog Isalnd	Maki, **41**
	Oyster Company, **8**	Maykadeh, **24**

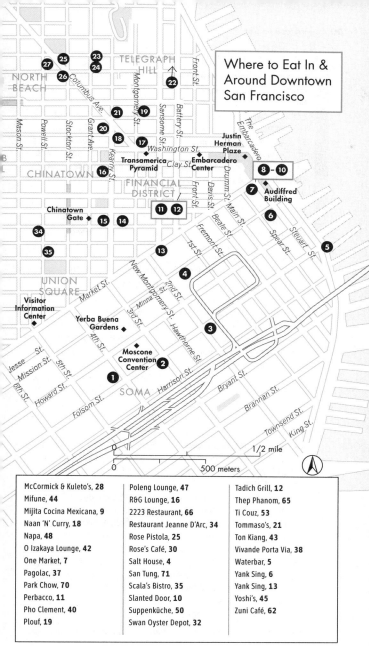

Where to Eat In & Around Downtown San Francisco

NORTH BEACH

TELEGRAPH HILL

Justin Herman Plaza

Embarcadero Center

CHINATOWN

Transamerica Pyramid

Washington St.
Clay St.

FINANCIAL DISTRICT

Audiffred Building

Chinatown Gate

UNION SQUARE

Visitor Information Center

Yerba Buena Gardens

Moscone Convention Center

SOMA

Market St.
Mission St.
Howard St.
Folsom St.
Harrison St.
Bryant St.
Brannan St.
Townsend St.
King St.

Mason St.
Powell St.
Stockton St.
Grant Ave.
Kearny St.
Columbus Ave.
Montgomery St.
Sansome St.
Battery St.
Front St.
Davis St.
Drumm St.
Main St.
Beale St.
Spear St.
Steuart St.
The Embarcadero

New Montgomery St.
2nd St.
3rd St.
4th St.
5th St.
6th St.
1st St.
Minna St.
Hawthorne St.
Fremont St.

Jesse St.

1/2 mile
0
500 meters

McCormick & Kuleto's, 28	Poleng Lounge, 47	Tadich Grill, 12
Mifune, 44	R&G Lounge, 16	Thep Phanom, 65
Mijita Cocina Mexicana, 9	2223 Restaurant, 66	Ti Couz, 53
Naan 'N' Curry, 18	Restaurant Jeanne D'Arc, 34	Tommaso's, 21
Napa, 48	Rose Pistola, 25	Ton Kiang, 43
O Izakaya Lounge, 42	Rose's Café, 30	Vivande Porta Via, 38
One Market, 7	Salt House, 4	Waterbar, 5
Pagolac, 37	San Tung, 71	Yank Sing, 6
Park Chow, 70	Scala's Bistro, 35	Yank Sing, 13
Perbacco, 11	Slanted Door, 10	Yoshi's, 45
Pho Clement, 40	Suppenküche, 50	Zuni Café, 62
Plouf, 19	Swan Oyster Depot, 32	

CLOSE UP

Picky Eaters?

If you're downtown for breakfast, stop at the venerable **Sears Fine Foods** (⊠ *439 Powell St., near Post St.* ☏ *415/986–0700*), home of "the world-famous Swedish pancakes." Eighteen of the silver-dollar-size beauties cost less than a movie ticket.

Nearby in Chinatown, **City View Restaurant** (⊠ *662 Commercial St., near Kearny St.* ☏ *415/398–2838*) serves a varied selection of dim sum, with tasty pork buns for kids and more exotic fare for adults.

Try **Pluto's** (⊠ *627 Irving St., between 7th and 8th Sts.* ☏ *415/753–8867*) after a visit to Golden Gate Park. Small kids love the chicken nuggets, which arrive with good-for-you carrot and celery sticks, whereas bigger kids will likely opt for one of the two-fisted sandwiches. Everyone will want a s'more for dessert.

Barney's Gourmet Burgers (⊠ *3344 Steiner St., near Union St.* ☏ *415/563–0307*), not far from Fort Mason and the Exploratorium, caters to older kids and their parents with mile-high burgers and giant salads. But Barney's doesn't forget "kids under 8," who have their own menu featuring a burger, an all-beef frank, chicken strips with ranch dressing, and more.

Nearly everybody loves pasta, and **Pasta Pomodoro** (⊠ *655 Union St., near Powell St.* ☏ *415/399–0300*), in North Beach, provides plenty of plates to choose from, including a kids-only menu that let's youngsters match up any one of three pasta shapes with five different sauces.

The Mission has dozens of no-frills taco-and-burrito parlors; especially worthy is the bustling, friendly **La Corneta** (⊠ *2731 Mission St., between 23rd and 24th Sts.* ☏ *415/252–9560*), which has a baby burrito.

In Lower Haight, the small **Rosamunde Sausage Grill** (⊠ *545 Haight St., between Steiner and Fillmore Sts.* ☏ *415/437–6851*) serves just that—a slew of different sausages, from Polish to duck to *weisswurst* (Bavarian veal). Carry your meal to nearby Duboce Park, with its charming playground.

Finally, both kids and adults love to be by the ocean, and the **Park Chalet** (⊠ *1000 Great Hwy., at Fulton St.* ☏ *415/386–8439*), hidden behind the two-story Beach Chalet, offers pizza, sticky ribs, a big banana split, and, on sunny days, outdoor tables and a wide expanse of lawn where kids can play while parents relax.

—Sharon Silva

come dinner, tableside service is usually in effect. **Family Matters:** With its quick service, this is a great choice if you have antsy kids who won't sit still for long, especially at lunch. ⊠*320 3rd St., SoMa* ☎*415/979–9946* ▭*MC, V.*

$$–$$$ ╳**LuLu.** *Mediterranean.* In its early years, LuLu was a magnet for dot-commers, who jammed the place every night. When the high-tech industry buckled, LuLu cooled, but never lost its appeal. Nowadays many of the same uncomplicated dishes—fried artichokes, fennel, and lemon slices; mussels roasted in an iron skillet; wood-oven roasted poultry, meats, and shellfish; a small selection of pizzas and pastas—fuel a more mixed clientele. There is a well-supplied raw bar, and main-course specials include a rotisserie-cooked main course that changes daily; Friday brings a succulent suckling pig. Sharing dishes is the custom here. Wine drinkers will appreciate the long list of choices by the glass. When LuLu is packed, service occasionally suffers. **Family Matters:** Locals know this is a good choice for groups. Though it's generally not a kids' kind of place, the high noise level makes it easy to duck in here for a meal with your family. ⊠*816 Folsom St., SoMa* ☎*415/495–5775* ▭*AE, D, DC, MC, V.*

$$$ ╳**Salt House.** *American.* A boisterous crowd—coworkers at the end of the day, folks in from the avenues, conventioneers from nearby Moscone Center—packs this high-ceilinged, brick-lined dining space that once housed a printing press. Rusted girders, chandeliers fashioned from old postcard racks, and water poured from vintage milk bottles set a casual mood. The small plates, like crisp shrimp atop spicy green beans, almonds, and serrano ham, are so appealing that most diners find it hard to move to the mains. Such flawed logic means missing out on a first-rate roast chicken with preserved lemon and garlic. Single diners can grab a seat at the big communal table. **Family Matters:** The "in-between" menu, available weekdays from 2–5:30, offers a few choices to stave off hunger until dinner—this is a good time to dine with kids "in between" the business lunches and twentysomething dinners. ⊠*545 Mission St., SoMa* ☎*415/543–8900* ▭*AE, MC, V* ⊘*No lunch weekends.*

HAYES VALLEY

$$$ ✕**Bar Jules.** *French.* An open kitchen, a counter lined with red-topped stools, a dozen or so small tables, and a generally young crowd are tucked into this cozy, bright eatery on the edge of trendy Hayes Valley. The daily-changing blackboard menu is small and invariably appealing, with dishes like leeks in vinaigrette dressed with sieved hard-cooked egg and capers, a buttery crab omelet, braised short ribs with pureed potatoes, and lamb chops with white beans. Desserts range from lemon tart to butterscotch pudding to apple crisp. Sunday brunch draws a neighborhood crowd to the sunny storefront. On the downside: service can be slow and sketchy, and the sea of hard surfaces can make quiet conversation impossible. **Family Matters:** Inside voices are not necessary here—in fact, you'll probably need to speak up to be heard. The walk-in-only policy can mean a wait, so try to arrive when the kitchen opens. ✉*609 Hayes St., Hayes Valley* ☎*415/621–5482* ✍*Reservations only for groups of six or more* ▭*AE, MC, V* ⊘*No lunch Sun. and Tues. No dinner Sun. Closed Mon.*

$$–$$$ ✕**Hayes Street Grill.** *Seafood.* Arrive here just as local music lovers are folding their napkins and heading off for the 8 PM curtain at the nearby opera house and you'll snag a table and some perfectly fresh seafood. Much of the fish—Pacific bluenose, yellowfin tuna, swordfish—is simply grilled and served with a choice of sauces from beurre blanc to tomato salsa. A pile of crisp, thin Belgian frites rides alongside the grilled offerings. Brass coat hooks, white tablecloths, a long bar, and a mix of banquettes and tables define the traditional San Francisco look of this three-decade-old seafood stronghold. Folks who eschew water-based fare will be happy to know grass-fed beef steak and thick pork chops are on the menu. **Family Matters:** With closely spaced tables—some so closely that diners are pinned in—this place is best if your kids are old enough to stay put through the entire meal. ✉*320 Hayes St., Hayes Valley* ☎*415/863–5545* ▭*AE, D, MC, V* ⊘*No lunch weekends.*

$–$$ ✕**Suppenküche.** *German.* Nobody goes hungry—and no beer drinker goes thirsty—at this lively, hip outpost of simple German cooking in the trendy Hayes Valley corridor. When the room gets crowded, which it regularly does, strangers sit together at unfinished pine tables. The food—bratwurst and red cabbage, potato pancakes with house-made applesauce, meat loaf, sauerbraten, schnitzel, strudel—is tasty and easy on the pocketbook, and the imported brews are first-rate. There's also a popular Sunday brunch, with appealing fare such as gravlax with mustard-dill sauce and pancakes with brandied raisins. **Family Matters:** The down-home cooking and friendly vibe make a meal at Suppenküche feel like dining at a friend's house—and bringing the kids is only natural. ✉ *601 Hayes St., Hayes Valley* ☎ *415/252-9289* ☐ *AE, MC, V* ☉ *No lunch.*

★ **Fodor'sChoice** ✕ **Zuni Café.** *Mediterranean.* After one bite of
$$$ chef Judy Rodgers' succulent brick-oven-roasted whole chicken with Tuscan bread salad, you'll understand why she's a national star. Food is served here on two floors; the rabbit warren of rooms on the second level includes a balcony overlooking the main dining room. The crowd is a disparate mix that reflects the makeup of the city: casual and dressy, young and old, hip and staid. At the long copper bar, trays of briny-fresh oysters on the half shell are dispensed along with cocktails and wine. The southern French–Italian menu changes daily (though the signature chicken, prepared for two, is a fixture). Rotating dishes include house-cured anchovies with Parmigiano-Reggiano, crostini with tuna confit, nettle and onion soup with a poached egg, and grilled grouper with artichokes and white beans. Desserts are simple and satisfying and include crumbly crusted tarts and an addictive cream-laced coffee granita. **Family Matters:** Lunchtime gives you the best chance of avoiding kid attitude. ✉ *1658 Market St., Hayes Valley* ☎ *415/552-2522* ☐ *AE, MC, V* ☉ *Closed Mon.*

VAN NESS/POLK

$–$$ ✕ **Bodega Bistro.** *Vietnamese.* With just one taste of his green papaya salad, you'll be hooked on the inspired cooking of North Vietnam–born Jimmy Kwok. His casual bistro, located on the mildly sketchy edge of the Tenderloin, brims at lunchtime with savvy eaters from Civic Center offices. For dinner, Kwok draws devotees from over the city who come not only for the salad, but also for his roast squab, *bun cha Hanoi* (broiled pork, herbs, rice vermicelli, and lettuce wrapped in rice paper), and salt-and-pepper Dungeness crab with garlic noodles. Kwok punctuates his Asian menu with a handful of French dishes. Cap your meal with crème caramel or a bowl of lemongrass ice cream. **Family Matters:** With excellent versions of familiar dishes like fried rice and fried noodles, along with its laid-back vibe, Bodega Bistro is a good choice for families with younger kids. ✉ *607 Larkin St., Van Ness/Polk* ☎ *415/921–1218* ▭ *MC, V.*

$–$$ ✕ **Helmand Palace.** *Middle Eastern.* In late 2007, this popular restaurant moved from a scruffy block of Broadway in North Beach (a rock slide forced its exit) to a smaller Van Ness address and added "Palace" to its name, but kept everything else—authentic Afghan cooking and a handsomely outfitted dining room—intact. Highlights of the reasonably priced menu include *aushak* (leek-filled ravioli served with yogurt and ground beef), pumpkin with yogurt-and-garlic sauce, and any of the lamb dishes, in particular the kebab strewn with yellow split peas and served on Afghan flatbread. Basmati rice pudding, perfumed with cardamom and pistachio, is an exotic—and satisfying—finish. **Family Matters:** Though Afghan food may not be familiar to your kids, if they're comfortable with anything beyond mac and cheese you won't have any trouble finding delicious options for them here—and families will feel welcome. ✉ *2424 Van Ness Ave., Van Ness/Polk* ☎ *415/362–0641* ▭ *AE, MC, V* ⊘ *No lunch.*

¢–$$ ✕ **Pagolac.** *Vietnamese.* Savvy diners know that Pagolac serves a great "seven-way beef" dinner, the classic south Vietnamese feast of seven different beef dishes, from soup to salad to spring rolls and more, for an unbelievable $16 per person. This is also a good place for lotus root salad with pink shrimp, all kinds of rolls (both fried and fresh), aromatic clay pots, and noodles or rice topped with protein of all types—pork, beef, shrimp, chicken—in all forms—fried, shredded, grilled. The narrow space is attractively decorated in dark wood tables and chairs and a few nice pieces of Vietnamese art, and the service, though sometimes a little ragged, is always friendly. Of course, such low prices and good food haven't remained a secret, so come before 6 or after 9 to avoid a long wait for a table. **Family Matters:** The great food, relaxed atmosphere, and warm welcome may not be enough to make some parents feel comfortable on this sketchy (though generally safe) block—with or without kids. ✉ *655 Larkin St., Van Ness/Polk* ☎ *415/776–3234* ▭ *No credit cards* ⊘ *Closed Mon. No lunch.*

★ Fodor'sChoice ✕ **Swan Oyster Depot.** *Seafood.* Here is old San **¢–$$** Francisco at its best. Half fish market and half diner, this small, slim seafood operation, open since 1912, has no tables, only a narrow marble counter with about a dozen and a half stools. Most people come in to buy perfectly fresh salmon, halibut, crabs, and other seafood to take home. Everyone else—locals and out-of-towners—comes to enjoy the excellent clam chowder—the only hot food served—a dozen oysters, half a cracked crab, a big shrimp salad, or a smaller shrimp cocktail. Come early or late to avoid a long wait. **Family Matters:** Kids will love hopping onto one of the rickety stools to enjoy a hot bowl of chowder. ✉*1517 Polk St., Van Ness/Polk* ☎*415/673–1101* ▭*No credit cards* ⊙*Closed Sun. No dinner.*

NORTH BEACH

$$–$$$ ✕**Capp's Corner.** *Italian.* One of North Beach's last family-style trattorias, Capp's is steadfastly old-fashioned. The men at the bar still roll dice for drinks, celebrity photos line the walls, and diners sit elbow-to-elbow at long, oilcloth-covered tables. The fare is packaged in bountiful five-course dinners for $20.50, with the roast lamb a good choice for the main (the tasty osso buco and polenta is $5 more). The food isn't award-winning, but a meal here won't break the bank either. A three-course option, good for smaller appetites—and smaller budgets ($18)—includes minestrone, salad, and choice of pasta. For $4 more, you can finish with an order of spumoni. Kids under 10 will be happy with their own menu priced at $13. **Family Matters:** You'll never be the only family with kids here, and yours will be welcomed. ✉*1600 Powell St., North Beach* ☎*415/989–2589* ▭*AE, DC, MC, V.*

$$$–$$$$ ✕**El Raigón.** *Steak house.* Gauchos—and beef eaters from everywhere—will feel right at home in this Argentine steak house, complete with cowhide bar and open wood-beam ceiling. The range-raised beef steaks are expertly charred over a wood and charcoal fire; diners add the traditional *chimichurri* sauce to taste. Truly serious carnivores will want to start with beef empanadas, grilled chorizo, or blood sausage. Sautéed spinach and grilled asparagus are good sides, pancakes filled with *dulce de leche* caramel is a decadent dessert, and the Argentine Malbecs go with everything. **Family Matters:** With a lively evening crowd, this is a good choice for carnivores 12 and up. ✉*510 Union St., North Beach* ☎*415/291–0927* ▭*AE, D, DC, MC, V* ⊙*Closed Sun. No lunch.*

★ Fodor's Choice ✕**L'Osteria del Forno.** *Italian.* A staff chattering in
$–$$ Italian and seductive aromas drifting from the open kitchen make customers who pass through the door of this modest

storefront, with its sunny yellow walls and friendly wait-staff, feel as if they've stumbled into a homey trattoria in Italy. The kitchen produces small plates of simply cooked vegetables, a few pastas, some daily specials, milk-braised pork, a roast of the day, creamy polenta, and thin-crust pizzas—including a memorable "white" pie topped with porcini mushrooms and mozzarella. At lunch try one of North Beach's best focaccia sandwiches. **Family Matters:** Come early and snag one of the few tables, or your gang will be among the hungry crowd hovering on the sidewalk outside. ⊠*519 Columbus Ave., North Beach* ☎*415/982–1124* ▭*No credit cards* ☉*Closed Tues.*

$$–$$$ ✕**Maykadeh.** *Middle Eastern.* Although it sits in an Italian neighborhood, this authentic Persian restaurant has a large and faithful following of homesick Iranian émigrés. Lamb dishes with rice are the specialties, served in an attractive but not showy dining room. Among the many appetizers are traditional dishes such as eggplant with mint sauce and spiced lamb tongue. Along with the requisite—and tasty—kebabs, the restaurant serves a variety of poultry and meats marinated in olive oil, lime juice, and herbs. Anyone looking for a hearty, traditional main dish should order *ghorme sabzee* (lamb shank braised with a bouquet of Middle Eastern spices). Give yourself plenty of time here, as service occasionally slows to a crawl. **Family Matters:** The delicious appetizers will keep the kids from starvation's door—and if you need to, you can always hold out the promise of a delicious North Beach treat afterward. ⊠*470 Green St., North Beach* ☎*415/362–8286* ▭*MC, V.*

$$–$$$$ ✕**Rose Pistola.** *Italian.* This busy spot is named for one of North Beach's most revered barkeeps, while the food celebrates the neighborhood's early Ligurian settlers. The menu changes daily, but a large assortment of antipasti—grilled octopus with butter beans and arugula; bruschetta with asparagus, prosciutto, and truffle oil—and pizzas from the wood-burning oven are favorites, as are the cioppino and the fresh fish of the day, served in various ways. A big bar area opens onto the sidewalk, and an exhibition kitchen lets you keep an eye on your order. Even though the kitchen has had trouble holding onto a good chef and the service sometimes arrives with attitude, the crowds keep coming. **Family Matters:** The lively street scene and good people-watching here are welcome distractions for young children. ⊠*532 Columbus Ave., North Beach* ☎*415/399–0499* ▭*AE, D, DC, MC, V.*

Need Some Caffeine?

North Beach may have the highest coffee profile, but fantastic brews can be found all over town. Tear yourself away from Columbus Avenue and head to Hayes Valley's **Blue Bottle Coffee** (✉ *315 Linden St., near Gough St.* ☎ *415/252–7535*), a modest kiosk where the organic beans (no more than two days from the roaster) are ground for each cup and the espresso is automatically *ristretto*—a short shot. (Although traditionalists stick to the quirky kiosk, in early 2008 Blue Bottle opened a "proper café" downtown in the newly minted Mint Plaza.) In the Mission District, the owners of the inviting **Ritual Coffee Roasters** (✉ *1026 Valencia, between 21st and 22nd Sts.* ☎ *415/641–1024*) have plunked their roaster in middle of the café, so you know where your beans—usually single-origin, rather than a blend—were roasted when you order your cap or latte. While you're sipping your inky strong cup at friendly **Farley's** (✉ *1315 18th St., at Texas* ☎ *415/648–1545*), a neighborhood institution on

sunny Potrero Hill, you can play chess, check out the eclectic magazine selection, or catch up on the local gossip. Cubans are serious coffee drinkers, and **Café Lo Cubano** (✉ *3401 California St., in Laurel Village* ☎ *415/831–4383*), with its *cafecito* (strong, sweet espresso) and other coffee drinks and grilled Cuban sandwiches, is the perfect introduction to a venerable tradition. In the Lower Haight, sun seekers grab an outside table at **Café du Soleil** (✉ *200 Fillmore St., at Waller* ☎ *415/934–8637*) and sip bowls of café au lait brewed from organic beans with their morning croissant. And anyone looking for a real cup of joe in a bare-bones pine shack should join the savvy dock workers, carpenters, and young suits at the 80-year-old **Red's Java House** (✉ *Pier 30, between Embarcadero and Bryant St.* ☎ *415/777–5626*), where the coffee typically follows a cheeseburger and a Bud and the gorgeous view of the East Bay is priceless.

—Sharon Silva

$$ ✕**Tommaso's.** *Pizza.* This is the site of San Francisco's first wood-fired-pizza oven, installed in the 1930s when the restaurant opened. The oven is still here, and the restaurant, with its coat hooks, boothlike dining nooks, and communal table running the length of the basement dining room, has changed little since those early days. The pizzas' delightfully chewy crusts, creamy mozzarella, and full-bodied house-made sauce—for sale in jars, too—have kept legions of happy eaters returning for decades. Pair one of the hearty pies with a salad of grilled sweet peppers or of broccoli dressed in lemon juice and olive oil and a bottle of the house wine. **Family Matters:** Local folks bring kids to Tommaso's every night—it's an honest-to-goodness North Beach family tradition. ⊠*1042 Kearny St., North Beach* ☎*415/398–9696* ▭*AE, D, DC, MC, V* ⊘*Closed Mon. No lunch.*

ON THE WATERFRONT

$$–$$$ ✕**B44.** *Spanish.* Going to restaurant-lined Belden Place is like visiting your favorite candy store: There are just too many choices. But this spare, modern Spanish restaurant, which draws locals and visitors alike with its Catalan tapas and paellas, won't disappoint. The open kitchen sends out appealing small plates: white anchovies with pears and Idiazabal cheese, sherry-scented fish cheeks, warm octopus with tiny potatoes, and blood sausage with white beans. The paellas, individually served in an iron skillet, bring together inviting combinations such as chicken, rabbit, and mushrooms, or mixed seafood with squid ink. **Family Matters:** The alley is hopping weekdays with the FiDi crowd and weekends with shoppers and locals—but the mid-afternoon lull here is made for kids with adventurous palates. ⊠*44 Belden Pl., Financial District* ☎*415/986–6287* ▭*AE, MC, V* ⊘*No lunch weekends.*

$$ ✕**Bocadillos.** *Spanish.* The name means "sandwiches," but that's only half the story here. You'll find 11 bocadillos at lunchtime: plump rolls filled with everything from serrano ham to Catalan sausage with arugula. But at night, chef-owner Gerald Hirigoyen, who also owns the high-profile Piperade, focuses on tapas, offering some two dozen choices, including a delicious grilled quail, an equally superb pig's trotters with herbs, and calamari with *romesco* (a thick combination of red pepper, tomato, almonds, and garlic) sauce. His wine list is well matched to the food. A youngish crowd typically piles into the modern, red-brick-walled dining space, so be prepared to wait for a seat. A large communal table is a good perch for singles. **Family Matters:** One of the few elegant and upscale eateries to be open breakfast through dinner, Bocadillos makes a great off-peak stop for families, and grownups with kids in tow can indulge in some sophistication without the crowd. ⊠*710 Montgomery St., Financial District* ☎*415/982–2622*

⚐*Reservations not accepted* ⊟*AE, MC, V* ⊘*Closed Sun. No lunch Sat.*

$$–$$$ ✕**Café Claude.** *French.* If you think this place looks like it could be in Paris, you're right. Nearly everything, from the zinc bar and the banquettes to the light fixtures and cinema posters, was shipped from a defunct café in the City of Light to this atmospheric downtown alley. Order a *croque monsieur* or niçoise salad at lunchtime. The francophone kitchen sends out even more French staples for dinner, like escargots, steak tartare, coquilles Saint Jacques, and roast lamb. Stop by Thursday, Friday, and Saturday nights to enjoy live music along with your food. **Family Matters:** The atmosphere here is not so much rarified as just French, and the table spacing makes for close quarters. ⊠*7 Claude La., Financial District* ☎*415/392–3515* ⊟*AE, DC, MC, V* ⊘*No lunch Sun.*

$$ ✕**Fog City Diner.** *American.* This fully chromed destination is a far cry from the no-frills diner of Edward Hopper's *Nighthawks.* Fog City has all the trappings of a luxurious railroad car: wood paneling, huge windows, and comfortable booths. The menu is both classic and contemporary and includes memorable mac and cheese made with Gouda, ham, and peas; fried salt-and-pepper squid with chili-lime sauce; red curry mussel stew; thick burgers with fries; a towering lemon-meringue pie; and a sinful rum coconut layer cake with cream cheese frosting. Locals complain of too many out-of-towners, but plenty of folks who call San Francisco home fill the booths at lunch and dinner. **Family Matters:** With so many familiar favorites to choose from, the little ones won't need a kids' menu. You'll likely see other families with children enjoying a meal here. ⊠*1300 Battery St., Embarcadero* ☎*415/982–2000* ⊟*D, DC, MC, V.*

$–$$$ ✕**Hog Island Oyster Company.** *Seafood.* Hog Island, a thriving oyster farm in Tomales Bay, north of San Francisco, serves up its harvest at this attractive raw bar and retail shop in the busy Ferry Building. The U-shaped counter and a handful of tables seat no more than three dozen diners, who come here for impeccably fresh oysters or clams (also from Hog Island) on the half shell. Other mollusk-centered options include a first-rate oyster stew, clam chowder, and Manila clams with white beans. The bar also turns out what is arguably the best grilled-cheese sandwich (with three artisanal cheeses on artisanal bread) this side of Wisconsin. You need to eat early, however, as the bar closes at 8 on weekdays and 6 on weekends. Happy hour, 5–7 on Monday and Thursday, is an oyster lover's dream: sweetwaters for a buck apiece and beer for $3.50. **Family Matters:** Always lively, this place fills up with FiDi denizens at happy hour, so bring your little (but not too little) oyster lovers during the afternoon. ⊠*Ferry Bldg., Embarcadero at Market St., Embarcadero* ☏*415/391–7177* ☐*AE, MC, V* ☺*Closed Sun.*

$$–$$$$ ✕**McCormick & Kuleto's.** *Seafood.* It sounds like a visitor's dream come true: a fabulous view of the bay from nearly every seat in the house, an Old San Francisco atmosphere, a menu that changes daily depending on what's fresh, and dozens of different fish and shellfish prepared in every imaginable fashion. But not everything is rosy at this seafood emporium, part of a nationwide chain. Food quality can be uneven, so stick with the simple preparations like oysters on the half shell and grilled fish. Or take in the bay view while fueling up on oyster shooters, ceviche, mussels, or bruschetta from the budget-friendly bar menu, all washed down with a cold beer. **Family Matters:** Given its location and vast dining room, the restaurant feeds plenty of kids, so you needn't be shy about bringing your brood here. ⊠*Ghirardelli Sq., Beach and Larkin Sts., Fisherman's Wharf* ☏*415/929–1730* ☐*AE, D, DC, MC, V.*

¢ ✕**Mijita Cocina Mexicana.** *Mexican.* Famed local chef Traci Des Jardins is the culinary powerhouse behind two of the city's best-known white-tablecloth restaurants, Jardinière and Acme Chophouse. But to honor her Latin roots, she chose Mexican hot chocolate over martinis when she opened this casual taquería and weekend brunch spot. The tacos feature handmade corn tortillas and fillings like *carnitas* (slow-cooked pork), mahimahi, and *carne asada* (grilled strips of marinated meat). The superb meatball soup and Oaxacan chicken tamales are served daily, and the weekend brings such favorites as *huevos rancheros,* fried corn tortillas topped with fried eggs and salsa. Kid-size burritos (beans and cheese) and quesadillas will keep your *niños* happy. Seating is simple—wooden tables and benches—but a perfect perch for watching gulls on the bay. Plan to eat dinner early; Mijita closes at 7 on weekdays, 8 on weekends. **Family Matters:** The sophisticated versions of familiar Mexican recipes throws some kids off, and the location—next to one of the Ferry Building's rear doors—means it may be hard to keep little ones in their seats. ⊠*Ferry Bldg., Embarcadero at Market St., Embarcadero* ☏*415/399–0814* ☐*MC, V* ☺*No dinner Sun.*

¢ ✕**Naan 'N' Curry.** *Indian.* You will find no frills here—and minimal service and housekeeping—but you will find food fresh off the fire at rock-bottom prices. This is just one location in a local minichain of Indian-Pakistani eateries that cater primarily to starving students, poorly paid office workers, local South Asians, and anyone else who likes spicy food but doesn't give a damn about ambience. The tandoor-fired chicken *tikka masala, bhindi* (okra with onion and spices), and tongue-scorching tandoori lamb chops are favorites. The Bollywood music is too loud, but the naan is the size of a hubcap and the chai (milk) tea is free. **Family Matters:** The super-casual, cafeteria-style dining works well for even the smallest children, and the noise level means you won't need to tell the kids to quiet down. ✉ *533 Jackson St., Financial District* ☎ *415/693–0449* ▭ *MC, V.*

$$–$$$$ ✕**One Market.** *American.* A giant among American chefs, Bradley Ogden runs an upscale mini-restaurant chain that stretches from Marin County to San Diego. This large space with a bay view and a grown-up ambience is his well-known San Francisco outpost. (He also boasts a steak house in the downtown Westfield Centre.) The two-tier dining room seats 170—many of them suits brokering deals—and serves a seasonal, wonderfully homey yet imaginative menu that might include tender bacon-wrapped pork tenderloin with dandelion greens, potato-crusted petrale sole, and duck breast with black trumpet mushrooms. Hearty appetites will appreciate the three-course market menu for just $48. Folks who want only a small sweet to finish can choose from a half dozen mini-desserts, such as chocolate toffee almond cake, mint-chip icecream bar, or butterscotch pudding. The wine list includes the best California labels, many by the glass. **Family Matters:** The staff will welcome families with children, and kids will certainly find plenty on the menu that appeals. Be aware, though, that at lunchtime One Market is the domain of the business crowd, and at night it's filled with couples and groups (of grownups). ✉ *1 Market St., Embarcadero* ☎ *415/777–5577* ⚓ *Reservations essential* ▭ *AE, DC, MC, V* ☺ *Closed Sun. No lunch Sat.*

$$–$$$ ✕**Perbacco.** *Italian.* With its long marble bar and open kitchen, this brick-lined two-story space oozes big-city charm. The arrival of skinny, brittle bread sticks is the first sign that the kitchen understands the cuisine of northern Italy, specifically Piedmont. And if the breadbasket doesn't convince you, try the antipasto of house-made cured meats or *burrata* (cream-filled mozzarella) with peppers

and anchovies, the delicate *agnolotti dal plin* (veal-stuffed pasta with a cabbage-laced meat sauce), or *pappardelle* with full-flavored short-rib *ragù*. The clientele, a mix of business types and Italian food aficionados, appreciates the big, smart wine list along with the superb food. **Family Matters:** This adult restaurant in the FiDi doesn't get a lot of young diners. Choose an off time if you're bringing the family, and expect great service and good, sophisticated food. ⊠*230 California St., Financial District* ☎*415/955–0663* ⊟*AE, D, DC, MC, V* ⊗*Closed Sun. No lunch Sat.*

$$–$$$ ✕**Plouf.** *French.* Plouf is a gold mine for mussel lovers, with seven preparations to choose from. Among the best are *marinière* (white wine, garlic, and parsley) and one combining coconut milk, lime juice, and chili. Add a side of the skinny fries and that's all most appetites need. The menu changes seasonally and includes roast lamb and steak to satisfy any unrepentant carnivores. Many of the appetizers—oysters on the half shell, calamari with fennel tempura, tuna tartare—stick to seafood, as well. The tables are squeezed together in the bright, lively dining room, so you might share in neighboring conversations. On temperate days and nights, try for one of the outdoor tables. **Family Matters:** And with kids, lunch at an alley table on a balmy day is your best bet. ⊠*40 Belden Pl., Financial District* ☎*415/986–6491* ⊟*AE, MC, V* ⊗*Closed Sun. No lunch Sat.*

$$–$$$$ ✕**Slanted Door.** *Vietnamese.* If you're looking for homey Vietnamese food served in a down-to-earth dining room at a decent price, *don't* stop here. Celebrated chef-owner Charles Phan has mastered the upmarket, Western-accented Vietnamese menu. To showcase his cuisine, he chose a big space with sleek wooden tables and chairs, white marble floors, a cocktail lounge, a bar, and an enviable bay view. Among his popular dishes are green papaya salad, cellophane crab noodles, chicken clay pot, and shaking beef (tender beef cubes with garlic and onion). Alas, the crush of fame means that no one speaking in a normal voice can be heard. To avoid the midday and evening crowds (and to save some bucks), stop in for the afternoon-tea menu (spring rolls, grilled pork over rice noodles), or visit Out the Door, Phan's take-out counter around the corner from the restaurant. **Family Matters:** Its mad popularity and cavernous Ferry Building location mean everyone comes to Slanted Door: tourists, hipsters, foodies . . . and sometimes even local families with kids. ⊠*Ferry Bldg., Embarcadero*

2

at Market St., Embarcadero ☎415/861–8032 ☜*Reservations essential* ▭*AE, MC, V.*

$$–$$$ ✕**Tadich Grill.** *Seafood.* Locations and owners have changed more than once since this old-timer started as a coffee stand on the waterfront in 1849, but the crowds keep coming. Generations of regulars advise that simple grills, sautés, and panfries are the best choices. Try the cioppino during crab season (November to May), and the Pacific halibut between January and May. Happily, the old-fashioned house-made tartar sauce doesn't change with the seasons. There's counter seating, a few tables, and private booths (complete with a bell to summon the waiter), and a long line of business types at noon is inevitable. The crusty, white-coated waiters are a throwback to another time, and the old-school bartenders serve up martinis as good as the mollusks. **Family Matters:** It's definitely *the* place to give older kids a taste of old San Francisco. ✉*240 California St., Financial District* ☎415/391–1849 ▭*MC, V* ⊙*Closed Sun.*

$$$–$$$$ ✕**Waterbar.** *Seafood.* When you walk in the door of Waterbar, there's no mistaking what's on the menu. The 200-seat dining room is dominated by sky-high aquariums filled with candidates—or at least cousins of candidates (the kitchen has its own aquariums)—for your dinner plate. Every fin and shell is sustainably sourced, so there's no guilt in sitting down to a plate of poached petrale sole, wood-oven-roasted striped bass, or seared haddock. Waterbar, like its next-door neighbor, Epic Roasthouse, is part of the steadily expanding empire of high-energy architect-restaurateur Pat Kuleto. Chef Parke Ulrich, who spent a decade at the city's celebrated seafood palace Farallon, dishes up the catch raw, cured, and cooked in dozens of ways, while nationally acclaimed pastry chef Emily Luchetti handles the sweet end of the menu. If you want to experience this watery world and not pay $50 for a whole lobster, grab a seat in the bar, where you can snack off the bar menu and take in the drop-dead bay view. **Family Matters:** Kids can choose from their own extensive menu, which also includes non-fish options such as grilled cheese and PB&J—in addition to fish-and-chips. ✉*399 Embarcadero (between Folsom and Harrison), Embarcadero* ☎415/284–9922 ▭*AE, D, DC MC, V.*

¢–$$ ✕**Yank Sing.** *Chinese.* This is the granddaddy of the city's dim sum teahouses. It opened in a plain-Jane storefront in Chinatown in 1959 but left its Cantonese neighbors behind for the high-rises of downtown by the 1970s. This brightly decorated location on quiet Stevenson Street (there's also a big, brassy branch in the Rincon Center) serves some of San Francisco's best dim sum to office workers—bosses and clerks alike—on weekdays and to big, boisterous families on weekends. The kitchen cooks up some 100 varieties of dim sum on a rotating basis, offering 60 different types daily. These include both the classic (steamed pork buns, shrimp dumplings, egg custard tartlets) and the creative (scallion-skewered prawns tied with bacon, lobster and tobiko roe dumplings, basil seafood dumplings). A take-out counter makes a meal on the run a satisfying and penny-wise compromise when office duties—or touring—won't wait. **Family Matters:** Either location works for kids, though Rincon Center has the added distraction of fountains and the cool WPA–era murals of California history. ⊠*49 Stevenson St., Financial District* ☎*415/541–4949* ⊟*AE, DC, MC, V* ⊙*No dinner* ⊠*1 Rincon Center, 101 Spear St., Embarcadero* ☎*415/957–9300* ⊟*AE, DC, MC, V* ⊙*No dinner.*

THE MARINA/COW HOLLOW

$$–$$$ ✕**Greens Restaurant.** *Vegetarian.* Owned and operated by the San Francisco Zen Center, this nonprofit vegetarian restaurant gets some of its fresh produce from the center's famous Green Gulch organic farm. Floor-to-ceiling windows give diners a sweeping view of the marina and the Golden Gate Bridge. Despite the lack of meat, hearty dishes like the Vietnamese yellow curry with cashew jasmine rice are designed to satisfy. Other standouts include thin-crust pizza with braised greens, sun-dried tomatoes, and three cheeses and fresh pea ravioli with saffron butter. An à la carte menu is offered on Sunday and weeknights, but on Saturday a $49 four-course prix-fixe dinner is served. Sunday brunch is a good time to watch boaters on the bay. A small counter just inside the front door stocks sandwiches, soups, and sweets for easy takeout. **Family Matters:** Greens attracts diners of all ages, from babies to grandparents. Brunch can be chaotic (which may dampen the sounds of unhappy babies); try for weekday lunch for a more relaxed meal. ⊠*Bldg. A, Fort Mason, enter across Marina Blvd. from Safeway, Marina* ☎*415/771–6222* ⊟*AE, D, MC, V* ⊙*No lunch Sun. or Mon.*

$$–$$$ ✕**Rose's Café.** *Italian.* Sleepy-headed locals turn up at Rose's for the breakfast pizza of ham, eggs, and fontina; house-baked scones and muffins; or soft polenta with mascarpone and jam. Midday is time for a roasted chicken and fontina sandwich; pizza with mushrooms, feta, and thyme; or pasta with clams. Evening hours find customers eating their way through more pizza and pasta, a sirloin steak, or maybe steamed mussels. Seating is in comfortable booths, at tables, and at a counter. At the outside tables, overhead heaters keep you toasty when the temperature dips. Expect long lines for Sunday brunch. **Family Matters:** Truly a neighborhood spot, Rose's welcomes diners of all ages (especially at breakfast, brunch, and lunch), so expect to see little ones you're not related to as well. ✉ *2298 Union St., Cow Hollow* ☎ *415/775–2200* ▤ *AE, D, DC, MC, V.*

RICHMOND

$–$$ ✕ **Katia's.** *Russian.* This bright Richmond District gem serves Russian food guaranteed to make former Muscovites smile. Order the deep-purple borscht, crowned with a dollop of sour cream. Small dishes of eggplant caviar, marinated mushrooms, blini and smoked salmon, and meat- or vegetable-filled *piroshki* are delicious ways to start a meal. Follow up with hearty beef Stroganoff, delicate chicken cutlets, or homey *pelmeni* (meat-filled dumplings in broth). If you can put together a group, make a reservation for one of Katia's afternoon tea parties, complete with sweets and savories and tea dispensed from a handsome samovar. **Family Matters:** This is a good spot for introducing the kids to Russian food, and you'll dine side-by-side with local families. ✉ *600 5th Ave., Inner Richmond* ☎ *415/668–9292* ▤ *AE, D, MC, V* ☉ *Closed Mon. and Tues. No lunch weekends.*

¢–$ ✕ **Pho Clement.** *Vietnamese.* The menu at this homey Formica-and-linoleum spot is big and remarkably cheap. You can order everything from sandwiches and salads to rice dishes and noodle plates. But the soups are what shine, from the two dozen varieties of *pho* (rice noodles in beef broth) to a dozen types of *hu tieu* (seafood and pork noodle soups). All of them are served in three sizes, small, medium, and large, with the sizes separated by just 50¢ and no bowl skimpy. Regulars, many of whom hail from Southeast Asia, favor the shrimp, fish ball, and pork slices soup with clear noodles and the special combo pho with rare steak, well-done brisket, tendon, and tripe. **Family Matters:** Even with small children, you'll feel comfortable at this family-friendly, neighborhood spot. ✉ *239 Clement St., Inner Richmond* ☎ *415/379–9008* ▤ *MC, V.*

$–$$$ ✕**Ton Kiang.** *Chinese.* This restaurant introduced the lightly seasoned Hakka cuisine of southern China, rarely found in this country and even obscure to many Chinese. Salt-baked chicken, stuffed bean curd, steamed fresh bacon with dried mustard greens, chicken in wine sauce, and clay pots of meats and seafood are among the hallmarks of the Hakka kitchen, and all of them are done well here, as the tables packed with local Chinese families and others prove. Don't overlook the excellent seafood offerings like salt-and-pepper shrimp, catfish in black bean sauce, or stir-fried crab, for example. Some of the finest dim sum in the city brings in the noontime rush (a small selection is available at night, too). **Family Matters:** The large space means there's no wait if you come off-peak. It's still a lively scene, and there's room for the littles to move around if they need to. ✉*5821 Geary Blvd., Richmond* ☎*415/387–8273* ▭*MC, V.*

SUNSET

¢–$$ ✕**Dragonfly.** *Vietnamese.* Refined Vietnamese fare draws droves of locals to this modestly decorated, bi-level restaurant each night. They return for intriguing dishes like rice and frogs' legs steamed in bamboo, fork-tender pork and egg in coconut juice, and crunchy lotus root salad. Even the rice offerings go beyond the ordinary, with four types offered: coconut, Hainan (cooked in chicken stock with ginger and garlic), white, or brown jasmine. Wash down the meal with one of three refreshing Vietnamese beers, and cap it all off with a cup of inky coffee. Lunchtime brings more casual dishes, including pho, rice plates, and noodles. The staff makes up for its inexperience and for the slow arrival of your order with a cheerful attitude. **Family Matters:** If you've got a hankering for Vietnamese fare but don't want to drag the kids to giant, crowded Slanted Door, Dragonfly gives that venerable restaurant a run for its money—and costs a lot less of yours. Plus, your family will be welcomed in this neighborhood spot. ✉*420 Judah St., Inner Sunset* ☎*415/661–7755* ▭*AE, MC, V.*

¢–$$ ✕**Park Chow.** *American.* What do spaghetti and meatballs, Thai noodles with chicken and shrimp, and big burgers have in common? They're all on the eclectic comfort food menu at Park Chow, and offered at unbeatable prices. This neighborhood favorite is also known for its desserts: fresh-fruit cobblers and ginger cake with pumpkin ice cream are standouts. In cool weather, there's a roaring fire in the dining room fireplace; in warm weather, get there early to snag an outdoor table. Up early? You can sit down to breakfast on weekdays and brunch on weekends. The original location is in the Castro neighborhood. **Family Matters:** Chow is definitely a top pick among local families. ⊠*1240 9th Ave., Inner Sunset* ☎*415/665–9912* ▭*MC, V.*

$–$$ ✕**San Tung.** *Chinese.* Many of the best chefs in Beijing's imperial kitchens hailed from China's northeastern province of Shandong. San Franciscans, with or without imperial ancestry, regularly enjoy dishes of the same province at this bare-bones storefront restaurant. Specialties include steamed dumplings—shrimp and leek dumplings are the most popular—and hand-pulled noodles, in soup or stir-fried. Among the typical accompaniments are a salad of jellyfish, seaweed, or sliced cucumbers and a plate of cold, poached chicken marinated in Shaoxing wine. Parents and kids regularly fight over platters of dry-fried chicken wings. To get a table without a wait, come before or after the noon rush. **Family Matters:** This linoleum diner is a nice alternative to the busy spots along 9th Avenue after a day in Golden Gate Park. If you park in the park, walk here unless you have really good parking karma. ⊠*1031 Irving St., Inner Sunset* ☎*415/242–0828* ▭*MC, V.*

THE HAIGHT

$–$$ ✕**Indian Oven.** *Indian.* This Victorian storefront draws diners from all over the city who come for the tandoori specialties—chicken, lamb, breads. The *saag paneer* (spinach with Indian cheese) and *bengan bartha* (roasted eggplant with onions and spices) are also excellent. On Friday and Saturday nights, famished patrons overflow onto the sidewalk as they wait for open tables. If you try to linger over a *lassi* on one of these nights, you'll invariably be hurried along by a waiter. For better service, come on a slower weeknight. **Family Matters:** Best option: bring your teens after shopping the Haight, as soon as the kitchen opens. ⊠*233 Fillmore St., Lower Haight* ☎*415/626–1628* ▭*AE, D, DC, MC, V* ☺*No lunch.*

$–$$$ ✕**Nopa.** *American.* In 2006, North of the Panhandle became the city's newest talked-about neighborhood in part because of the big, bustling Nopa, which is cleverly named after it. This casual space, with its high ceilings, concrete floor, long bar, and sea of tables, suits the high-energy crowd of young suits and neighborhood residents that fills it every night.

They come primarily for the rustic fare, like an irresistible flatbread topped with bacon, caramelized leeks, and cheese; duck with *farro* (an ancient cereal grain similar to wheat) and vegetables; smoky, crisp-skinned rotisserie chicken; and a juicy grass-fed hamburger with thick-cut fries; and pecan pie with salted-caramel ice cream. But they also love the lively spirit of the place. Unfortunately, that buzz sometimes means raised voices are the only way to communicate with fellow diners. **Family Matters:** That makes Nopa a great choice for families—if parents can handle the hipster vibe. ✉*560 Divisidero St., Haight* ☎*415/864–8643* ▭*MC, V* ⊗*No lunch.*

¢–$$ ✕**Poleng Lounge.** *Asian.* At once a restaurant, nightclub, and tearoom, this captivating space hosts a young, diverse crowd that is happy to graze on Poleng's two dozen modern pan-Asian small plates. The food delivers a satisfying mix that keeps you ordering more: panfried vegetable-filled dumplings dusted with green tea powder, spicy-sweet adobo chicken wings, crab noodles, and crispy salt-and-pepper squid with green chili sauce. No one goes thirsty here, with dozens of cocktails, teas (including alcohol-infused teas), sakes, and wines to choose from. The dining space, with a communal table, batik accents, and water gently flowing down a limestone-tile wall, is comfortably separated from the nightclub, which doesn't tune up until 10. **Family Matters:** Grab a table when the doors open at 4 PM and you'll have quick service and time to get some yummy food before the happy-hour crowd arrives; dinner service officially begins at 5:30, but the appetizer offerings are solid. ✉*1751 Fulton St., Haight* ☎*415/441–1751* ▭*MC, V* ⊗*Closed Mon. No lunch.*

$–$$ ✕**Thep Phanom.** *Thai.* Long ago, local food critics and restaurant-goers began singing the praises of Thep Phanom. The tune hasn't stopped, except for an occasional sour note on rising prices. Duck is deliciously prepared in several ways—atop a mound of spinach, in a fragrant curry, minced for salad. Seafood (in various guises) is another specialty, along with warm eggplant salad, stuffed chicken wings, spicy beef salad, fried quail, and rich Thai curries. The lengthy regular menu is supplemented by a list of daily specials, which makes it only harder to make a decision. At least you'll be pondering your choices in comfortable surroundings: the cozy dining room is lined with Thai art and artifacts that owner Pathama Parikanont has collected over the years. **Family Matters:** Though it's more elegant (and more expensive) than your typical Thai joint, Thep Phanom is a great splurge with kids who love Thai food—especially if you arrive at 5:30 and can slip right in. ✉*400 Waller St., Lower Haight* ☎*415/431–2526* ▭*AE, D, DC, MC, V* ⊗*No lunch.*

THE CASTRO

$$–$$$$ ✕**2223 Restaurant.** *American.* Slip into the urbane 2223 on Tuesday when every main course is just 12 bucks. The menu changes seasonally, with tandoori-spiced salmon with squash curry, herb-roasted chicken with garlic mashed potatoes, and a luscious sour-cherry bread pudding among possible offerings. For its popular Sunday brunch, the restaurant spins out old favorites like buttermilk pancakes and cinnamon French toast with caramelized bananas with a light touch, so you won't be tempted to slink back to your hotel for a nap. **Family Matters:** With young ones, brunch offers the benefit of yummy, kid-friendly dishes, a lively room, and electricity instead of candlelight. ✉*2223 Market St., Castro* ☎*415/431–0692* ▭*AE, DC, MC, V* ⊗*No lunch.*

$–$$ ✕**Chow.** *American.* Wildly popular and consciously unpretentious, Chow is a funky yet savvy diner where soporific standards like hamburgers, pizzas, and spaghetti and meatballs are treated with culinary respect. A magnet for penny pinchers, the restaurant has built its top-notch reputation on honest fare made with fresh local ingredients priced to sell. Salads, pastas, and mains come in two sizes to accommodate big and small appetites, there's a daily sandwich special, and kids can peruse their mini-menu. Because reservations are restricted to large parties, folks hoping to snag seats usually surround the doorway. Come early (before 6:30) or late (after 10) to reduce the wait, and don't even think about leaving without trying the ginger cake with caramel sauce. **Family Matters:** Along with its sister restaurant Park Chow, near Golden Gate Park, Chow is on every local parent's Top 10 list—a great place to bring the kids and relax. ✉*215 Church St., Castro* ☎*415/552–2469* ▭*MC, V.*

$–$$ ✕**Home.** *American.* If you're hungry for home cooking but don't want to stir the pots yourself, this big, noisy eatery is a good solution. Service can be sluggish, but the fresh, all-natural ingredients and classic fare compensate heartily. Happiest at Home are comfort-food seekers who dream of macaroni and cheese, corn dogs, sloppy joes with cole-slaw, Cobb salad, and meat loaf and potatoes. The lively Backyard Bar, a heated rear patio, roars until late in the night. On weekends, there are ham and eggs, brisket hash, and serious Bloody Marys for brunch-goers. Every night, the thrifty can sit down to the early-bird special—three courses and a glass of wine for $12—while the late-night crowd can dine until midnight. **Family Matters:** The dishes here are familiar enough to make kids happy and sophisti-cated enough to please grownups. Though you won't see many children dining here, the simultaneously trendy and friendly atmosphere makes this a decent choice for every-one. ⊠ *2100 Market St., Castro* ☎ *415/503–0333* ⊟ *AE, D, MC, V* ☺ *No lunch.*

NOE VALLEY

$$ ✕ **La Ciccia.** *Italian.* Chef Massimiliano Conti quickly won a loyal following after opening this charming neighborhood trattoria serving Sardinian food. The island's classics are all represented—seafood salad dressed with olive oil and lemon, seared lamb chops, pasta with *bottarga* (salted mul-let roe); and *fregola* (pebble-shaped pasta) with an aromatic tomato sauce—and recommended. The space came with a pizza oven, so Conti also turns out a quartet of respectable thin-crusted pies. Opt for one of the Sardinian gems on the large wine list. **Family Matters:** Given its Stroller Valley location and the graciousness of the ever-present owners, you'll be welcomed here if you have children—though the restaurant (and its clientele) is decidedly grown up. ⊠ *291 30th St., Noe Valley* ☎ *415/550–8114* ⊟ *MC, V* ☺ *Closed Mon. No lunch.*

THE MISSION

¢–$ ✕ **Angkor Borei.** *Cambodian.* Aromatic Thai basil, lemon-grass, and softly sizzling chiles perfume this modest neigh-borhood restaurant, opened by Cambodian refugees in the late 1980s. The menu includes an array of curries, salads of squid or cold noodles with ground fish, a crisp, pork-and-sprout-filled crepe, and lightly curried fish mousse cooked in a banana leaf. Chicken grilled on skewers and served with mild pickled vegetables is a house specialty, as are the green-papaya salad and the panfried catfish. Vegetarians will be happy to discover two full pages of selections. Service is friendly though sometimes languid, so don't stop here when you're in a hurry. **Family Matters:**

More elegant than your average ethnic eatery (though still accessible), Angkor Borei is a good lunch stop if you have kids in tow. ✉*3471 Mission St., Mission* ☎*415/550–8417* ▤*MC, V* ⊘*No lunch Sun.*

¢ ✕**Burger Joint.** *Burger.* Cross the threshold here and you're back in the days of sock hops and big Chevy sedans. Dressed in red and turquoise, with checkered floors and comfy booths, the retro Burger Joint serves Niman Ranch beef burgers, thick and creamy milk shakes, big root-beer floats, and crisp, stocky fries. Every burger comes with tomatoes, lettuce, onion, and pickles, a toasted sesame bun, and a pile of fries. Cheeseburger partisans can dress up their patties with American, cheddar, Swiss, or Monterey jack. Non–beef eaters can opt for veggie or chicken-breast burgers. **Family Matters:** Even the simplest palates and pickiest eaters will be happy with the reliably good fare here. ✉*807 Valenica St., Mission* ☎*415/824–3494* ▤*No credit cards.*

$–$$ ✕**Charanga.** *Latin American.* It's hard to resist the tropical vibe that weaves its way through this animated tapas depot, with its eclectic mix of Caribbean-inspired flavors. Some tapas stay true to their Spanish ancestry, like *patatas bravas,* which are twice-fried potatoes with roast-tomato sauce. Others, like fried yucca with chipotle aioli, are a mix of the Old and the New World, and some, like *picadillo* (Cuban-style minced beef dish studded with green olives and raisins) are firmly rooted on this side of the Atlantic. The dining room, with walls of exposed brick and soothing green, is small and friendly, so grab—or make—some friends, order a pitcher of sangria or a round of margaritas, and enjoy yourselves. **Family Matters:** The volume level means no one will be staring daggers at your kids, but the late-evening vibe turns decidedly hipster. ✉*2351 Mission St., Mission* ☎*415/282–1813* ⌕*Reservations not accepted* ▤*AE, D, MC, V* ⊘*Closed Sun. and Mon. No lunch.*

¢–$$ ✕**Dosa.** *Indian.* Like Indian food but crave more than tandoori chicken and naan? Dosa is your answer. This temple of south Indian cuisine, done in cheerful tones of tangerine and turmeric, serves not only the large, thin savory pancake for which it is named, but also curries, *uttapam* (open-faced pancakes), and various starters, breads, rice dishes, and chutneys. You can select from about 10 different *dosa* fillings, ranging from traditional potatoes, onions, and cashews to nontraditional cheddar, mozzarella, and onion.

Each comes with tomato and fresh coconut chutneys and *sambar* (lentil curry) for dipping. Lamb curry with fennel and potatoes and prawn coconut masala are popular, as are starters like Chennai chicken (chicken marinated in yogurt and spices and lightly fried), fried chile-dusted prawns, and mung sprout salad. The wine and beer lists are top drawer and both include some Indian labels. **Family Matters:** When the kids need to eat *now* but you want something more than a quick burrito, Dosa's a fine choice—it's one of the few good, sit-down spots in the Mission that always seems to have an available table. ⊠*995 Valencia St. at 21st St., Mission* ☎*415/642–3672* ⌕*Reservations only for five or more* ⊟*AE, D, MC, V* ⊘*No lunch.*

$$–$$$ ✕**Foreign Cinema.** *American.* Forget popcorn. In this hip, loftlike space, "dinner and a movie" become one joyous event. Classic and contemporary films like Fellini's *Nights of Cabiria* and Schnabel's *The Diving Bell and the Butterfly* are projected on a wall in a large inner courtyard while you're served oysters on the half shell, house-cured sardines, grilled squid with peppers and garlic, or steak with Argentine salsa. Fussy filmgoers should call ahead to find out what's playing and arrive in time for a good seat. Kids aren't forgotten, with celery and carrot sticks, pasta with butter and cheese, and two scoops of ice cream for just $7. The weekend brunch brings big crowds. **Family Matters:** Foreign Cinema is a dream come true—albeit a rather expensive one—for hipster parents. ⊠*2534 Mission St., Mission* ☎*415/648–7600* ⊟*AE, MC, V* ⊘*No lunch.*

¢–$ ✕**La Santaneca de la Mission.** *Latin American.* Lots of El Salvadorans live in the Mission, and here they find the *pupusa,* a stuffed cornmeal round that is more or less the hamburger of their homeland. It usually comes filled with beans, cheese, or meat—sometimes in combination—and is eaten with seasoned shredded cabbage. The kitchen at this friendly, family-run place also makes the more unusual rice-flour pupusa, as well as other dishes popular in Central America, including fried plantains, seafood soup, tamales filled with chicken or pork, *chicharrones* (fried pork skins), and yucca. Accompany your meal with *horchata,* a cooling rice-based drink flavored with cinnamon. **Family Matters:** You'll likely dine with El Salvadoran families at this neat and casual spot, where no one will bat an eye if your toddler needs to take a lap or two around the tables. ⊠*2815 Mission St., Mission* ☎*415/285–2131* ⊟*MC, V.*

$$–$$$ ✕ **Limón.** *Peruvian.* Cooks in Peru and Ecuador have long argued over which country invented *ceviche,* a dish consisting of raw fish marinated in citrus juices. Most diners at Limón would probably line up with the Peruvians after eating the myriad, delicious versions here (try the impeccably fresh halibut or prawn with red pepper varieties), all accompanied by yucca and corn, and prepared by chef-owner Martin Castillo. They also like the *empanadas* (flaky pastries filled with minced beef, olives, and raisins), the hearty *lomo saltado* (beef strips sautéed with onions, tomatoes, and potatoes), the *arroz con mariscos* (mixed seafood with saffron rice), and the crispy whole snapper with coconut rice. Choose from a list of Peruvian beers for sipping with your meal. **Family Matters:** Bustling and trendy at dinner, at lunch Limón is, well, bustling and trendy—perfect for a celebratory meal with older kids. ✉*524 Valencia St., Mission* ☎*415/252–0918* ▤*MC, V* ✆*No lunch Mon.*

¢–$ ✕ **Los Jarritos.** *Mexican.* A *jarrito* is an earthenware cup used for drinking tequila and other beverages in Mexico. You'll see plenty of these small traditional mugs hanging from the ceiling and decorating the walls in this old-time, sun-filled, family-run restaurant. At brunch, try the hearty *chilaquiles,* made from day-old tortillas cut into strips and cooked with cheese, eggs, chiles, and sauce. Or order eggs scrambled with cactus or with *chicharrones* (crisp pork skins) and served with freshly made tortillas. Soup offerings change daily, with Tuesday's *albondigás* (meatballs) comfort food at its best. On weekend evenings adventurous eaters may opt for *birria* (a spicy goat stew) or *menudo* (a tongue-searing soup made from tripe, calf's foot, and hominy). The latter is a time-honored hangover cure. Bring plenty of change for the jukebox loaded with Latin hits. **Family Matters:** Huge portions, low prices, and cheery service make this casual eatery a good stop in a less-traveled area of the Mission. ✉*901 Van Ness Ave., Mission* ☎*415/648–8383* ▤*MC, V.*

$–$$$ ✕ **Luna Park.** *American.* It's a tight fit on weekend nights in this clangorous American bistro in the trendy Mission District. The youngish crowd is here to sip mojitos and Long Islands and nosh on steamed mussels or goat cheese fondue with apple wedges. Most of the mains are homey—mac and cheese, barbecued spareribs with fries and slaw, grilled hanger steak—and easy on the pocketbook. An order of s'mores includes cups of melted chocolate and marshmallows and a handful of house-made graham crackers to customize the campfire classic. On weekends, a slew of popular brunch dishes are added to the weekday lunch list of salads and sandwiches. **Family Matters:** The menu definitely has its share of kid pleasers, and the volume level can reach playground intensity; it's a good family choice for lunch, before the mad dinner rush. ⊠*694 Valencia St., Mission* ☎*415/553–8584* ⊟*MC, V.*

¢–$ ╳**Ti Couz.** *French.* Big, thin, square buckwheat crepes just like those found in Brittany are the specialty here, filled with everything from ham to Gruyère to ratatouille to sausage to scallops. You can begin with a green salad, oysters on the half shell, a plate of charcuterie, or a bowl of soup. Then, order a savory crepe from the long list of possibilities—you create your own filling combination—and end with a divine white chocolate or chestnut crepe. Or, you can skip the sweet crepe and order a gelato doused with espresso or liqueur. The self-consciously rustic dining room—sturdy wood tables, mismatched cutlery, whitewashed walls—welcomes an eclectic crowd late into the night. A full bar serves mixed drinks, but the best—and the traditional—beverage is French hard cider, served in pottery bowls. **Family Matters:** Pretty much everything on the menu here is kid-friendly, and the casual vibe is just right for family dining. ⊠*3108 16th St., Mission* ☎*415/252–7373* ⊟*MC, V.*

PACIFIC HEIGHTS

$$–$$$ ╳**Florio.** *French.* San Franciscans have always had a weakness for little French bistros, which helped make Florio a hit from the day it opened. It had all the elements: a space that looked like a Paris address, classic charcuterie and roast chicken, and reasonably priced French wines. Since then, this neighborhood favorite has picked up an Italian accent, with ravioli stuffed with butternut squash lining up next to steamed mussels and *steak frites* on the menu. Save room for the kitchen's crème caramel, a neighborhood favorite. The room can get noisy, so don't come here hoping for a quiet tête-à-tête. **Family Matters:** The bistro itself is casual enough to bring older kids, though the Pac Heights crowd that dines here tends to leave the little ones at home. ⊠*1915 Fillmore St., Lower Pacific Heights* ☎*415/775–4300* ⊟*AE, MC, V* ⊗*No lunch.*

$$-$$$ ×**Vivande Porta Via.** *Italian.* The secret of how this quarter-century-old Italian delicatessen-restaurant, operated by well-known chef and cookbook author Carlo Middione, has outlasted many of its competitors is simple: authentic, carefully made trattoria dishes served by an engaged staff. The regularly changing menu includes simple fare at lunchtime—frittatas, sandwiches, pastas—and classier plates at night—prosciutto with figs, grilled Belgian endive wrapped in pancetta with lemon vinaigrette, fresh fettuccine with house-made fennel sausage, and risotto with shrimp and lemon. Counter seating lets you enjoy an antipasto and a glass of wine, or one of the excellent house-made desserts—lemon tart, cannoli, biscotti—and an espresso before or after a movie at the nearby Clay Theater. **Family Matters:** Casual and low key, this deli is a fine choice for lunch with the kids (though you'll pay restaurant prices). ⊠ *2125 Fillmore St., Lower Pacific Heights* ☎ *415/346–4430* ☰ *AE, D, DC, MC, V.*

JAPANTOWN

$–$$$ ×**Maki.** *Japanese. Wappa-meshi* (rice topped with meat or fish and steamed in a bamboo basket) is the specialty at this diminutive restaurant featuring the refined Kansai cuisine of Osaka and Kyoto. The sashimi, sukiyaki, and freshwater eel on rice in a lacquer box are also first-rate. Everything is served on beautiful tableware, from the smallest *sunomono* salad to a big lunchtime *donburi* (protein-topped rice). Maki stocks an impressive assortment of sakes, which it serves in exquisite decanters. If you don't know your sake, the helpful staff will lead you in the right direction. **Family Matters:** If your kids are Japanese-cuisine epicures, definitely bring them here. For neophytes, one of the less pricey Japan Center options is probably a better way to go. ⊠ *Japan Center, Kinokuniya Bldg., 1825 Post St., Japantown* ☎ *415/921–5215* ☰ *MC, V* ⊘ *Closed Mon.*

¢–$$ ×**Mifune.** *Japanese.* Thin brown soba and thick white udon are the stars at this long-popular North American outpost of an Osaka-based noodle empire. A line regularly snakes out the door, but the house-made noodles, served both hot and cold and with a score of toppings, are worth the wait. Seating is at wooden tables, where diners of every age can be heard slurping down big bowls of such traditional Japanese combinations as *nabeyaki udon* (wheat noodles topped with tempura, chicken, and fish cake) and *tenzaru* (cold noodles and hot tempura with gingery dipping sauce) served on lacquered trays. **Family Matters:** Pack some toys to distract the kids while you wait for a table, but once you're in you won't need them—this is definitely a place to fill up, not to linger. ⊠*Japan Center, Kintetsu Bldg., 1737 Post St., Japantown* ☏*415/922–0337* ▭*AE, D, DC, MC, V.*

¢–$$ ✕**O Izakaya Lounge.** *Japanese.* San Francisco has been hit by a mini-tsunami of *izakaya* spots, Japanese-style pubs where folks gather to drink and share small plates. The good-looking O Izakaya delivers that tradition plus big flat-screen TVs so that no one misses an inning. The walls are covered with oversize baseball cards, and seating is a mix of booths and tall communal tables. The menu is a wild ride of noodles (soba, yam), skewers (pork belly, hamachi belly, chicken), tempura, dumplings, salads, raw and cooked fish—even burgers. Sake aficionados will find plenty to choose from, including a trio of flights, plus there's lots of beer, *shochu* (a distilled spirit made from sweet potato, rice, or barley; similar to vodka), and cocktail choices to ensure no one goes thirsty. **Family Matters:** The more boisterous tables by the TV-lined bar offer both distraction and volume, perfect for families with younger kids. ⊠*1625 Post St., in the Hotel Kabuki,Japantown* ☏*415/614–5431* ▭*AE, D, DC, MC, V* ⊙*No lunch weekdays.*

$$–$$$ ✕**Yoshi's.** *Japanese.* San Franciscans were long envious of Oakland jazz lovers who had Yoshi's restaurant and nationally known jazz club at their doorstep. But with the 2007 opening of Yoshi's in San Francisco's slowly rising jazz district on the edge of Japantown, that envy quickly became history. While talented musicians do their thing in a separate space, the equally talented chef Shotaro Kamio serves some of the city's finest—and priciest—Japanese food: exquisite sashimi, memorable robata, crisp tempura, exotic maki-sushi (rolls), pristine nigiri sushi. A wood-burning oven delivers an unforgettable big-eye red snapper, a tender rib eye, cedar paper–wrapped vegetables, and more. The big, handsome restaurant harbors stylish booths, a sushi bar, small tables, a tatami room, a mezzanine lounge, and a bar, ensuring a comfortable perch for every diner. **Family Matters:** Sunday at 2 the jazz club hosts a kids' matinee, with world-class jazz and kid-friendly meals. Kids' tickets are a steal at $5. ⊠*1300 Fillmore St., Japantown* ☏*415/655–5600* ▭*AE, D, C, MC, V* ⊙*No lunch.*

Where to Stay

WORD OF MOUTH

"I personally feel like the Clift, location wise, is better than anything on Nob Hill. Remember, the Fairmont is on top of a hill so anywhere you go on foot means that you are inevitably going to be walking two to three blocks UPHILL back to the hotel. If you are not used to the hills, this could be an issue —it was for some of my guests. The Clift is also closer to the many public transportation options near Union Square."

—SanFrancisco Native

Updated
by Denise
M. Leto

SAN FRANCISCO IS ONE OF the country's best hotel towns, offering a rich selection of properties that satisfy most tastes and budgets. Whether you're seeking a cozy inn, a kitschy motel, a chic boutique, or a grande dame hotel, this city has got the perfect room for you.

Now is a great time to go: upgrades and renovations are taking place at properties throughout the city. Ritz-Carlton just finished a $12.5 million renovation, W Hotel is undergoing an extensive update, the Palace is planning a 60-story condo tower, and the new Intercontinental just opened its doors near Moscone Center. Both new and established properties are trending toward the eco-friendly, and San Francisco hotels are "going green" in a big way. Although the Orchard Garden boasts San Francisco's first all-new green construction, the Ritz-Carlton and many other local properties are installing ecological upgrades. Most of the city's hotels are nonsmoking—or will be soon.

Wherever you stay, be sure to ask what's included in your room rate. And when you settle into your perfect room, remember this tip: When in doubt, ask the concierge. This holds true for almost any request, whether you have special needs or burning desires (if anyone can get you tickets to a sold-out show or reservations at a fully booked restaurant, it's the concierge). You'll likely be impressed by the lengths hoteliers are willing to go to please their guests.

FAMILY TRAVEL

San Francisco has gone to great lengths to attract family vacationers, and hotels have followed the family-friendly trend. Some properties provide diversions like in-room video games; others have suites with kitchenettes and fold-out sofa beds. Most full-service San Francisco hotels provide roll-away beds, babysitting, and stroller rentals, but be sure to make arrangements when booking the room, not when you arrive.

RESERVATIONS

Reservations are always advised, especially during the peak seasons—May through October and weekends in December. The San Francisco Convention and Visitors Bureau publishes a free lodging guide with a map and listings of San Francisco and Bay Area hotels. You can reserve a room, by phone or via the Internet, at more than 60 bureau-recommended hotels. San Francisco Reservations, in business since 1986, can arrange reservations at more than 200 Bay Area hotels, often at special discounted rates. Hotellocators.com also offers online and phone-in reservations at special rates.

Booking: **Hotellocators.com** (☎*800/576–0003* 🖳*858/581–1730* ⊕*www.hotellocators.com*). **San Francisco Convention and Visitors Bureau** (☎*415/391–2000 general information, 415/283–0177, 888/782–9673 lodging service* ⊕*www.sfvisitor.org*). **San Francisco Reservations** (☎*800/677–1500* ⊕*www.hotelres.com*). **Bed & Breakfast San Francisco** (☎*415/899–0060* ⊕*www.bbsf.com*).

PARKING

Several properties on Lombard Street and in the Civic Center area have free parking (but not always in a covered garage). Hotels in the Union Square and Nob Hill areas almost invariably charge $23–$50+ per day for a spot in their garages. Some hotel package deals include parking. Some bed-and-breakfasts have limited free parking available, but many don't and require you to park on the street. Depending on the neighborhood and the time, this can be easy or difficult, so ask for realistic parking information when you call. Some hotels with paid parking offer a choice of valet parking with unlimited in-out privileges or self-parking (where the fee is less expensive and there's no tipping).

FACILITIES

In each review, we list what facilities are available, but we don't specify whether they cost extra. When pricing accommodations, always ask what's included and what entails an additional charge. All the hotels listed have private baths, central heating, and private phones unless otherwise noted. Many places don't have air-conditioning, but you probably won't need it. Even in September and October, when the city sees its warmest days, the temperature rarely climbs above 70°F.

Many hotels now have wireless Internet (Wi-Fi) available, although it's not always free. Larger hotels often have video- or high-speed checkout capability, and many can arrange babysitting. Pools are a rarity, but most properties have gyms or health clubs, and sometimes full-scale spas; hotels without facilities usually have arrangements for guests at nearby gyms, sometimes for a fee.

PRICES

San Francisco hotel prices, among the highest in the United States, may come as an unpleasant surprise. Weekend rates for double rooms in high season average about $132 a night citywide. Rates may vary widely according to room availability; always inquire about special rates and packages when making reservations; call the property directly, but also check its Web site and try Internet booking agencies.

The lodgings we list are the cream of the crop in each price category. Assume that prices are based on the European Plan (EP, with no meals) unless we specify that hotels operate on the Continental Plan (CP, with a continental breakfast), Breakfast Plan (BP, with a full breakfast), Modified American Plan (MAP, with breakfast and dinner), or the Full American Plan (FAP, with all meals).

WHAT IT COSTS				
¢	$	$$	$$$	$$$$
under $90	$90–$149	$150–$199	$200–$250	over $250

Prices are for two people in a standard double room in high season, excluding 14% tax.

CIVIC CENTER/VAN NESS

$$$ 🌐**Hotel Kabuki.** This pagoda-style hotel is next door to Japantown and two blocks from Fillmore Street and Pacific Heights. Rooms are located in the tower and the garden wing, which has a traditional Japanese garden and waterfall. Japanese-style rooms have futon beds with tatami mats, whereas the Western variety have traditional beds. All rooms are decorated with gorgeous Asian furniture and original artwork, and most have their own soaking rooms, which come with a bucket, stool, and a Japanese-style tub (1 foot deeper than Western tubs). The O Izakaya Lounge serves breakfast and dinner daily, and the bar hosts karaoke on some nights. A club level offers complimentary breakfast as well as free appetizers and cocktails during happy hour. **Pros:** Japanese style, serene environment. **Cons:** Popular with the business crowd. **Family Matters:**Family suites bring together Japanese and Western styles: parents have a traditional king-size bed, and the kids get their own futons and tatami mats behind a shoji screen. Little ones will be entranced by the hotel's koi ponds. ✉1625 Post St., at

TOP 5 FAMILY HOTELS

Cow Hollow Motor Inn & Suites: With rooms as big as apartments—including fully loaded kitchens—you'll be tempted to stay in. But then you'd miss Cow Hollow's lively street scene, great restaurants, and fun, fancy shopping.

Westin St. Francis, Union Square: This pedigreed hotel has it all: a cool welcome kit for the children; fine, kid-friendly dining at Michael Mina; a scandalous history; and a prime spot directly on Union Square.

Omni San Francisco Hotel, Financial District: Splurge on a family suite here and the kids will have bunk beds and stylish kids' furniture in their own room, where they

can watch movies and explore their welcome goodies while you enjoy your own private attached room.

Hilton San Francisco, Financial District: One of the few downtown hotels with an outdoor swimming pool, the Hilton has crazy-fantastic views and urbane dining for the grownups, and a library full of games and toys for its lucky young guests.

Seal Rock Inn, Lincoln Park: Get away from it all on the city's Western Shoreline, where you can enjoy the beach, stunning coastal views, and the hotel's pool, Ping-Pong table, and badminton court.

Laguna St., Japantown ☎*415/922–3200 or 800/533–4567* 🖷*415/921–0417* ⊕*www.jdvhotels.com* 🛏*204 rooms, 14 suites* ⊘*In-room: Internet, Wi-Fi. In-hotel: restaurant, bar, gym, laundry service, Internet terminal, parking (paid), no-smoking rooms* ⊟*AE, D, DC, MC, V.*

$–$$ 🖼 **Seal Rock Inn.** About as far west as you can go in San Francisco without falling into the Pacific, this hotel within easy walking distance of the Cliff House and Ocean Beach is a welcome refuge from the hubbub of downtown. A recreation area with a small pool, Ping-Pong table, and badminton court—plus large rooms with accordion-style dividers separating a queen bed from two twins—makes it a good choice for families with kids. Recent improvements include two ADA–compliant rooms, new furniture and mattresses, renovated bathrooms, and a new patio. Second-story rooms enjoy ocean views, some have kitchenettes, and a little restaurant serves breakfast and lunch. **Pros:** Close to the beach, lots of activities for kids. **Cons:** No air-conditioning, no pets allowed. **Family Matters:**Neighborhood families like breakfast (and lunch) at the on-site restaurant; another option is taking the kids across the street—and back to the 1970s—to Louies' Restaurant. Just a block away you can enjoy breathtaking views and give the kids room to run at Sutro Heights Park; look for the lion statue marking the entrance. ⊠*545 Point Lobos Ave., Lincoln Park* ☎*415/752–8000 or 888/732–5762* ⊟*415/752–6034* ⊕*www.sealrockinn.com* ⇄*27 rooms* ⌂*In-room: no a/c, kitchen (some), refrigerator, Internet. In-hotel: restaurant, pool, parking (free), no-smoking rooms* ⊟*AE, DC, MC, V* ⦿*EP.*

FINANCIAL DISTRICT

$$$ 🍸**Hilton San Francisco Financial District.** A $45 million transformation has taken place at this stylish, luxurious hotel adjacent to Chinatown and the Financial District. The lobby's minimalist decor has a distinctly Asian flavor, while the Grille at Seven Fifty offers a regional twist on comfort food. For personal pampering, sample the Tru day spa which provides a range of packages. Tastefully decorated, airy rooms come with blond wood Signature Serenity beds, Wi-Fi, flat-screen TVs, and large work desks with ergonomic chairs. **Pros:** Abundant parking, bay and city views. **Cons:** Congested area. **Family Matters:** In the kids' column, the best thing about this hotel is its Chinatown location, directly above the hustle and bustle (and playground) of Portsmouth Square. ⊠*750 Kearny St., Financial District* ☎*415/433–6600* ⊟*415/765–7891* ⊕*www.sanfranciscohiltonhotel.com* ⇄*549 rooms, 7 suites* ⌂*In room: safe, Internet, Wi-Fi. In-hotel: room service, bar, laundry service, parking (paid)* ⊟*AE, D, DC, MC, V* ⦿*BP.*

$$$$ 🍸**Hyatt Regency.** This seminal 20-story gray concrete structure—designed by influential architect John Portman, who launched the trend toward indoor–outdoor hotel environments—is the focal point of the Embarcadero Center, where more than 100 shops and restaurants cater to the Financial District. The spectacular 17-story atrium lobby (listed by Guinness World Records as the largest hotel lobby in the world) is a marvel, with water elements, sprawling trees, a shimmering stream, a huge fountain, and a sleek bar. All rooms have city or bay views; 134 come with bay-view balconies. (At this writing, renovation of suites on the top two floors were expected to be completed by early 2009.) The Ferry Building—a hub of activity, great

shopping, excellent eateries, and a burgeoning weekend farmers' market—is a short walk away. **Pros:** Convenient location, elegant modernist design. **Cons:** Some may find it cool rather than cozy, geared toward business travelers. **Family Matters:** Though you won't find any special services or programs for children here—the majority of guests here are businesspeople—the hotel's location near the Embarcadero and on top of public transit makes it a good choice for families with older kids. ⊠*5 Embarcadero Center, Embarcadero* ☎*415/788–1234 or 888/591–1234* ☎*415/398–2567* ⊕*sanfranciscoregency.hyatt.com* ⇩*802 rooms, 51 suites* ⌂*In-room: safe, Internet, Wi-Fi. In-hotel: restaurant, room service, bar, gym, laundry service, parking (paid), no-smoking rooms* ⊟*AE, D, DC, MC, V.*

$$$–$$$$ 🔲**Le Méridien.** Across Battery Street from the Embarcadero Center complex, this hotel (formerly the Park Hyatt) has completely renovated its lounge and lobby area (and has completed a style-makeover of its standard rooms and suites) in an effort to attract both leisure and business visitors. Australian lacewood paneling, polished granite sinks, stylish contemporary furniture, and fresh flowers outfit the spacious guest rooms. The in-room safes have interior outlets for recharging laptops and cell phones. The Park Grill serves excellent, high-end California cuisine, and the popular Bar 333 off the lobby has a Mediterranean menu and an extensive list of wines and other libations. **Pros:** Excellent service, ultraconvenient, spacious rooms, great views, top-notch concierge. **Cons:** New Age elevator soundtrack. **Family Matters:** No milk and cookies, welcome gifts, or kids' menus at this mostly business hotel—but the friendly staff will make you feel welcome, and you're likely to run into other families staying here. ⊠*333 Battery St., Financial District* ☎*415/296–2900* ☎*415/296–2901* ⊕*www.lemeridien.com/sanfrancisco* ⇩*351 rooms, 9 suites* ⌂*In-room: safe, Internet, Wi-Fi. In-hotel: 2 restaurants, room service, bars, gym, laundry service, Internet terminal, parking (paid), no-smoking rooms* ⊟*AE, MC, V.*

★ **Fodor's**Choice 🔲**Mandarin Oriental, San Francisco.** Two towers
$$$$ connected by glass-enclosed sky bridges compose the top 11 floors of one San Francisco's tallest buildings. Spectacular panoramas grace every room, and windows open so you can hear that trademark San Francisco sound, the "ding-ding" of the cable cars some 40 floors below. The rooms, corridors, and lobby areas are decorated in rich hues of red, gold, and chocolate brown. The Mandarin Rooms have

Chestnut St.
Lombard St.

Van Ness Ave.
Polk St.
Larkin St.
Hyde St.

RUSSIAN
HILL

Green St.
Vallejo St.
Broadway
Pacific St.
Jackson St

Leavenworth St.

Steiner St.
Fillmore St.
Webster St.
Buchanan St.
Laguna St.
Laguna St.
Octavia St.
Gough St.
Franklin St.

Broadway

PACIFIC
HEIGHTS

Alta
Plaza

Lafayette
Park

Washington St.
Clay St.
Sacramento St.

California St.

Pine St.

Bush St.

Sutter St.

Post St.

Geary St.

O'Farrell St.
Ellis St.
Eddy St.
Turk St.

JAPANTOWN

TENDERLOIN

Laguna St.
Gough St.
Franklin St.
Van Ness Ave.
Polk St.
Larkin St.
Hyde St.

Golden Gate Ave.

McAllister St. HAYES VALLEY

Alamo
Square

United Nations
Plaza

City Hall
CIVIC
CENTER

Fulton St.

Grove St.

9th St.
8th St.

0   1/2 mile

0   500 meters   Hayes St.

Andrews Hotel, **41**	Cow Hollow Motor Inn and Suites, **2**	Hotel Beresford Arms, **13**
Argonaut Hotel, **50**	Executive Hotel Vintage Court, **32**	Hotel Bohème, **48**
Best Western Hotel California, **14**	Four Seasons Hotel San Francisco, **21**	Hotel Del Sol, **3**
Best Western Tuscan Inn, **51**	Golden Gate Hotel, **36**	Hotel Diva, **39**
Campton Place, **29**	Harbor Court, **23**	Hotel Kabuki, **11**
Chancellor Hotel on Union Square, **33**	Hilton San Francisco, **16**	Hotel Majestic, **12**
Clift, **15**	Hilton San Francisco Financial District, **46**	Hotel Milano, **18**
Coventry Motor Inn, **4**	Hotel Beresford, **42**	Hotel Nikko, **17**
		Hotel Rex, **35**
		Hotel Triton, **28**

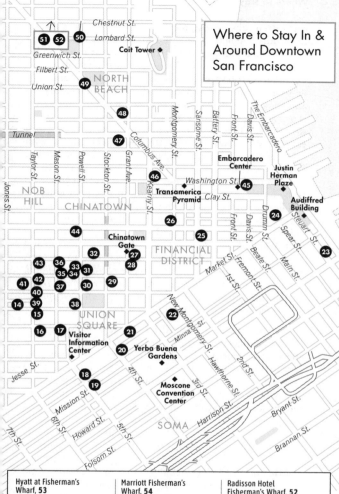

Where to Stay In & Around Downtown San Francisco

Chestnut St.
Lombard St.
Coit Tower ◆
Greenwich St.
Filbert St.
NORTH
BEACH
Union St.

Tunnel

Montgomery St.
Sansome St.
Battery St.
Front St.
Davis St.
The Embarcadero

Columbus Ave.

Embarcadero
Center

Justin
Herman
Plaze

Washington St.

Grant Ave.
Stockton St.
Powell St.
Mason St.
Taylor St.
Jones St.

Transamerica
Pyramid
Clay St.

Audiffred
Building

NOB
HILL

CHINATOWN

Kearny St.
Front St.
Davis St.
Drumm St.
Steuart St.
Spear St.
Main St.

Chinatown
Gate

FINANCIAL
DISTRICT

Market St.
Fremont St.
Beale St.
1st St.

UNION
SQUARE

Visitor
Information
Center

Yerba Buena
Gardens

New Montgomery St.
Minna St.
Hawthorne St.
2nd St.

Jesse St.

4th St.

Moscone
Convention
Center

3rd St.

SOMA

Bryant St.

Mission St.
6th St.
5th St.
Howard St.
Harrison St.
Brannan St.

7th St.
Folsom St.

Hyatt at Fisherman's Wharf, **53**
Hyatt Regency, **24**
Jackson Court, **8**
JW Marriott San Francisco, **37**
Larkspur Union Square, **34**
Laurel Inn, **9**
Le Méridien, **45**
Mandarin Oriental, San Francisco, **25**
Marina Inn, **5**

Marriott Fisherman's Wharf, **54**
Omni San Francisco Hotel, **26**
Orchard Garden Hotel, **27**
Orchard Hotel, **31**
Pacific Heights Inn, **7**
Palace Hotel, **22**
Petite Auberge, **43**
Pickwick, **19**
Prescott Hotel, **40**

Radisson Hotel Fisherman's Wharf, **52**
San Francisco Marriott, **20**
Seal Rock Inn, **10**
Sir Francis Drake Hotel, **30**
The Stanford Court, **44**
SW Hotel, **47**
Town House Motel, **6**
Travelodge at the Presidio, **1**
Washington Square Inn, **49**
Westin St. Francis, **38**

extra deep tubs next to picture windows enabling guests to literally and figuratively soak up what one reader called "unbelievable views from the Golden Gate to the Bay Bridge and everything in between." Pamper yourself with luxurious Egyptian-cotton sheets, two kinds of robes (terry and waffle-weave), and terry slippers. A lovely complimentary tea and cookie tray delivered to your room upon your arrival is one among many illustrations of the hotel's commitment to service. The pricey mezzanine-level restaurant, Silks, earns rave reviews for innovative American cuisine with an Asian flair. **Pros:** Spectacular "bridge-to-bridge" views, attentive service. **Cons:** Located in a business area that's quiet on weekends, restaurant is excellent but expensive (as is the hotel). **Family Matters:** Upon arrival your children will be greeted with their own backpack—perfect for toting crayons and paper around town—and a selection of kids' movies and video games. ✉*222 Sansome St., Financial District* ☎*415/276–9600 or 800/622–0404* ✉*415/276–9304* ⊕*www.mandarinoriental.com/sanfrancisco* ⤶*151 rooms, 7suites* ⌂*In-room: safe, DVD, Internet, Wi-Fi. In-hotel: restaurant, room service, bar, gym, laundry service, Internet terminal, parking (paid), some pets allowed (paid), no-smoking rooms* ▤*AE, D, DC, MC, V.*

$$$–$$$$ ⌕**Omni San Francisco Hotel.** Although the lobby's glittering crystal chandeliers, dark mahogany paneling, and iron-and-marble staircase may hark back to an old-fashioned gentility, this 1926 red-brick-and-stone building is home to a modern luxury hotel. Rooms have 9-foot-high ceilings with crown moldings and carved-mahogany furniture; sliding doors open to reveal bathrooms with marble floors and green-and-black granite basins. Daylight floods the corner suites, each of which has six tall windows. More expensive Signature Rooms offer extra amenities such as complimentary fresh seasonal fruit daily, bottled water, and assorted business tools including color printer-copiers and personal phone numbers. Bob's Steak and Chop House, more elegant than the name implies, is off the lobby. **Pros:** Outstanding personalized service, cookies and milk for the kids, immaculately clean. **Cons:** Some may find the air-conditioning inadequate, rooftop views are less than inspiring. **Family Matters:** Even if you don't opt for the luxurious family suite—with bunk beds and kid-sized furniture in a kids' room attached to a spacious bedroom for you—your kids will enjoy the toy- and book-filled suitcase and goodie bags they receive here. ✉*500 California*

St., Financial District ☎415/677–9494 🖷415/273–3038 ⊕www.omnisanfrancisco.com ⇝347 rooms, 15 suites ♿In-room: safe, DVD (some), Internet, Wi-Fi. In-hotel: restaurant, room service, bar, gym, laundry service, Internet terminal, parking (paid), some pets allowed (paid), no-smoking rooms ☰AE, D, DC, MC, V.

FISHERMAN'S WHARF/NORTH BEACH

3

★ Fodor's Choice 🏨**Argonaut Hotel.** When the four-story Haslett
$$$–$$$$ Warehouse was a fruit-and-vegetable canning complex in 1907, boats docked right up against the building. Today, it's a hotel with a nautical decor—anchors, ropes, compasses, and a row of cruiseship deck chairs in the lobby—that reflect its unique partnership with the San Francisco Maritime National Historical Park. Spacious rooms, many with a sofa bed in the sitting area, have exposed-brick walls, wood-beamed ceilings, and whitewashed wooden furniture reminiscent of a summer beach house. Windows open to the sea air and the sounds of the waterfront, and many rooms have straight ahead views of Alcatraz and the Golden Gate Bridge. Suites come with extra deep whirlpool tubs and telescopes for close-up views of passing ships. **Pros:** Bay views; bright, clean rooms; near Hyde Street cable car; sofa beds; toys for the kids. **Cons:** Nautical theme isn't for everyone, cramped public areas, service can be hit or miss, location is a bit of a hike from other parts of town. **Family Matters:** Your kids will be greeted with genuine warmth by a staff that knows all the fun kid options in town, from parks to classes. Kids will love the plush, animal-print robes so much you might have to buy one to take home. ✉495 Jefferson St., at Hyde St., Fisherman's Wharf ☎415/563–0800 or 866/415–0704 🖷415/563–2800 ⊕www.argonauthotel. com ⇝239 rooms, 13 suites ♿In-room: safe, refrigerator, VCR, Internet. In-hotel: restaurant, room service, bar, gym, laundry service, Wi-Fi, parking (paid), some pets allowed, no-smoking rooms ☰AE, D, DC, MC, V.

$$–$$$ 🏨**Best Western Tuscan Inn.** Described by some Fodors.com users as a "hidden treasure," this hotel's red-brick facade barely hints at the Tuscan country villa that lies within. Each small, Italianate room has white-pine furniture, floral bedspreads and curtains, a completely mirrored wall, and a newly refurbished bathroom. Complimentary beverages and biscotti are laid out mornings near the fireplace

in the oak-panel lobby, where a convivial wine hour is held nightly. There's free morning limousine service to the Financial District. Café Pescatore, the Italian seafood restaurant off the lobby, provides room service for breakfast. **Pros:** Wine/beer hour, down-home feeling. **Cons:** Congested touristy area, small rooms. **Family Matters:** Kids can grab a pizza or choose a meal from the kids' menu at the café, where the sidewalk tables make for great people-watching. ⊠*425 Northpoint St., at Mason St., Fisherman's Wharf* ☎*415/561–1100* ⎙*415/561–1199* ⊕*www.tuscaninn. com* ⇨*209 rooms, 12 suites* ⌂*In-room: Wi-Fi. In-hotel: restaurant, room service, bar, laundry service, Internet terminal, parking (paid), some pets allowed, no-smoking rooms* ⊟*AE, D, DC, MC, V.*

$$ ⊞**Hotel Bohème.** This small hotel in historic North Beach takes you back in time with cast-iron beds, large mirrored armoires, and memorabilia recalling the Beat generation—whose leading light, Allen Ginsberg, often stayed here (legend has it that in his later years he could be seen sitting in a window, typing away on his laptop computer). Screenwriters toiling nearby at Francis Ford Coppola's dream factory, American Zoetrope Studio, as well as sundry poets and artists are frequent patrons. Rooms have a bistro table, two chairs, and tropical-style mosquito netting over the bed; bathrooms have cheerful yellow tiles and tiny showers. Rooms in the rear are a refuge from the noisy crush, especially on weekends. Complimentary sherry is served in the lobby. **Pros:** North Beach location with literary pedigree. **Cons:** Street parking is scarce, lots of traffic congestion, no air-conditioning. **Family Matters:** Be sure to book ahead: the few rooms that will accommodate a family of 4 get snapped up quickly. The hotel provides folding futons for smaller kids, who may enjoy the "campout" feeling of bedding down on the floor. ⊠*444 Columbus Ave., North Beach* ☎*415/433–9111* ⎙*415/362–6292* ⊕*www.hotelboheme. com* ⇨*15 rooms* ⌂*In-room: no a/c, Internet, Wi-Fi. In-hotel: no-smoking rooms* ⊟*AE, D, DC, MC, V.*

$$–$$$ ⊞**Hyatt at Fisherman's Wharf.** The location is key to this hotel's popularity: it's within walking distance of tourist hot spots such as Ghirardelli Square, the Cannery, Pier 39, Aquatic Park, and Alcatraz ferries; bay cruises dock nearby; and it's across the street from a cable-car turnaround. The double-pane windows of the moderately sized, predominantly nonsmoking rooms—which have flat-screen TVs and dark-wood furniture—keep out the considerable street noise. Each floor has a laundry room. In the North Point Lounge, a domed Tiffany skylight with a seashore motif crowns a large, comfy lounge area with a fireplace and fountain. The guest rooms, fitness center, and lobby have all been recently upgraded. **Pros:** Primo sightseeing location, close to cable car. **Cons:** Street noise, crowds. **Family Matters:** In addition to the frenzy of family-friendly activities in the neighborhood, the kids will enjoy the outdoor pool and indoor game room, complete with video games and Foosball. ⊠ *555 N. Point St., Fisherman's Wharf* ☎ *415/563–1234 or 800/233–1234* ☐ *415/486–4444* ⊕ *www.fishermanswharf.hyatt.com* ↪ *313 rooms, 8 suites* ⚐ *In-room: safe, refrigerators (some), Wi-Fi. In-hotel: restaurant, bar, room service, pool, gym, laundry facilities, laundry service, Internet terminal, parking (paid), no-smoking rooms* ⊟ *AE, D, DC, MC, V.*

$$$–$$$$ ▥**Radisson Hotel Fisherman's Wharf.** Directly facing Alcatraz, this city-block-size hotel and shopping area at Fisherman's Wharf has vast, unobstructed views of the bay. Contemporary rooms, most of which have water vistas, are decorated with cherrywood furniture and black-and-tan-striped drapes. Radisson's signature Sleep Number beds allow you to adjust the firmness of each side of the bed individually. A landscaped courtyard and heated pool are in the center of the hotel complex, which provides the closest accommodations to Pier 39 and baycruise docks. **Pros:** Good views, close to Pier 39 and docks. **Cons:** Touristy area. **Family Matters:** Your kids won't lack for company here: many families with children choose this hotel, and the entire area is crawling with little ones. Though the hotel lacks a restaurant, there are plenty of kid-friendly dining options in the neighborhood, such as the giant Boudin Sourdough Bakery & Café around the corner on Jefferson. ⊠ *250 Beach St., Fisherman's Wharf* ☎ *415/392–6700 or 800/333–3333* ☐ *415/986–7853* ⊕ *www.radisson.com/sanfranciscoca_wharf* ↪ *355 rooms* ⚐ *In-room: safe, refrigerator (some), Internet, Wi-Fi. In-hotel: pool, gym, laundry service, parking (paid), no-smoking rooms* ⊟ *AE, D, DC, MC, V.*

$$$ ▥**Marriott Fisherman's Wharf.** Behind the hotel's sand-color facade is a lavish, low-ceiling lobby with marble floors, a double fireplace, and English club–style furniture. Rooms—which are expected be fully remodeled by mid-2009—have either a king-size bed or two double beds; all are triple-sheeted, and the abundance of extra pillows allows for lots of luxurious lounging. One hundred rooms, designed with business travelers in mind, have an extra-large desk, ergonomic chair, speakerphone, and two data ports. Restaurant Spada serves breakfast and dinner, and lunch is available all day in the lounge. Complimentary limo service to the Financial District is available weekday mornings. **Pros:** Near tourist hot spots, comfortable bedding. **Cons:** Touristy area. **Family Matters:** Cribs and rollaways are provided for families in what is essentially a business hotel (despite the Fisherman's Wharf location). ✉*1250 Columbus Ave., Fisherman's Wharf* ☎*415/775–7555* ☎*415/474–2099* ⊕*www. marriott.com* ⟋*269 rooms, 16 suites* ♿*In-room: safe, refrigerator, Internet. In-hotel: restaurant, room service, bar, gym, spa, laundry facilities, laundry service, Internet terminal, Wi-Fi, parking (paid), some pets allowed (paid), no-smoking rooms* ☰*AE, D, MC, V.*

$–$$ 🏨 **SW Hotel.** Opened in 1913 as the Columbo Hotel, this lodging on the bustling border between Chinatown and North Beach has rooms and suites decorated in a blend of Italian and Chinese styles, with Florentine wall coverings and Ming-style furniture. Old-fashioned wooden Venetian blinds cover the windows, and baths have polished granite countertops. Top-floor rooms have nice views of Coit Tower and North Beach. Be warned: The smallest rooms have teensy closets and bathrooms, so ask for the most spacious accommodations available. A multilingual staff serves morning pastries and beverages in the mezzanine area. **Pros:** Top-floor views of Coit Tower, multilingual staff, self-serve parking under building. **Cons:** Cramped closets and bathrooms. **Family Matters:** The lack of public space to hang out with small kids means this well-located hotel is best for families with older children. Be aware that in addition to terrific restaurants and cafés, some of the neighborhood's strip joints and adult stores are nearby. ✉*615 Broadway, Chinatown/North Beach* ☎*415/362–2999 or 888/595–9188* ☎*415/362–1808* ⊕*www.swhotel.com* ⟋*105 rooms, 2 suites* ♿*In-room: no a/c (some), kitchen (some), Internet, Wi-Fi. In-hotel: Internet terminal, parking (paid), no-smoking rooms* ☰*AE, DC, MC, V* ⦿*CP.*

$$$ 🏨 **Washington Square Inn.** Overlooking the tree-lined park of its namesake and surrounded by fine shops and cafés, this gracious corner B&B sits at the foot of Telegraph Hill in the heart of North Beach. Both large and small rooms are individually decorated with Venetian and French accents; upgraded bathrooms are done in imported marble and tiles. Most rooms have gas fireplaces and beds with 400- to

600-thread-count sheets. The lobby, which has a gleaming mahogany fireplace and brass chandeliers, is the setting for free wine and antipasti in the evening. An expanded continental breakfast is served by the front windows. **Pros:** Nice rooms, fun location. **Cons:** Some guests complain about gruff management, no air-conditioning, street parking is difficult to come by. **Family Matters:** This grownup B&B is best for families with older kids; the least expensive rooms are quite small. A terrific breakfast awaits at Mama's, just down the street. ⊠*1660 Stockton St., at Filbert St., North Beach* ☎*415/981–4220 or 800/388–0200* 🖷*415/397–7242* ⊕*www.wsisf.com* ➲*15 rooms* ⊘*In-room: no a/c, Internet, Wi-Fi. In-hotel: restaurant, Internet terminal, parking (paid), no-smoking rooms* ⊟*AE, D, DC, MC, V* ⏀*BP.*

NOB HILL

$$ 🏨**Executive Hotel Vintage Court.** This Napa Valley–inspired hotel two blocks from Union Square has inviting rooms named after California wineries. Some have sunny window seats, and all have large writing desks, dark-wood Venetian blinds, and steam heat. Bathrooms are small; some have tub-showers, whereas others have stall showers. The Wine Country theme extends to complimentary local vintages served nightly in front of a roaring fire in the chocolate-color lobby, where long couches encourage lingering. For a superior gastronomic experience, book a table at the adjoining Masa's, one of the city's most celebrated French restaurants. **Pros:** Complimentary local wines. **Cons:** Small bathrooms, far from downtown and many tourist spots. **Family Matters:** In-room Nintendo and a cable-car stop across the street are big bonuses for families. ⊠*650 Bush St., Nob Hill* ☎*415/392–4666 or 800/654–1100* 🖷*415/433–4065* ⊕*www.executivehotels.net/vintagecourt* ➲*106 rooms, 1 suite* ⊘*In-room: refrigerator, Internet, Wi-Fi. In-hotel: restaurant, bar, laundry service, Internet terminal, parking (paid), no-smoking rooms* ⊟*AE, D, DC, MC, V* ⏀*CP.*

$$–$$$ 🏨**The Stanford Court.** A stained-glass dome and a sweeping 360-degree mural depicting scenes of early San Francisco and the gold rush dominate the lobby of this stately-but-comfortable Marriott-operated hotel. Rooms achieve understated elegance with a mix of English-country-manor-style furnishings accented with Asian artwork and accessories. Nice touches include 300-thread-count Frette sheets, plush robes, heated towel racks, bathroom TVs, and nightly turn-down service. The brand-new Aurea restaurant serves a seasonal menu and is casual enough to be kid-friendly. Complimentary coffee or tea is delivered to your room each morning upon request. **Pros:** Focus on comfort, classic elegance. **Cons:** Far from most popular tourist sights, some guests complain that rooms are small. **Family Matters:** If you have kids in strollers, the walk up steep Nob Hill may prove to be a challenge. Also be aware that crowded cable cars don't easily accommodate folded strollers. ⊠ *905 California St., Nob Hill* ☎*415/989–3500* 🖷*415/391–0513* ⊕*www.stanfordcourt.com* ⤳*393 rooms, 9 suites* ⌂*In-room: Internet, Wi-Fi. In-hotel: restaurant, room service, bar, gym, laundry service, Internet terminal, parking (paid), some pets allowed, no-smoking rooms* ⊟*AE, D, DC, MC, V.*

PACIFIC HEIGHTS, COW HOLLOW & THE MARINA

¢–$ 🖳**Coventry Motor Inn.** Among the many motels on busy Lombard Street, this is one of the cleanest, friendliest, and quietest—especially the rooms that don't face Lombard. The oak-paneled lobby is decorated with leather furniture and photographs of historic San Francisco, and the unusually spacious rooms have cheery yellow wallpaper, gold drapes, oak furniture, and well-lit dining and work areas. Many rooms have bay windows, and some on the upper floors have views of the Golden Gate Bridge. **Pros:** Clean, friendly, good value, lots of eateries nearby, free parking under building. **Cons:** Busy street, few amenities. **Family Matters:** The size of the rooms here is the big bonus for families. Cow Hollow and Marina shopping and dining are just around the corner. ⊠*1901 Lombard St., Cow Hollow* ☎*415/567–1200* 🖷*415/921–8745* ⊕*www.coventrymotorinn.com* ⤳*69 rooms* ⌂*In-room: Internet, Wi-Fi. In-hotel: parking (free), no-smoking rooms* ⊟*AE, MC, V.*

¢–$ 🖳**Cow Hollow Motor Inn and Suites.** Rooms at this large, family-owned modern motel are more spacious than average, with sitting-dining areas, dark-wood traditional furniture, and wallpaper with muted yellow, brown, and green patterns. Resembling typical San Francisco apartments, expansive rooms feature hardwood floors, Oriental rugs, antique furnishings, marble wood-burning fireplaces, big living rooms, and fully equipped kitchens; some have views of the Golden Gate Bridge. Huge, lovely suites, overlooking the eclectic mix of shops, coffeehouses, and neighborhood businesses on Chestnut Street, have one or two bedrooms and baths. **Pros:** Rooms are the size of apartments, covered parking under building. **Cons:** Congested neighborhood has a fratty feeling. **Family Matters:** Cook for the family in your own kitchen, or head out to one of the neighborhood's many kid-friendly eateries. ✉ *2190 Lombard St., Marina* ☎ *415/921–5800* 🖷 *415/922–8515* ⊕ *www.cowhollowmotorinn.com* ➷ *117 rooms, 12 suites* ⚿ *In-room: kitchen (some), Wi-Fi. In-hotel: restaurant, parking (free), no-smoking rooms* ═ *AE, DC, MC, V.*

$$ ⊤**Hotel Del Sol.** Go tropical in the Marina District at this colorfully restored three-story 1950s motor lodge. Summer barbecues by the courtyard pool and the hotel's proximity to Funston playground make this place kid-friendly, as do free toys, games, a "pillow library," and evening cookies and milk. Since the Del Sol is only two blocks from Union Street shopping and restaurants, with easy access off Lombard Street, it will please adults, too. **Pros:** Kid friendly, plenty of nearby places to eat and shop. **Cons:** Congested area, street parking is elusive. **Family Matters:** After the kids have taken a dip in the heated pool and played with the hotel's toys and games, they can check out the selection of family-friendly movies in the hotel's video library. ✉ *3100 Webster St., Marina* ☎ *415/921–5520 or 877/433–5765* 🖷 *415/931–4137* ⊕ *thehoteldelsol.com* ➷ *42 rooms, 15 suites* ⚿ *In room: kitchen (some), refrigerator (some), DVD, Wi-Fi. In hotel: room service, pool, children's programs (ages toddler–10), laundry service, parking (free), no-smoking rooms* ═ *AE, D, DC, MC, V* ⦿*CP.*

$$–$$$ ⊤**Hotel Majestic.** Built in 1902 as a private residence, this five-story white Edwardian building, the city's oldest continually operating hotel, turned into a residence club two years later—movie star sisters Joan Fontaine and Olivia de Havilland, symbols of Old Hollywood royalty, once lived here. Nicolas Cage, his uncle August Coppola, and the crew of *Sweet November* are among the more contemporary moviemakers who have visited the hotel's elegant lobby, appointed with antique chandeliers, plush Victorian chairs, and hundreds of antiquarian French books. Most rooms—which have either hand-painted, four-poster or two-poster twin beds—have gas fireplaces and claw-foot tubs. The hotel, which survived both of San Francisco's major 20th-century earthquakes, is legendary for its friendly ghost, the

newly renovated Café Majestic, and the largest collection of exotic butterflies in Northern California—on display at the café bar, where you can also order light fare. **Pros:** Quintessential San Francisco hotel, destination café, Victorian flavor, quiet neighborhood, perfect for a romantic getaway. **Cons:** You'll need a cab to get downtown or to tourist hot spots. **Family Matters:** This house of old-time elegance—best for older children—isn't in much of a walking neighborhood, so prepare to drive or take public transportation. ⊠*1500 Sutter St., Pacific Heights* ☎*415/441–1100 or 800/869–8966* 🖷*415/673–7331* ⊕*www.thehotelmajestic. com* ⌕*49 rooms, 9 suites* ♿*In-room: refrigerator (some), Wi-Fi. In-hotel: restaurant, room service, bar, laundry service, Internet terminal, parking (paid), no-smoking rooms* ⊟*AE, D, DC, MC, V* ⋈*CP.*

$$–$$$ 🖵**Jackson Court.** This B&B and time-share is a converted 1900 brownstone mansion on a tony residential block. Light, spacious rooms, some with fireplaces and window seats, blend antiques with contemporary furnishings and fresh flowers. An unusual hand-carved fireplace with gentle faces (said to depict the original owners) is the centerpiece of the parlor, where afternoon tea and cookies are served. The adjacent wood-paneled game room is stocked with local information, books, and games. Free continental breakfast served in the upstairs breakfast room can also be taken on trays back to your room or downstairs to the parlor. **Pros:** Pleasant residential area, games for the kids. **Cons:** No TV, no air-conditioning. **Family Matters:** Just two blocks away is Lafayette Park, where kids can get a workout hiking to the top and relax in the company of the neighborhood's pampered pooches. ⊠*2198 Jackson St., Pacific Heights* ☎*415/929–7670* 🖷*415/929–1405* ⊕*www. jacksoncourt.com* ⌕*10 rooms* ♿*In-room: no a/c, VCR (some), no TV, Internet, Wi-Fi. In-hotel: laundry service, no-smoking rooms* ⊟*AE, MC, V* ⋈*CP.*

$$–$$$ 🖵**Laurel Inn.** The blue-and-tan Googie-style facade of this stylish inn suggests its 1963 urban motel origins. Rooms, newly renovated and decorated in modern gray and bold primary blues, reds, and yellows, are spacious and clean; all have ceiling fans, some have desks and fold-out sofas, and 18 offer convenient kitchenettes. Adjoining rooms can be connected to create a kid-friendly suite. Accommodations in the rear have cityscape views and tend to be quieter. Day passes are available to the extensive exercise facilities at the Jewish Community Center of San Francisco, located

directly across the street. The young, hip G-bar cocktail lounge boasts the best martini in town. Diverse shops and restaurants are one block away on Sacramento Street. **Pros:** Clean, spacious, kid-friendly rooms, close to Sacramento Street. **Cons:** No air-conditioning, far from downtown. **Family Matters:** The location has two big family bonuses: the Presidio's Julius Kahn Playground—one of the best playgrounds in the city—is a few blocks north, and terrific brunch awaits at Ella's, just across the street from the hotel. ⊠*444 Presidio Ave., Pacific Heights* ☎*415/567–8467 or 800/552–8735* 🖷*415/928–1866* ⊕*thelaurelinn.com* ⇨*49 rooms* ⌂ *In-room: no a/c, kitchen (some), refrigerator (some), Wi-Fi. In-hotel: bar, laundry service, Internet terminal, parking (paid), some pets allowed, no-smoking rooms* ⊟*AE, D, DC, MC, V* ⍥*CP.*

¢–$ 🏨**Marina Inn.** Five blocks from the Marina, this four-story 1924 building feels like a B&B but is priced like a motel. English country-style rooms with vivid floral wallpaper and bedspreads are simply appointed with queen-size two-poster beds, private baths, small pinewood writing desks, and armoires. Some rooms have daybeds appropriate for a small child. The rooms facing Octavia and Lombard streets have bay windows with window seats, but they are noisier than the inside rooms. A simple continental breakfast is served in the central sitting room. **Pros:** Cheap, daybed option for kids. **Cons:** Street-side rooms are noisy. **Family Matters:** Ask for a rollaway bed or crib for your little ones; kids 5 and under stay for free. ⊠*3110 Octavia St., at Lombard St., Marina* ☎*415/928–1000 or 800/274–1420* 🖷*415/928–5909* ⊕*www.marinainn.com* ⇨*40 rooms* ⌂*In-room: no a/c, Internet, Wi-Fi. In-hotel: no-smoking rooms* ⊟*AE, DC, MC, V* ⍥*CP.*

¢–$ 🏨**Pacific Heights Inn.** One of the most genteel-looking motels in town, this two-story motor court near the busy intersection of Union and Van Ness is dressed up with wrought-iron railings and benches, hanging plants, and pebbled exterior walkways facing the parking lot. Rooms, with floral bedspreads and brass beds, are on the small side; however, about half have kitchenettes, and several units are two-bedroom suites. Two rooms come with special Duxiana beds, which are especially kind to weary backs. Morning pastries and coffee are served in the lobby, along with a free newspaper. **Pros:** Kitchenettes, reasonable rates. **Cons:** Small rooms, noisy, crowded parking area. **Family Matters:** Check out the surrounding neighborhood's myriad kid-friendly dining options when the kitchenette cupboards are empty. ⊠*1555 Union St., Pacific Heights* ☎*415/776–3310 or 800/523–1801* 🖷*415/776–8176* ⊕*www.pacificheightsinn.com* ⤳*35 rooms, 5 suites* ⚒*In-room: no a/c, kitchen (some), refrigerator, Wi-Fi. In-hotel: parking (free), some pets allowed (paid), no-smoking rooms* ▭*AE, DC, MC, V* ⦿*CP.*

¢–$ 🆃**Town House Motel.** This modest motel in the heart of the Marina District may lack luxury and atmosphere, but it makes up for its shortcomings in value. Rooms with contemporary blond-wood furniture, floral bedspreads, and plantation-style shutters have radios, irons and ironing boards, and hair dryers. **Pros:** Kids under 14 stay free. **Cons:** Bare-bones accommodations. **Family Matters:** In addition to great dining on nearby Union Street, the kids will enjoy walking to see the yachts docked next to Fort Mason (just a few blocks north), where they can also run around and watch the kites at the Marina Green. ⊠*1650 Lombard St., Marina* ☎*415/885–5163 or 800/255–1516* 🖷*415/771–9889* ⊕*www.sftownhousemotel.com* ⤳*23 rooms* ⚒*In-room: no a/c, refrigerator, Internet. In-hotel: parking (free), no-smoking rooms* ▭*AE, D, DC, MC, V* ⦿*CP.*

¢–$ 🆃**Travelodge at the Presidio.** Next to one of the entrance gates of the Presidio's woodsy national parkland is a terrific location for this freshly painted green and tan three-story motel. Rooms have blond-wood furniture and standard motel amenities such as coffeemakers. Resident manager Debra Hodges is friendly and informative, pointing out that there are "six bus lines within six blocks" of the hotel. **Pros:** Professional service, near public transportation and natural beauty. **Cons:** No frills. **Family Matters:** Stock the in-room fridge with snacks to take along to the nearby Exploratorium, Palace of Fine Arts, and the gorgeous parkland of the Presidio. ⊠*2755 Lombard St., Cow Hollow* ☎*415/931–8581 or 800/578–7878* 🖷*415/776–0904* ⊕*www.presidiotravelodge.com* ⤳*27 rooms* ⚒*In-room: refrigerator, Internet, Wi-Fi. In-hotel: parking (free), no-smoking rooms* ▭*AE, D, DC, MC, V.*

SOMA

★ **Fodor's**Choice 🆃**Four Seasons Hotel San Francisco.** Occupying
$$$$ floors 5 through 17 of a new skyscraper, this luxurious hotel, designated as the "heart of the city," is sandwiched between multimillion-dollar condos, elite shops, and a

premier sports-and-fitness complex. Elegant rooms with contemporary artwork and fine linens have floor-to-ceiling windows that overlook either Yerba Buena Gardens or the historic downtown. All have deep soaking tubs, glass-enclosed showers, and flat-screen TVs. Seasons restaurant serves high-end California cuisine, with a strong focus on seasonal and locally produced ingredients. Various packages offer focuses on art, shopping, and cooking. **Pros:** Near museums, galleries, restaurants, and clubs; terrific fitness facilities. **Cons:** Pricey. **Family Matters:** Parents of toddlers and young children will appreciate the baby-proofing service (call ahead), and kids of all ages will be tickled by the age-appropriate welcome packages. ✉ *757 Market St., SoMa* ☎*415/633–3000 or 800/819–5053* 🖷*415/633–3001* ⏛*www.fourseasons.com/sanfrancisco* ⮑*231 rooms, 46 suites* ⟐*In-room: safe, DVD, Internet, Wi-Fi. In-hotel: restaurant, room service, bar, pool, gym, spa, laundry service, Internet terminal, parking (paid), some pets allowed, no-smoking rooms* ▭*AE, D, DC, MC, V.*

$$–$$$ ▣**Harbor Court.** Exemplary service and a friendly staff earn high marks for this cozy hotel, which overlooks the Embarcadero and is within shouting distance of the Bay Bridge. Guest rooms are on the small side, but have double sets of soundproof windows and include nice touches such as wall-mounted 27-inch flat-screen TVs. Brightly colored throw pillows adorn beds with 320-thread-count sheets, and tub-showers have curved shower-curtain rods for more elbow room. Some rooms have views of the Bay Bridge and the Ferry Building. Complimentary evening wine and late-night cookies and milk are served in the lounge, where coffee and tea are available mornings. The hotel provides free use of the adjacent YMCA and free weekday limo service within the Financial District. **Pros:** Convenient location, quiet, friendly service, cozy. **Cons:** Small rooms. **Family Matters:** Your kids will receive a warm welcome and a welcome gift; after bathtime they can snuggle into fluffy KimptonKids leopard-print robes. Be sure to ask the concierge about nearby kid-friendly fun. ✉ *165 Steuart St., SoMa* ☎*415/882–1300 or 866/792–6283* 🖷*415/882–1313* ⏛*www.harborcourthotel.com* ⮑*130 rooms, 1 suite* ⟐*In-room: Internet. In-hotel: bar, laundry service, Internet terminal, Wi-Fi, parking (paid), some pets allowed, no-smoking rooms* ▭*AE, D, DC, MC, V.*

$$ ▤**Hotel Milano.** Adjacent to the new Westfield San Francisco Shopping Centre—whose tenants include Bloomingdales and Nordstrom—and close to many of the museums and attractions south of Market Street, this hotel is a shopping and culture maven's delight. The eight-story hotel's stately 1913 neoclassical facade gives way to a warm, stylish lobby with a large Alexander Calder–style mobile over the lounge area. Warm earth tones complement the spacious, attractive guest rooms, which have contemporary Italian furnishings. Too much sightseeing or shopping? Ease your fatigue in the split-level fitness center on the seventh and eighth floors. **Pros:** Good value, great location close to shopping/museums, comfy beds, responsive front desk, stylish arty environs. **Cons:** Lots of hubbub and traffic, air-conditioning is inconsistent. **Family Matters:** If your little ones are light sleepers, ask for a room on one of the higher floors. The downstairs Thai restaurant serves yummy, cheap food all day, and casual Café Venue is next door. ✉55 5th St., SoMa ☎415/543–8555 ≈415/543–5885 ⊕www.hotelmilanosf. com ➷108 rooms ⚘In-room: safe, refrigerator, Internet, Wi-Fi. In-hotel: restaurant, room service, bar, gym, laundry service, parking (paid), no-smoking rooms ▭AE, D, DC, MC, V.

★ Fodor'sChoice ☵**Palace Hotel.** "Majestic" is the word that best
$$$$ sums up this landmark hotel, which was the world's largest and most luxurious when it opened in 1875. It was completely rebuilt after the 1906 earthquake and fire, and the carriage entrance reemerged as the grand Garden Court restaurant. Today the hotel is still graced with architectural details that recall a bygone era, like chandeliers, tall mirrored glass doors, and eight pairs of turn-of-the-century, bronze filigreed marble columns supporting a magnificent domed ceiling filtering natural light; it's a refined environment ideally suited for the high tea served on weekends and daily during holiday periods. Rooms, with twice-daily maid service and nightly turndown, have soaring 14-foot ceilings, traditional mahogany furnishings, flat-screen TVs, and marble bathrooms. The wood-paneled Pied Piper Bar is named after the delightful 1909 Maxfield Parrish mural behind the bar. **Pros:** Gracious service, close to Union Square, near BART. **Cons:** Older design, small rooms with even smaller baths, many nearby establishments closed on weekends, west-facing rooms can be warm and stuffy. **Family Matters:** The fourth-floor indoor pool, beneath a glass ceiling, is a highlight for kids and adults alike; if you have a hard time tearing yourself away, you can order poolside snacks and refreshments. ✉2 New Montgomery St.,

SoMa ☎415/512–1111 *or* 888/627–7196 ⊞415/243–8062
⊕*www.sfpalace.com* ⇝*518 rooms, 34 suites* ⌂*In-room:
safe, refrigerator, Internet. In-hotel: 3 restaurants, room
service, bar, pool, gym, spa, laundry service, Wi-Fi, parking
(paid), no-smoking rooms* ⊟*AE, D, DC, MC, V.*

$$$ 🏨**Pickwick.** This terra-cotta-clad neo-Gothic hotel, built in
1926, is decked out with a can't-miss-it, seven-story corner
sign straight out of film noir. Next door to the Westfield San
Francisco Centre, which houses Bloomingdales and Nor-
dstrom, and convenient to Moscone Center, Yerba Buena
Center, and Union Square, the hotel caters to both business
and leisure travelers. Some rooms have flat-screen TVs.
Little Joe's offers Italian cuisine as well a traditional break-
fast and lunch. Courteous multilingual staff and 24-hour
concierge service offer welcome assistance. **Pros:** Multilin-
gual staff, helpful concierge, close to Metreon and Yerba
Buena District. **Cons:** Not as opulent as some other options.
Family Matters: Kids under 18 can stay in a room with
their parents for free, making this an especially good bar-
gain for the neighborhood (and one tight fit). ⊠*85 5th St.,
SoMa* ☎415/421–7500 *or* 800/227–3282 ⊞415/243–8066
⊕*www.thepickwickhotel.com* ⇝*186 rooms, 3 suites* ⌂*In-
room: refrigerator (some), Wi-Fi. In-hotel: restaurant, bar,
laundry service, Wi-Fi, parking (paid), no-smoking rooms*
⊟*AE, D, DC, MC, V.*

$$$$ 🏨**San Francisco Marriott.** The distinctive design of this
40-story hotel has been compared to a parking meter and
a jukebox. Inside, a five-story, glass-top atrium encloses a
dining court lush with palm trees, tropical plants, a cascad-
ing fountain, and a Starbucks in the lobby. Contemporary
cherry furniture fills the rooms, which have gold-and-orange
bedspreads and curtains. Several hundred rooms also have
writing desks and ergonomic chairs. The top-floor View
lounge has huge, fan-shaped windows with stunning views
of the city. Look for artwork by Richard Diebenkorn and
other major artists installed throughout the hotel, which
is close to the San Francisco Museum of Modern Art and
the Yerba Buena Gardens complex. **Pros:** Stunning views
from some rooms, in cultural district. **Cons:** Pricey parking.
Family Matters: The drinks and snacks may be pricey, but
it's worth a visit to the View lounge to enjoy the fantastic
vista over the city and the bay (mom and dad can enjoy
a cocktail while the kids play spot-the-landmark). ⊠*55
4th St., SoMa* ☎415/896–1600 ⊞415/486–8101 ⊕*www.
marriott.com* ⇝*1,498 rooms, 134 suites* ⌂*In-room: Inter-*

3

*net, Wi-Fi. In-hotel: 2 restaurants, room service, bars, pool,
gym, laundry service, parking (paid), no-smoking rooms*
=*AE, D, DC, MC, V.*

UNION SQUARE/DOWNTOWN

$ ⬚**Andrews Hotel.** Two blocks west of Union Square, this
Queen Anne–style abode began its life in 1904 as the Sultan
Turkish Baths. The lobby is dominated by a huge Elliott
grandfather clock and the original cage-style elevator.
Rooms and bathrooms are small, but well decorated with
Victorian reproductions, old-fashioned flower curtains
with lace sheers, iron bedsteads, ceiling fans, and large
closets. Complimentary wine is served each evening in the
lobby. Fino, the hotel restaurant, has been praised for its
pizza and spaghetti carbonara. **Pros:** Intimate, decor has
character, moderately priced. **Cons:** Smallish rooms and
baths. **Family Matters:** Considering the coziness of the
rooms, families will do well to choose one of the suites.
Breakfast magically appears in the hallway each morning,
a boon for parents with very little ones (a good idea: pack
your breakfast to go and head to more open spaces). ⊠*624
Post St., Union Square* ☎*415/563–6877 or 800/926–3739*
⬚*415/928–6919* ⊕*www.andrewshotel.com* ⮐*48 rooms,
5 suites* ♿*In-room: no a/c, DVD, Wi-Fi. In-hotel: restaurant, laundry service, Internet terminal, parking (paid),
no-smoking rooms* =*AE, DC, MC, V* ⦿*CP.*

$$–$$$ ⬚**Best Western Hotel California.** A highly polished mahogany
facade beckons you into the former Savoy Hotel, a 1913
building whose Western-style lobby with yellow-paned windows and oversize red leather chairs recalls Gold Country
hotels. Traditional and modern comforts abound, including
goose-down pillows and puffy featherbeds with 400-thread-
count sheets. Suites have parlor rooms with a sofa and chair,
a marble-top coffee table, and a large desk. Although all
rooms at this Best Western property have been updated with
amenities like flat-screen TVs and modern window shutters,
they can still feel a bit closed in; small, dated baths and tiny
closets add to this sensation. Complimentary afternoon
wine and cheese are served in the lobby, and the food at
the hotel's Millennium Restaurant is so delicious that it's
hard for many to believe that it's vegan (no meat or dairy).
Pros: Reasonably priced, just a few blocks from Union
Square. **Cons:** Somewhat dicey area—especially at night;
smallish dark rooms; tight baths. **Family Matters:** Opt for

a room away from busy Geary Street—less street noise will help the little ones sleep, and you'll save a few bucks to boot. ✉*580 Geary St., Union Square* ☎*415/441–2700 or 800/780–7234* 📠*415/441–0124* ⊕*www.hotelca.com/ sanfrancisco* ➦*70 rooms, 12 suites* △*In-room: safe, refrigerator, Wi-Fi. In-hotel: restaurant, bar, laundry service, Internet terminal, parking (paid), no-smoking rooms* ⊟*AE, D, DC, MC, V.*

$$$$ ⬚**Campton Place.** Aesthetic beauty and highly attentive service remain the hallmarks of this exquisite jewel-like, top-tier hotel. The pampering—from unpacking assistance to nightly turndown—begins the moment the doormen greet you outside the marble lobby, a spare, sophisticated, yet comfortable space furnished with cognac leather chairs and a corduroy couch. Fresh-cut orchids and Japanese floral arrangements, placed strategically throughout, bring natural beauty inside a hotel where you'll feel sheltered from the teeming crowds on the street. The hotel's atrium, rooms, and outdoor fitness terrace are flooded with natural light. Rooms can be small but are well-laid out and elegantly decorated in a contemporary Italian style, with sandy earth tones and handsome pearwood paneling and cabinetry. Limestone baths have deep soaking tubs; double-paned windows keep city noises at bay, a plus in this active neighborhood. If you're feeling flush, rent the Presidential Suite, which starts at $3,000 per night. The Campton Place Restaurant, whose new Indian chef serves French-infused contemporary cuisine at dinner, is famed for its lavish breakfasts. The lounge, where you can order from the restaurant menu if you so choose, is a popular cocktail hour hangout for the downtown crowd. **Pros:** Attentive service, first-class restaurant, abundant natural light. **Cons:** Smallish rooms, pricey (but worth it). **Family Matters:** Well-heeled families are regular visitors at Campton Place. Be aware that although the kids will receive a small gift upon arrival, the hotel is first and foremost a business property. ✉*340 Stockton St., Union Square* ☎*415/781–5555 or 866/332–1670* 📠*415/955–5585* ⊕*www.camptonplace. com* ➦*101 rooms, 9 suites* △*In-room: safe, Internet. In-hotel: restaurant, room service, bar, gym, laundry service, Wi-Fi, parking (paid), some pets allowed (paid), no-smoking rooms* ⊟*AE, DC, MC, V.*

$–$$ ⬚**Chancellor Hotel on Union Square.** Built to accommodate visitors to the 1915 Panama Pacific International Exposition, this busy hotel is considered by many to be one of the best buys on Union Square for comfort without extravagance. Floor-to-ceiling windows in the modest lobby overlook cable cars on Powell Street. The moderate-size Edwardian-style rooms, some with huge walk-in closets, have high ceilings and were recently remodeled. Though a bit dated, the small clean bathrooms have deep tubs—rubber ducky included. The pleasant Restaurant Luques serves American breakfast and lunch, and complimentary coffee, tea, apples, and cookies are available round-the-clock in the lobby. This is a completely nonsmoking property. **Pros:** Huge walk-in closets, great value for Union Square, clean rooms. **Cons:** Older building with dark hallways and rooms, small bathrooms, noise from cable cars. **Family Matters:** At some hotels families can squeeze into regular rooms, but this is one place where you'll be glad you opted for a suite (the hotel will strongly discourage you from bunking together in a regular room). ✉ *433 Powell St., Union Square* ☎ *415/362–2004 or 800/428–4748* ☎ *415/362–1403* ⊕ *www.chancellorhotel.com* ⬇ *135 rooms, 2 suites* ⌂ *In-room: no a/c, safe, Wi-Fi. In-hotel: restaurant, room service, bar, laundry service, Internet terminal, parking (paid), no-smoking rooms* ☰ *AE, D, DC, MC, V.*

$$$$ ⌐**Clift.** A favorite of hipsters, music industry types, and celebrities fleeing the media onslaught—security discreetly keeps photographers and other heat-seekers away—this sexy hotel, whose entrance is so nondescript you can walk right past it without a hint of what's inside, is the brainchild of Entrepreneur Ian Schrager and artist-designer Philippe Starck, known for his collection of eccentric chairs. The moody, dramatically illuminated lobby is dominated by a gigantic Napoleonic chair that could accommodate Shrek, with room to spare. This theatrical staging is enhanced by surreal seating options like a leather love seat with buffalo tusks and a miniature "drink me" chair, all surrounding a floor-to-ceiling, pitch-black fireplace. Spacious rooms—as light as the lobby is darkly intriguing—have translucent orange Plexiglas tables, high ceilings, and two huge "infinity" wall mirrors. Some visitors have remarked on the thin walls and advise booking a room on an upper-level floor to avoid street noise. The art-deco Redwood Room bar, paneled with wood from a 2,000-year-old tree, is known for its "beautiful people." Asia de Cuba restaurant prepares an artful fusion of Asian and Latino cuisines. **Pros:** Good rates compared to similar top-tier hotels in San Francisco, surreal moody interior design, ideal location for shopping

and theaters, close to public transportation, discreet and helpful staff. **Cons:** Some guests note thin walls, street noise. **Family Matters:** Upon arrival, some families are unpleasantly surprised by the additional per-person charge for each guest beyond two (even children) staying in one room, so be sure to confirm the total price when you book. Given the hipness quotient, most people save this one for adults-only time. ⊠495 Geary St., Union Square ☎415/775–4700 or 800/697–1791 ☐415/441–4621 ⊕www.clifthotel.com ⬅337 rooms, 26 suites ♿In-room: safe, DVD, Internet, Wi-Fi. In-hotel: restaurant, room service, bar, gym, laundry service, Internet terminal, parking (paid), some pets allowed (paid), no-smoking rooms ☐AE, D, DC, MC, V.

$ ☷**Golden Gate Hotel.** Families looking for accommodations in the Union Square area will delight in this homey, family-run B&B. Built in 1913, the four-story Edwardian has front and back bay windows and an original "birdcage" elevator that transports you to hallways lined with nostalgic historical photographs. Freshly painted and carpeted guest rooms are decorated with antiques, wicker pieces, and Laura Ashley bedding and curtains. Fourteen rooms have private baths, some with claw-foot tubs. Sit in the cozy parlor by the fire and savor afternoon tea and homemade cookies. **Pros:** Friendly staff, spotless rooms, comfortable bedding, good location if you're a walker. **Cons:** Only half of the rooms have private baths. **Family Matters:** At this warm and welcoming B&B, you may well meet other families. You'll certainly appreciate the genuine hospitality children receive here, as well as the hotel's charm. ⊠775 Bush St., Union Square ☎415/392–3702 or 800/835–1118 ☐415/392–6202 ⊕www.goldengatehotel.com ⬅25 rooms, 14 with bath ♿In-room: no a/c, Internet, Wi-Fi. In-hotel: Internet terminal, parking (paid), some pets allowed, no-smoking rooms ☐AE, DC, MC, V ☺CP.

$$$ ☷**Hilton San Francisco.** With 1,908 renovated rooms and suites, this is the largest hotel on the West Coast. Its silvery tower rises 46 floors to a penthouse event space with awe-inspiring 360-degree panoramic views that rank among the finest in San Francisco. Handsome rooms, many with balconies and superlative views of their own, are either in the original 16-story building or in the tower, which was built in 1971. Accommodations on the 44th floor afford the most stunning views of the city and the bay. Seventy-eight ADA–compliant rooms have roll-in showers. Thirty-five executive cabana-style rooms surround a

sheltered courtyard by an outdoor heated swimming pool and whirlpool. "Sight and Sound" guest rooms feature plasma televisions and a custom connectivity panels for digital cameras, iPods, and video downloads. In 2008, the hotel added 13,600 square feet of event space, a Starbucks, and a new restaurant. As the hotel is located near the dicey Tenderloin area, guests are directed toward Union Square (two blocks away) when venturing out on foot after dark. **Pros:** Super views, excellent service, full-service spa. **Cons:** Area is dodgy after dark. **Family Matters:** This is one of the few downtown hotels with an outdoor pool; when the kids are done swimming they can check out toys and games from the hotel's lending library. ⊠ *333 O'Farrell St., Union Square* ☎ *415/771–1400* 🖷 *415/771–6807* ⊕ *www. sanfrancisco.hilton.com* ⊅ *1,824 rooms, 84 suites* ♿ *In-room: safe, refrigerator, DVD (some), Internet. In-hotel: restaurant, room service, bars, pool, gym, spa, laundry service, Wi-Fi, parking (paid), no-smoking rooms* ⊟ *AE, D, DC, MC, V.*

$–$$ ⌧ **Hotel Beresford.** At this relatively inexpensive hotel less than two blocks from Union Square, a white wooden horse marks the entrance to the White Horse Restaurant and pub, an authentic reproduction of an English establishment. Well-maintained rooms with traditional furniture have clean, bright bathrooms. The friendly staff assists with sightseeing arrangements, and the front desk has a large video library. **Pros:** Reasonably priced, close to Union Square, friendly staff. **Cons:** No air-conditioning, no in-room Internet access. **Family Matters:** Kids under 12 stay free, so an already good deal gets even better. Two-bed rooms, while not as large as suites, are adequate for four people. ⊠ *635 Sutter St., Union Square* ☎ *415/673–9900 or 800/533–6533* 🖷 *415/474–0449* ⊕ *www.beresford. com* ⊅ *114 rooms* ♿ *In-room: no a/c, refrigerator, VCR (some). In-hotel: restaurant, bar, laundry service, Internet terminal, parking (paid), some pets allowed, no-smoking rooms* ⊟ *AE, D, DC, MC, V* ⦿*CP.*

$–$$ ⌧ **Hotel Beresford Arms.** Surrounded by fancy molding and 10-foot-tall windows, the red-carpeted lobby of this ornate brick Victorian explains why the building is on the National Register of Historic Places. Rooms with dark-wood reproduction-antique furniture vary in size and setup: junior suites have sitting areas and either a wet bar or kitchenette; full suites have two queen beds, a Murphy bed, and a kitchen. All suites have a bidet in the bathroom. Continental breakfast, afternoon tea, and wine are served beneath a crystal chandelier in the lobby. **Pros:** Moderately priced, suites with kitchenettes and Murphy beds are a plus for families with kids. **Cons:** No air-conditioning. **Family Matters:** You won't find a better deal on a suite with kitchenette in this neighborhood. ✉701 Post St., Union Square, ☎415/673–2600 or 800/533–6533 ☏415/929–1535 ⊕www.beresford.com ↪83 rooms, 12 suites ♦In-room: no a/c, kitchen (some), refrigerator, VCR, Internet, Wi-Fi. In-hotel: laundry service, Internet terminal, parking (paid), some pets allowed, no-smoking rooms ⊟AE, D, DC, MC, V ⊚CP.

$$$–$$$$ ☷**Hotel Diva.** Entering this hotel requires stepping over footprints, handprints, and autographs embedded into the sidewalk by visiting stars. With two major theaters, the Curran and Geary (home of the acclaimed American Conservatory Theater company), just across the street, this hotel has long been a magnet for actors, musicians, writers, and artists. It's definitely a hip place, and the updated rooms, especially the suites, feel urban and modern. A new digital movie system plays on flat-screen TVs. Cobalt-blue carpets and brushed-steel headboards echoing the shape of ocean waves lend a nautical touch to the white-walled rooms, which have silver bedspreads and sleek steel light fixtures. Bathrooms are tiny but well equipped. A Starbucks and Colibri Mexican Bistro are in the lobby. **Pros:** Clean, safe, in the heart of the theater district, accommodating service. **Cons:** No frills, tiny bathrooms. **Family Matters:** Children have their own check-in at the Diva, where they'll receive an iPod Shuffle to use during their stay. In the Kids' Suite, budding performers will find a karaoke machine, family movies, and a trunk full of dress-up clothes. ✉440 Geary St., Union Square ☎415/885–0200 or 800/553–1900 ☏415/346–6613 ⊕www.hoteldiva.com ↪115 rooms, 1 suite ♦In-room: safe, refrigerator (some), DVD, Wi-Fi. In-hotel: gym, laundry service, Internet terminal, parking (paid), some pets allowed (paid), no-smoking rooms ⊟AE, D, DC, MC, V ⊚CP.

$$$$ ☷**Hotel Nikko.** The vast gray-flecked white marble and gurgling fountains in the neoclassical lobby of this business traveler hotel has the sterility of an airport. Crisply designed rooms in muted tones have modern bathrooms with sinks that sit on top of black vanities and "in-vogue" separate showers and tubs. Look for gold drapes, wheat-color wall coverings, and ingenious window shades that screen the sun while allowing partial views of the city. The excellent, 10,000-square-foot Club Nikko fitness facility has traditional *ofuros* (Japanese soaking tubs), his-and-hers *kama-burso* (Japanese meditation rooms), and a glass-enclosed 16-meter rooftop pool and a whirlpool. Restaurant Anzu combines European and Japanese cuisines, and Executive Chef Barney Brown continually updates the menu. A multilingual staff provides attentive, sincere service throughout the hotel. **Pros:** Friendly multilingual staff, some rooms have ultramodern baths, very clean. **Cons:** Rooms and antiseptic lobby lack color, some may find the atmosphere cold, expensive parking. **Family Matters:** You might be surprised at the reasonable rates that are sometimes available for families, especially through the hotel's Web site. When the weather is harsh or the kids have had enough touring, take them to the lovely indoor pool, where you can also enjoy snacks and drinks. ⊠ *222 Mason St., Union Square* ☎ *415/394–1111 or 800/248–3308* 🖷 *415/394–1106* ⊕ *www.hotelnikkosf.com* ➫ *510 rooms, 22 suites* ⚴ *In-room: refrigerator, Internet, Wi-Fi . In-hotel: restaurant, room service, bar, pool, gym, laundry service, executive floor, Internet terminal, Wi-Fi, parking (paid), some pets allowed (paid), no-smoking rooms* ▭ *AE, D, DC, MC, V.*

★ Fodor's Choice 🖻 **Hotel Rex.** If this stylish literary-themed hotel—
$$ named after San Francisco Renaissance poet, translator, and essayist Kenneth Rexroth and frequented by artists and writers—had a kindred spirit, it would be *The New Yorker* magazine. Paintings and shelves of antiquarian books line the "library," a homey lobby lounge where book readings and roundtable discussions take place. Although the small, somewhat dark, cramped rooms with restored period furnishings and striped carpeting evoke the spirit of salon society—excerpts from historic San Francisco social registers paper the elevator—they also have modern touches like CD players, complimentary Aveda hair and skin products, and a study decorated with a collection of vintage typewriters (and two high-tech workstations). Some Fodors.com users have found the service inconsistent and noted that their rooms were unclean—but these problems may be remedied by the new GM, formerly of the chichi W Hotel. Breakfast, lunch, and dinner featuring California seasonal cuisine and local wines are served in the hotel's petite bistro, Andrée. **Pros:** Convenient location, literary pedigree. **Cons:** Cramped airless rooms, tiny baths and closets, musty hallways, some guests have experienced

inconsistent service. **Family Matters:** If your kids aren't inclined to sit still for a meal at Café Andrée, take them to casual Theatre Too Café, on the same block, for quick, delicious sandwiches and Mediterranean wraps. ✉*562 Sutter St., Union Square* ☎*415/433–4434 or 800/433–4434* 📠*415/433–3695* ⊕*www.thehotelrex.com* 🛏*92 rooms, 2 suites* ⚒*In-room: refrigerator, Wi-Fi. In-hotel: restaurant, room service, bar, laundry service, Internet terminal, parking (paid), no-smoking rooms* ⊟*AE, D, DC, MC, V.*

$$–$$$ 🏨**Hotel Triton.** The spirit of fun has taken up full-time residence in this Kimpton property, which has a youngish, super-friendly staff; pink and blue neon elevators; and a colorful psychedelic lobby mural depicting the San Francisco art and music scene—think flower power mixed with Andy Warhol. Playful furniture includes a green/gold metallic couch and striped carpeting, a whimsical and far-out setting for free morning coffee and tea, fresh afternoon cookies, evening wine events, and the on-call tarot reader. Smallish rooms are painted silver gray and tomato-soup red and come with ergonomic desk chairs, flat-screen TVs, and oddball light fixtures; sinks are positioned outside the bathrooms, European style. The hotel's ardent devotees, an eclectic group that includes CEOs, musicians, and Humboldt County hippies, feel right at home here. Fashion and entertainment industry regulars often request one of the celebrity-theme suites, named in honor of Carlos Santana, Jerry Garcia, and, yes, Häagen-Dazs; one was designed by Kathy Griffin for her Bravo TV show, *My Life on the D List.* Twenty-four "environmentally sensitive" rooms have water- and air-filtration systems and biodegradable soap. A 24-hour yoga channel will help you find that elusive path to inner peace. **Pros:** Attentive service, refreshingly funky atmosphere, hip arty environs, good location. **Cons:** Rooms and baths are on the small side. **Family Matters:**In addition to its fun vibe, the Triton has the added advantage of being less than a block from the Chinatown gate—near tons of kid-friendly dining options—and next door to Café de la Presse, where you can enjoy excellent coffee, a snack, and fantastic people-watching. ✉*342 Grant Ave., Union Square* ☎*415/394–0500 or 800/433–6611* 📠*415/394–0555* ⊕*www.hoteltriton.com* 🛏*133 rooms, 7 suites* ⚒*In-room: refrigerator, DVD (some), Wi-Fi. In-hotel: restaurant, bar, gym, laundry service, parking (paid), some pets allowed, no-smoking rooms* ⊟*AE, D, DC, MC, V.*

$$$–$$$$ ⊞ **JW Marriott San Francisco.** Guests here are whisked skyward in bullet elevators from the rose-and-gray-marble foyer into this John Portman–designed, former Pan Pacific hotel. A graceful Matisse-inspired bronze sculpture encircles the fountain in the dramatically reconfigured 21-story lobby atrium. Guest rooms have new gold, olive, and maroon bedding, flat-screen TVs, and versatile desks for dining or working; elegant bathrooms boast new vanities and deep soaking tubs, which many guests rave about. **Pros:** Recently renovated, convenient location, large rooms, luxurious bathrooms. **Cons:** Comfortable but lacking character. **Family Matters:** The hotel's new bar/restaurant, Level III, allows guests to choose where they eat: in the elegant dining room, in the casual bar next to the massive TV, or at one of the tables scattered around the large-scale, eye-catching sculpture (this system works well for families with kids who don't stay in one place for long). ⊠*500 Post St., Union Square* ☎*415/771–8600* ☎*415/398–0267* ⊕*www. marriott.com/sfojw* ⚓*329 rooms, 9 suites* ⌂*In-room: safe, VCR (some), Internet, Wi-Fi. In-hotel: restaurant, room service, bar, gym, laundry service, Wi-Fi, parking (paid), some pets allowed (paid), no-smoking rooms* ☐*AE, D, DC, MC, V.*

$–$$ ⊞ **Larkspur Union Square.** This compact boutique hotel, housed in a 1913 Edwardian building near Union Square, is now managed by the Larkspur Hospitality Company. Complimentary amenities include breakfast buffet in the Garden Room, a morning paper, and a nightly wine reception in the lobby. Rooms come with Featherborne beds, Lather natural bath and body products, and flat-screen TVs. A computer and printer are available in the library. A recent remodeling project updated 10 rooms, all of the hotel's suites, and the lobby. ADA–compliant rooms will also be available. Note that this is a historic building, so rooms and baths can feel cramped and claustrophobic—but for travelers who want to be near Union Square, it's a relatively inexpensive option. **Pros:** Good location, moderately priced. **Cons:** Dark, airless rooms and hallways; small baths. **Family Matters:** If your children have outgrown their cribs, consider a suite; if you go the roll-away route, you'll be tripping over each other. ⊠*524 Sutter St., Union Square* ☎*415/421–2865 or 800/919–9779* ☎*415/398–6345* ⊕*www.larkspurhotelunionsquare.com* ⚓*109 rooms, 5 suites* ⌂*In-room: Internet, Wi-Fi, refrigerator (some). In-hotel: laundry ser-*

vice, Wi-Fi, parking (paid), some pets allowed, no-smoking rooms ⊟*AE, D, DC, MC, V* ⧗*BP.*

$$$–$$$$ ⊡**Orchard Garden Hotel.** Feel virtuous and environmentally sensitive at the first San Francisco hotel built to environmentally stringent LEED specifications, exacting standards which mandate the use of eco-friendly features such as chemical-free cleaning agents, recycling bins, and a custom guest-room key card energy-control system. Local artist Archie Held's glass water sculpture in the lobby sets the stage for the hotel's high aesthetics. The owner's collection of original artwork is scattered throughout the hotel—and rooftop garden. Amenities include complimentary car service to the Financial District and a buffet breakfast at the restaurant Roots, supplied by organic and local purveyors (lunch and dinner are also available). The simply styled rooms offer low-flow toilets, washable textiles in soothing hues of green and gold, and natural woods. **Pros:** Environmentally sensitive. **Cons:** A bit of a hike from Union Square. **Family Matters:** If the kids aren't up for fine dining at pricey Roots, head across the street into the warren of Chinatown for your pick of family-friendly restaurants. ✉*446 Bush St., Union Square* ☎*415/399–9807, 888/717–2881* 🖷*415/393–9917* ⊕*www.theorchardgardenhotel.com* ⇆*82 rooms, 4 suites* ♿*In-room: safe, refrigerator, DVD, Wi-Fi. In-hotel: restaurant, parking (paid)* ⊟*AE, D, DC, V, MC* ⧗*BP.*

$$$–$$$$ ⊡**Orchard Hotel.** Unlike most other boutique hotels in the area, which sometimes occupy century-old buildings, the strictly 21st-century Orchard was built in 2000. The hotel embraces state-of-the-art technology—from CD and DVD players in each room to Wi-Fi access throughout the building—mixing cutting-edge Silicon Valley chic with classic European touches. The hotel's marble lobby, where the bronze statue *Spring Awakening* greets visitors, previews the dramatic architectural embellishments, like arched openings, vaulted ceilings, and stone floors that are found throughout the hotel. With just 12 rooms per floor, the hotel feels quite intimate; some guests have compared it to a cozy (decidedly upscale) mountain inn. Rooms, sizable by boutique hotel standards, are done in a soft palette of relaxing colors, a balm for harried shoppers returning from a busy day of retail therapy in Union Square. The hotel's restaurant, Daffodil, serves seasonal California fare for breakfast and dinner. Like its "green sister," the Orchard Garden, this one is also going for its

LEED certification, giving San Francisco visitors yet another ecofriendly option. **Pros:** Cutting-edge technology. **Cons:** Can be a bit pricey. **Family Matters:** Be aware that you'll have to pay extra for each guest beyond two, even if you book a suite—a reminder that this hotel is designed for adults. ⊠*665 Bush St., Union Square* ☎*415/362–8878 or 888/717–2881* ☎*415/362–8088* ⊕*www.theorchardhotel. com* ⌖*104 rooms, 9 suites* ⚲*In-room: safe, DVD, Wi-Fi. In-hotel: restaurant, room service, laundry service, parking (paid), some pets allowed, no-smoking rooms* ☐*AE, D, DC, MC, V.*

$$$ ☗**Petite Auberge.** The teddy bears in the reception area may seem a bit too precious, unlike the provincial decor of the rooms in this re-creation of an intimate French country inn. Small rooms each have bright flowered wallpaper, an old-fashioned writing desk, and a much-needed armoire (there's little or no closet space). Many rooms have gas fireplaces, and the suite has a whirlpool tub. Afternoon tea, wine, and hors d'oeuvres are served in the lobby by the fire, and there's a full-breakfast buffet in the downstairs dining room. **Pros:** European charm. **Cons:** Virtually no closet space, some guests complain that rooms are in need of an update. **Family Matters:** If you value European ambience—and size—above amenities and convenience, you'll like the Petite Auberge. ⊠*863 Bush St., Union Square,* ☎*415/928–6000 or 800/365–3004* ☎*415/673–7214* ⊕*www.jdvhotels.com* ⌖*25 rooms, 1 suite* ⚲*In-room: no a/c, VCR (some), Internet, Wi-Fi. In-hotel: restaurant, laundry service, Wi-Fi, parking (paid), no-smoking rooms* ☐*AE, DC, MC, V* ☉*BP.*

$$–$$$ ☗**Prescott Hotel.** This relatively small establishment providing extremely personalized service prides itself on offering "good taste on Union Square." One guest described the hotel as making "you feel welcomed at every point of your stay." Postrio, Wolfgang Puck's award-winning restaurant, one of the most breathtaking dining rooms in the city, is attached to the lobby. The casual Postrio café bar offers three-cheese pizza, delectable sandwiches, and soups. The rooms, which were renovated in 2001, are filled with cherry furniture, handsomely decorated in dark autumn colors, and have bathrooms with marble-top sinks. Free coffee and evening wine are offered by a flickering fireplace in the living room. Executive Club Level rooms include a free continental breakfast and afternoon cocktails with Puck's pizza in the private Executive Club

Level lounge. **Pros:** Good location; excellent café, bar, and restaurant on premises. **Cons:** Off-site valet service can be slow, some guests complain of street noise. **Family Matters:** Little ones receive special treatment and welcome gifts, and kids all the way up to 17 stay here for free. ✉545 *Post St., Union Square* ☎415/563–0303 *or* 866/271–3632 🖷415/563–6831 ⊕*www.prescotthotel.com* ⇆*132 rooms, 32 suites* ♿*In-room: safe, VCR (some), Wi-Fi. In-hotel: restaurant, room service, bar, gym, executive floor, Internet terminal, parking (paid), some pets allowed, no-smoking rooms* ⊟*AE, D, DC, MC, V.*

$$$$ 🖩**Sir Francis Drake Hotel.** Beefeater-costumed doormen welcome you into the regal, dimly lit, and slightly run-down lobby of this 1928 landmark property, decked out with boldly striped banners, wrought-iron balustrades, chandeliers, Italian marble, and leather and velvet furnishings that are a little on the tired side. The cumulative effect is of a Scottish castle that's seen better days. The lobby bar, guest rooms, bathrooms, public spaces, gym, and meeting rooms are somewhat shopworn or downright shabby despite a recent $20 million renovation. Be advised: service can sometimes be unresponsive. The trade-off is a first-rate location and an establishment steeped in history, including Harry Denton's Starlight Room, on the hotel's top floor. A tribute to faded 1920s glory, it's one of the city's best known skyline bars. The hotel's surprisingly affordable restaurant, Scala's Bistro, serves better than average food in its somewhat noisy bi-level dining room. **Pros:** Can't beat the location, free in-room Wi-Fi, on-site restaurant and bar are moderately priced. **Cons:** Small baths and dated decor, some complaints about unresponsive service and cleanliness. **Family Matters:** You'll see plenty of families with kids here—this is definitely a tourist hotel. If you have little light sleepers, ask for a quiet room; those with lovely views—especially the higher rooms—tend to funnel noise from the Starlight Room. ✉*450 Powell St., Union Square* ☎415/392–7755 *or* 800/795–7129 🖷415/391–8719 ⊕*www.sirfrancisdrake. com* ⇆*412 rooms, 5 suites* ♿*In-room: DVD, Wi-Fi. In-hotel: restaurant, bar, gym, room service, laundry service, Internet terminal, parking (paid), some pets allowed, no-smoking rooms* ⊟*AE, D, DC, MC, V.*

$$$$ 🖩**Westin St. Francis.** Since its 1904 opening, this historic hotel has hosted the likes of Hirohito, Queen Elizabeth II, several U.S. presidents and a roster of international luminaries. The site of sensational, banner headline scandals,

the hotel's past is shrouded in as much infamy as stardust. This is the place where Sara Jane Moore tried to assassinate Gerald Ford, where Al Jolson died playing poker; suite 1219–1221 was the scene of massive scandal, which erupted when a 30-year-old aspiring actress died after a night of heavy boozing in the close company of silent-film comedian Fatty Arbuckle. (The incident destroyed his career.) The hotel is comprised of the original building (Empire-style furnishings, Victorian moldings) and a modern 32-story tower (Asian-inspired lacquered furniture, glass elevators); guests are divided when it comes to the virtues of the modern addition vs. the historic building. The imposing facade, black-marble lobby, and gold-top columns form an impressive public space. Adding to the air of upscale sophistication is the cool chic of Michael Mina restaurant and the Oak Room Restaurant and Lounge. **Pros:** Fantastic beds, prime location, spacious rooms, some with great views. **Cons:** Some guests commented on the long wait at check-in, rooms in original building can be small, glass elevators are not for the faint of heart. **Family Matters:** Young explorers will be greeted with a bag full of goodies to help them discover San Francisco: a city map, compass, postcard-making kit, and more. The fabulous Michael Mina is one fine-dining restaurant you won't have to pass up because you're traveling with children: with two little foodies of his own, Mina offers a thoughtful—if expensive—kids' menu. ⌧*335 Powell St., Union Square* ☎*415/397–7000 or 800/917–7458* ⎙*415/774–0124* ⊕*www.westinstfrancis. com* ⟳*1,155 rooms, 40 suites* ⏚*In-room: safe, refrigerator (some), Internet, Wi-Fi. In-hotel: 3 restaurants, room service, bars, spa, laundry service, Internet terminal, parking (paid), some pets allowed, no-smoking rooms* ⊟*AE, D, DC, MC, V.*

The Performing Arts

4

WORD OF MOUTH

"Teatro ZinZanni was so much fun! We loved it and had a really good time. It's a dinner/show that combines cabaret, vaudeville, comedy, circus acts and singing. There's lots of audience participation . . . I would highly recommend it for something completely different."

—mycatmiko

Updated
by Denise
M. Leto

SAN FRANCISCO HAS A FULL arts calendar of events that will appeal to kids, from special family matinees at the San Francisco Symphony and San Francisco Ballet to traditional family performances such as the *Nutcracker* and *A Christmas Carol*. During summer—and especially in September and October—city stages come alive with free music festivals. Your kids might get the chance to try their hand at taiko drumming, dance on stage at a Senegalese concert, or learn hula moves from a master at the city's beloved Stern Grove Festival, the San Francisco Jazz Festival, or any number of other offerings.

THE 4-1-1

Entertainment information is printed in the pink Sunday "Datebook" section (*www.sfgate.com/datebook*) and the more-calendar-based Thursday "96 Hours" section (*www.sfgate.com/96hours*) in the *San Francisco Chronicle*; the site also has a customizable kids' events search feature (*www.sfgate.com/listings/pages.php?events,kids*). Also consult any of the free alternative weeklies, notably the *SF Weekly* (*www.sfweekly.com*), which blurbs nightclubs and music, and the *San Francisco Bay Guardian* (*www.sfbg.com*), which lists neighborhood, avant-garde, and budget events. GoCityKids.com has an up-to-date calendar of entertainment goings-on.

TICKETS

The opera, symphony, the San Francisco Ballet's *Nutcracker,* and touring hit musicals are often sold out in advance. Tickets are usually available for other shows within a day of the performance.

City Box Office (✉*180 Redwood St., Suite 100, off Van Ness Ave. between Golden Gate Ave. and McAllister St., Civic Center* ☎*415/392–4400* ⊕*www.cityboxoffice.com*), a charge-by-phone service, offers tickets for many performances and lectures. You can buy tickets in person at its downtown location weekdays 9:30–5:30. You can charge tickets for everything from jazz concerts to Giants games by phone or online through **Tickets.com** (☎*800/955–5566* ⊕*www.tickets.com*). Half-price, same-day tickets for many local and touring stage shows go on sale (cash only) at 11 AM Tuesday through Saturday at the **TIX Bay Area** (✉*Powell St. between Geary and Post Sts., Union Square* ☎*415/433–7827* ⊕*www.theatrebayarea.org*) booth on Union Square. TIX is also a full-service ticket agency for theater and music events around the Bay Area, open 11–6

TOP 5 PERFORMING ARTS PICKS

Stern Grove Festival, Sunset: Come out to the eucalyptus grove on the city's west side any Sunday during summer to join San Francisco families enjoying an afternoon of world-class music or dance and a picnic at the granddaddy of the city's free festivals.

ODC/San Francisco's Velveteen Rabbit Ballet, SoMa: Local kids adore this holiday-inspired dance version of the story of the lovable stuffed rabbit that became real.

San Francisco Jazz Festival: Dream of seeing your child on stage with Wynton Marsalis?

At special family performances throughout the city, kids are encouraged to join in.

San Francisco Shakespeare Festival, Presidio: Free Shakespeare in the park is a great way to introduce even the youngest kids to the Bard's work.

Yerba Buena Festival, SoMa: Soaking up culture in the museum district and need a break? On many afternoons throughout the year you can catch free concerts and dance performances outdoors at the lovely Yerba Buena Gardens—many designed especially for a young audience.

Tuesday through Thursday, Friday 11–7, Saturday 10–7, and Sunday 10–3.

DANCE

San Francisco is gaining recognition for its exciting modern and experimental dance companies. Local groups such as Alonzo King's Lines Ballet and ODC/San Francisco tour extensively and are well regarded by national dance critics. The San Francisco Ballet excels at both traditional and contemporary repertoires.

ODC/San Francisco. Popular with kids, this 10-member group's annual Yuletide version of *The Velveteen Rabbit* (mid-November to mid-December), at the Yerba Buena Center for the Arts, ranks among the city's best holiday-season performances. The group's main repertory season generally runs intermittently between January and June. ☎415/863–6606 ⊕*www.odcdance.org.* 3+up

San Francisco Ballet. Under artistic director Helgi Tomasson, the San Francisco Ballet's works—both classical and contemporary—have won admiring reviews. The primary season runs from February through May. Its repertoire includes full-length ballets such as *Don Quixote* and *Sleeping Beauty*; the December presentation of the *Nutcracker* is one of the most spectacular in the nation. The company also performs bold new dances from star choreographers such as William Forsythe and Mark Morris, alongside modern classics by George Balanchine and Jerome Robbins. Tickets and information are available at the **War Memorial Opera House.** If you're interested in seeing a performance other than the *Nutcracker* with your younger children, call and ask about community matinees. Offered occasionally throughout the year, these shorter, less formal performances are designed to entertain children while introducing them to ballet. ✉ *War Memorial Opera House, 301 Van Ness Ave., Civic Center* ☎ *415/865–2000* ⊕ *www.sfballet.org* ☉ *Weekdays 10–4.* 3+up

FESTIVALS

Ethnic Dance Festival. About 30 of the Bay Area's ethnic dance companies and soloists perform at this event, which takes place over four weekends in June. Ticket prices start at $22; all matinee tickets are half-price for children under 16 years of age. You'll need to leave tots with a sitter: children under 2 years are not permitted. ✉ *Palace of Fine Arts Theatre, Bay and Lyon Sts., Marina* ☎ *415/474–3914* ⊕ *www.worldartswest.org/edf.* 3+up

FILM

The San Francisco Bay Area, including Berkeley and Marin County, is considered one of the nation's most savvy movie markets. Films of all sorts find an audience here. The area is also a filmmaking center, where documentaries and experimental works are produced on modest budgets and feature films and television programs are shot on location. In San Francisco, about a third of the theaters regularly show foreign and independent films.

San Francisco Cinematheque (☎ *415/552–1990* ⊕ *www.sfcinematheque.org*) showcases experimental film and digital media, with most screenings at the Yerba Buena Center for the Arts or Artists' Television Access.

MOVIE THEATERS

Many San Francisco theaters screen high-quality independent and foreign-language films (Friday and Saturday evening shows often sell out, so consider buying tickets in advance via ⊕ *www.moviefone.com* or ☎ *777–FILM* [*preceded by the local area code*]).

★ Fodor'sChoice **Castro Theatre.** Designed by art-deco master Timothy Pfleuger and opened in 1922, the most dramatic movie theater in the city hosts revivals as well as foreign and independent engagements and the occasional sing-along movie musical. Parking is limited in the Castro district, so taking public transportation is advised. Be sure to check the calendar: the Castro hosts plenty of kid-friendly events, but some programming is definitely adults only. ⊠*429 Castro St., near Market St., Castro* ☎*415/621–6120* ⊕*www. castrotheatre.com.* 5+up

---

MUSIC

San Francisco's symphony and opera perform in the Civic Center area, but musical ensembles can be found all over the city: in churches, museums, restaurants, and parks—not to mention in Berkeley and on the Peninsula.

Noontime Concerts at St. Patrick's Catholic Church. This Gothic revival church, completed in 1872 and rebuilt after the 1906 earthquake, hosts a notable chamber-music series on Wednesday at 12:30; suggested donation is $5. A show here is a nice add-on to a day in the Yerba Buena Arts District: the church is next to the Contemporary Jewish Museum and across the street from Yerba Buena Gardens (which makes a nice stop if the kids need to run around). ⊠*756 Mission St., between 3rd and 4th Sts., SoMa* ☎*415/777–3211* ⊕*www. noontimeconcerts.org.* 9+up

San Francisco Symphony. One of America's top orchestras, the San Francisco Symphony performs from September through May, with additional summer performances of light classical music and show tunes; visiting artists perform here the rest of the year. Music director Michael Tilson Thomas, who is known for his innovative programming of 20th-century American works (most notably his Grammy Award–winning Mahler cycle), and the orchestra often perform with soloists of the caliber of Andre Watts, Gil Shaham, and Renée Fleming. Just to illustrate the more adventuresome side of the organization, this symphony once collaborated with the heavy-metal group Metallica. Tickets run about $15–$100.

Many members of the San Francisco Symphony perform in the **Summer in the City** (☎*415/864–6000* ⊕*www.sfsymphony. org*) concert series, held in the 2,400-seat Davies Symphony Hall. The schedule includes light classics and Broadway, country, and movie music. A series of weekend matinees for families is designed to introduce kids (and their parents) to the pleasure of live orchestral music. Tickets start at $15 for adults and $7.50 for kids. ✉ *Davies Symphony Hall, 201 Van Ness Ave., at Grove St., Civic Center* ☎ *415/864–6000* ⊕ *www.sfsymphony.org.* 7+up

MUSIC FESTIVALS

Hardly Strictly Bluegrass Festival. The city's top free music event, as well as one of the greatest gatherings for bluegrass, country, and roots music fans in the country, takes place from late September to early October. Roughly 50,000 folks turn out to see the likes of Willie Nelson, Emmylou Harris, Jimmie Dale Gilmore, and Del McCoury at Speedway Meadows in Golden Gate Park. Lots of parents bring their kids to this feel-good festival—though some are put off by the huge crowd and hippie vibe. ☎ *No phone* ⊕ *www. strictlybluegrass.com.* 3+up

San Francisco Blues Festival. Billed as the country's oldest ongoing blues festival, SFBF has hosted a hall of fame's worth of blues legends over the years, including John Lee Hooker, B. B. King, Buddy Guy, and James Cotton. It's also a great place to catch rising Bay Area blues stars like J. C. Smith and Tommy Castro. The festival, which was founded by local blues historian Tom Mazzolini in 1973, is held each September at Fort Mason's Great Meadow, which has stunning views of the Golden Gate Bridge and the bay. Kids under 10 are free—those 11 and up pay full price. ☎ *415/979–5588* ⊕ *www.sfblues.com.* 5+up

San Francisco Jazz Festival. Every year starting in October, concert halls, clubs, and churches throughout the city host this acclaimed two-week festival. The popular event, which got its start in 1983, has featured such big-name acts as Ornette Coleman, Sonny Rollins, and McCoy Tyner, as well as talked-about up-and-comers like Brad Mehldau and Chris Botti. At hour-long family matinees, children not only get to hear world-class music they're encouraged to participate by dancing on stage, asking the artists questions . . . and sometimes even trying their hands at the instruments. ☎ *415/398–5655* ⊕ *www.sfjazz.org.* 9+up

★ **Fodor'sChoice Stern Grove Festival.** The nation's oldest continual free summer music festival hosts Sunday-afternoon performances of symphony, opera, jazz, pop music, and dance. The amphitheater is in a beautiful eucalyptus grove below street level, perfect for picnicking before the show. (Dress for cool weather.) The festival is a tradition for thousands of San Francisco families. In addition to wonderful performances, there's a full program of events for kids. On Kids' Days, children may get to try taiko drumming or hula with the week's artists; Kidstage is a pre-performance, hands-on art project, available before each Sunday's show. ✉*Sloat Blvd. at 19th Ave., Sunset* ☎*415/252–6252* ⊕*www.sterngrove.org.* 3+up

THEATER

San Francisco's theaters are concentrated on Geary Street west of Union Square, but a number of additional commercial theaters, as well as resident companies that enrich the city's theatrical scene, are within walking distance of this theater row. The three major commercial theaters—Curran, Golden Gate, and Orpheum—are operated by the Shorenstein-Nederlander organization, which books touring plays and musicals, some before they open on Broadway. Theatre Bay Area (*www.theatrebayarea.org*) lists most Bay Area performances online.

American Conservatory Theater. Not long after its founding in the mid-1960s, the city's major nonprofit theater company became one of the nation's leading regional theaters. During its season, which runs from early fall to late spring, ACT presents approximately eight plays, from classics to contemporary works, often in rotating repertory. In December ACT stages a much-loved version of Charles Dickens's *A Christmas Carol.* The **ACT ticket office** (✉*405 Geary St., Union Square* ☎*415/749–2228*) is next door to the theater. With a running time of almost two hours, *A Christmas Carol* is best suited to kids above the running-around stage. ✉*425 Geary St., Union Square* ⊕*www.act-sf.org.* 5+up

Curran Theater. Some of the biggest touring shows mount productions at this theater, which has hosted classical music, dance, and stage performances since its 1925 opening. Shows are of the long-running Broadway musical variety, such as *Stomp* and *Jersey Boys,* and the seasonal *A Christmas Carol.* The policy on children varies from show to show, but in general kids under 5 are not allowed. Be sure to check age limits before you invest in tickets. ✉*445 Geary St., at Mason St., Union Square* ☎*415/551–2000* ⊕*www.shnsf.com.* 5+up

San Francisco Mime Troupe. The politically leftist, barbed satires of this Tony Award–winning troupe are hardly mime in the Marcel Marceau sense. The group performs afternoon musicals at area parks from the July Fourth weekend through September, and taking one in is a perfect way to spend a sunny summer day. Many of the jokes will go over kids' heads, but there's enough humor and physical comedy keep them (and you) entertained. ☎*415/285–1717* ⊕*www.sfmt.org.* 5+up

★ Fodor'sChoice **Teatro ZinZanni.** Contortionists, chanteuses, jugglers, illusionists, and circus performers ply the audience as you're served a surprisingly good five-course dinner in a fabulous antique Belgian traveling-dance-hall tent. Be ready to laugh, and arrive early for a front-and-center table. Reservations are essential; tickets are $116–$156. Dress fancy. A three-hour performance, however entertaining, can make for one long evening for (and with) kids. Even if yours are at least 5—and therefore permitted—be sure to consider how much entertainment they can take. Also note that neither a children's menu nor discounted tickets are available. ⊠*Pier 29, Embarcadero at Battery St., Embarcadero* ☎*415/438–2668* ⊕*www.zinzanni.org.* 5+up

Yerba Buena Center for the Arts. Across the street from the Museum of Modern Art and abutting a lovely urban garden, this performing arts complex schedules interdisciplinary art exhibitions, dance, music, film programs, and contemporary theater events. You can depend on the quality of the productions at Yerba Buena. The Yerba Buena Gardens Festival brings an eclectic menu of free performances to the gardens, including half-hour shows Friday and Saturday for even the youngest children. The festival runs May through October. ⊠*3rd and Howard Sts., SoMa* ☎*415/978–2787* ⊕*www.ybca.org.* All ages

ARTS FESTIVALS

San Francisco Shakespeare Festival. Free weekend performances of the Bard's works take place in September at the Presidio. Though free Shakespeare in the park performances are certainly family-friendly events, the festival offers at least one matinee performance especially for folks with kids. These days include a craft related to the performance and a bit of education about the show. ☎*800/978–7529 or 415/558–0888* ⊕*www.sfshakes.org.* 3+up

Sports & the Outdoors

WORD OF MOUTH

"Saw a thread about biking over the [Golden Gate] Bridge into Sausalito and taking a ferry back. Anyone out there done this?"

—schmidtrossi

"Yes! Did it, loved it, and would do it again. I rented from Blazing Saddles, Pier 39. They were very helpful in mapping out the trail for me. I went past Sausalito and on to Tiburon, then took the ferry to Angel Island . . . then took another ferry back to SF."

—suzanne

Updated
by Denise
M. Leto

SAN FRANCISCO'S SURROUNDINGS—BAY, OCEAN, MOUNTAINS, and forests—make getting outdoors outside the city a no-brainer. Muir Woods, Point Reyes, and Stinson Beach in Marin County offer dozens of opportunities for exploring the natural beauty of the Bay Area. But the peninsular city—with its many green spaces, steep inclines, and catch-your-breath views—has plenty to offer itself.

Getting outdoors in San Francisco isn't all about daunting grades and pounding surf, though. Even with young children you'll be able to enjoy the city's natural bounty. Bikers and hikers traverse the majestic Golden Gate Bridge, bound for the Marin Headlands or the winding trails of the Presidio. Runners, strollers, in-line skaters, and cyclists head for Golden Gate Park's wooded paths, and water lovers satisfy their addictions by kayaking, sailing, or kite-surfing in the bay and along the rugged Pacific coast.

BASEBALL

★ **Fodor's Choice** The National League's New York Giants became the **San Francisco Giants** when they moved to California in 1958, the same year that the Brooklyn Dodgers moved to Los Angeles. Today, the beautiful yet classic design of the Giants' AT&T Park has created a new legion of fans—some more interested in the baseball experience than the Giants, per se. Still, buy your tickets in advance—nearly every game sells out.

GETTING THERE
Parking is pricey ($25 and up), and 5,000 spaces for 43,000 seats doesn't add up. Take public transportation. MUNI line N (to CalTrain/Mission Bay) stops right in front of the park, and MUNI bus lines 10, 15, 30, 42, 45, and 47 stop a block away. Or you can arrive in style—take the ferry from Jack London Square in Oakland (⊕*www. eastbayferry.com*).

AT&T Park (⊠*24 Willie Mays Plaza, SoMa* ☎*415/972–1800* ⊕ *sanfrancisco.giants.mlb.com*).

Park Tours (⊠*$10 adults*, $6 children 2–12 ☉*Daily at 10:30 and 12:30*).

The giant Coca-Cola bottle and mitt you see beyond the outfield are part of the **Coca-Cola Fan Lot, a free playground that's open during games and on weekdays when the team is away.** The bottle is a slide, and the mitt actually has decent

TOP 5 SPORTS & OUTDOORS

Take Me Out to the Ball-game: Have a hot dog and a soda at retro AT&T Park, and during the 7th-inning stretch kids can slide down the huge Coca-Cola bottle in the fan lot.

Bike the Bridge: Grab a bike and head down the lovely, painlessly flat Embarcadero all the way to the Golden Gate Bridge. Up for an adventure? Head over the bridge to Mediterranean-style Sausalito, then return to the city on a sunset cruise.

Set Sail in Golden Gate Park: Even the littlest sailors will enjoy tooling around Stow Lake in a paddle boat,

passing under stone bridges and watching turtles lazing in the sun.

Head to the End of the World: Hike the stunning Coastal Trail, starting in the Outer Richmond, along steep cliffs all the way to Lands End. Time it right and you might spy migrating gray whales or the reclining masts of sunken ships.

A Day on the Shore: End-less adventure awaits at the Presidio's Crissy Field, hugging the bay shoreline: watch local crab fishermen on the pier, play in the sand, see sea lions frolicking in the water, and visit a science center.

views of the field. Kids can also test their batting skills at a miniature version of AT&T Park.

GETTING TICKETS

The park is small and there are 30,000 season ticket hold-ers (for 43,000 seats), so Giants tickets for popular games routinely sell out the day they go on sale, and other games sell out quickly. If tickets aren't available at Tickets.com, try the Double Play Ticket Window, or even showing up on game day—there are usually plenty of scalpers, some selling at reasonable prices.

Tickets.com (☎*877/473–4849* ⊕*www.tickets.com*) sells game tickets over the phone and charges a per-ticket fee of $2–$10, plus a per-call processing fee of up to $5. The **Giants Dugout** (✉*AT&T Park, 24 Willie Mays Plaza, SoMa* ☎*415/972–2000* ✉*4 Embarcadero Center, Embarca-dero* ☎*415/951–8888*) sells tickets in any of its stores (check the Web site, sanfrancisco.giants.mlb.com/sf/ballpark/dugout_stores.jsp, for all locations); a surcharge is added at all but the ballpark store.

The Giants' Web-only **Double Play Ticket Window** (⊕*sanfrancisco.giants.mlb.com*) allows season ticket holders to resell their unused tickets. You won't always find a deal, but you might get a seat at an otherwise sold-out game. Click the "Tickets" menu on the home page.

BICYCLING

San Francisco is known for its treacherously steep hills, so it may be surprising to see so many cyclists. This is actually a great city for biking—there are ample bike lanes, it's not hard to find level ground with great scenery (along the water), and if you're willing to tackle a challenging uphill climb, you're often rewarded with a fabulous view—and a quick trip back down.

■ TIP➔**Streetcar tracks can wreak havoc on skinny bike tires—and the bicyclist perched above them. Watch the ground and cross the tracks perpendicularly.**

Don't want to get stuck slogging up 30-degree inclines? Then be sure to pick up a copy of the foldout *San Francisco Bike Map and Walking Guide* ($4), which indicates street grades by color and delineates bike routes that avoid major hills and heavy traffic. You can pick up a copy in bicycle shops, select bookstores, or at the San Francisco Bicycle Coalition's Web site (*see below*).

The **San Francisco Bicycle Coalition** (☎415/431–2453 ⊕*www.sfbike.org*) has extensive information about the policies and politics of riding a bicycle in the city and lists local events for cyclists on its Web site. You can also download (but not print) a PDF version of the *San Francisco Bike Map and Walking Guide.*

WHERE TO RENT

Bike and Roll. You can rent bikes here for $7 per hour or $27 per day ($5 or $20, respectively, for kids' bikes); discounted weekly rates are available. They also have complimentary maps. Kids' bikes are available for $5 per hour or $20 per day, and trailers and tandem bikes area also available. ✉*899 Columbus Ave., North Beach* ☎*866/736–8224 or 415/229–2000* ⊕*www.bicyclerental.com.*

Blazing Saddles. This outfitter rents bikes for $7 an hour or $28 a day, and shares tips on sights to see along the paths. Children's bikes start at $20 per day; trailers, tag-alongs, and baby seats are also $20 per day. This is the only place in town that rents a triple tandem ($105 per day). ✉2715 *Hyde St., Fisherman's Wharf* ✉465 Jefferson St., at Hyde *St., Fisherman's Wharf* ✉Pier 43½, near Taylor St., Fisher-*man's Wharf* ✉Pier 41, at Powell St., Fisherman's Wharf ☎415/202–8888 ⊕www.blazingsaddles.com.

From April through October, you can rent mountain bikes on **Angel Island** (☎415/435–1915 ⊕www.angelisland.org) for $10 an hour or $30 a day.

THE EMBARCADERO

A completely flat, sea-level route, the Embarcadero hugs the eastern and northern bay and gives you a clear view of open waters, the Bay Bridge, and sleek high-rises. The route from Pier 40 to Aquatic Park takes about 30 minutes, and there are designated bike lanes the entire way. Along the way you can see—from east to west—the Ferry Building, the Bay Bridge, a view of Coit Tower near Pier 19 (look inland), and various ferries and historic ships. At Aquatic Park, there's a nice view of Golden Gate Bridge. If you're not tired yet, continue along the Marina and through the Presidio's Crissy Field. You may want to time your ride so you end up at the Ferry Building, where you can refuel with a sandwich, a gelato, or—why not?—fresh oysters.

■TIP➔Be sure to keep your eyes open along this route—cars **move quickly here, and streetcars and tourist traffic can cause congestion. Near Fisherman's Wharf you can bike on the promenade, but take it slow—we've seen more than one near miss between bicyclist and pedestrian.**

GOLDEN GATE PARK

A beautiful maze of roads and hidden bike paths criss-crosses San Francisco's most famous park, winding past rose gardens, lakes, waterfalls, museums, horse stables, bison, and, at the park's western edge, spectacular views of the Pacific Ocean. John F. Kennedy Drive is closed to motor vehicles on Sunday (and sometimes Saturday), when it's crowded with people-powered wheels. ■TIP➔**Get a map of the park before you go—it's huge.**

From the eastern entrance of the park between Oak and Fell streets, veer right to begin a 30- to 45-minute, 3-mi ride down John F. Kennedy Drive through the park to the Great Highway, where land meets ocean. Take a break and watch the waves roll in at Ocean Beach, or cross the street for a drink or a bite to eat at the casual, tree-shrouded Park Chalet (behind the Beach Chalet). Extend your ride a few more miles by turning left, riding a few blocks, and connecting with a raised bike path that runs parallel to the Pacific, winds through fields of emerald-green ice plants, and, after 2 mi, leads to Sloat Boulevard and the San Francisco Zoo. ■TIP➔**On exceptionally windy days, expect to encounter blowing sand along this route**.

THE MARINA GREEN & GOLDEN GATE BRIDGE

The Marina Green, a vast lawn at the edge of the northern bayfront, stretches along Marina Boulevard, adjacent to Fort Mason. It's the starting point of a well-trod, paved bike path that runs through the Presidio along Crissy Field's waterfront wetlands, then heads for the Golden Gate Bridge and beyond. To do this ride, first take the path from Aquatic Park through Fort Mason to the Marina Green. Continue into the Presidio, and you'll eventually reach the base of the bridge, a 60-minute ride round-trip. To view the bridge from underneath, stay at water level and ride to Fort Point (where Kim Novak leaped into the drink in the film *Vertigo*).

If you want to cross the bridge, take Lincoln Boulevard to reach the road-level viewing area and continue across the bridge (signs indicate which side you must use). Once you're across, turn right on the first road leading northeast, Alexander Avenue. After a 10-minute all-downhill ride, you'll arrive on Bridgeway in downtown Sausalito, where you can rest in a café. After a little shopping, board the Blue & Gold Fleet's ferry (the ferry terminal is at the end of Bridgeway) with your bike for the half-hour ride back to Fisherman's Wharf. ■TIP➔**If it's overcast, foggy, or windy, don't bother doing the Golden Gate Bridge bike ride—the wind can feel downright dangerous on the bridge, and the trip is only awe-inspiring when you can take in the view.**

THE MARIN HEADLANDS

After crossing the Golden Gate, the super-fit can ride alongside triathletes and hardcore cyclists in the Marin Headlands. Take the Alexander Avenue exit off the bridge as if you were going to Sausalito, but turn left instead and double back under the freeway. Just before the road merges with San Francisco–bound traffic, bear right and ascend the steep, rolling hills of the Marin Headlands. Follow the road to the top, where it becomes one-way and drops toward the ocean. Loop around the backside of the hills and through the tunnel, back to the bridge. On a clear day, the views along this route are stunning.

ANGEL ISLAND STATE PARK

★ A former military garrison and a beautiful wildlife preserve, Angel Island has some steep roads and great views of the city and the bay. Bicycles must stay on roadways; there are no single-track trails on the island. A ferry operated by **Blue & Gold Fleet** (☎415/705–8200 ⊕*www.blueandgoldfleet. com*) runs to the island from Pier 41 at Fisherman's Wharf and takes about 20 minutes one way; the fare is $15 round-trip (children ages 6–12 $8.50, children 5 and under free), which includes park admission. Ferries leave once a day at 10 AM weekdays and 10:35 AM weekends, returning at around 3:20 PM weekdays, 3:50 PM weekends; schedules change, so call for up-to-date info. Twenty-five bicycles are permitted on-board on a first-come, first-served basis. The café is closed mid-November through February, so bring your own grub. Rangers lead great historic programs, and special events like Civil War Days dot the calendar; check the schedule as you leave the ferry. ☎415/435–1915 ⊕*www.angelisland.org*.

BOATING & SAILING

San Francisco Bay has year-round sailing, but tricky currents and strong winds make the bay hazardous for inexperienced navigators. Boat rentals and charters are available throughout the Bay Area and are listed under "Boat Renting" in the Yellow Pages.

Near Fisherman's Wharf, from spring through fall, **Adventure Cat Sailing** (✉*Pier 39, Fisherman's Wharf* ☎415/777–1630 or 800/498–4228 ⊕*www.adventurecat.com*) takes passengers aboard a 55-foot-long catamaran. The kids can play on the trampoline-like net between the two hulls while you sip drinks on the wind-protected sundeck. A 90-minute bay cruise costs $30; sunset sails with drinks and hors d'oeuvres are $45 ($15 for children 6–12; free for children 5 and under). **Rendezvous Charters** (✉*Pier 40, South Beach Harbor* ☎415/543–7333 ⊕*www.rendezvouscharters.com*) offers individually ticketed trips on large sailing yachts, including sunset sails ($25, children 11 and under $20) and Sunday brunch cruises on a schooner ($40, children 11 and under $35). **Spinnaker Sailing** (✉*Pier 40, South Beach Harbor* ☎415/543–7333 ⊕*www.spinnaker-sailing.com*) offers sailing instruction and charters private sailboats with or without a skipper (bring your logbook if you want to captain a boat yourself). Both Rendezvous and Spinnaker

WACKY WEATHER

San Francisco's unique weather can be a blessing and a curse. On the positive side, there's hardly any rain between June and October, and there are warm days even in the rainy winter months. But although daytime temperatures rarely drop below 50°F, they seldom get *above* 70°F—and the famous fog often makes the "real feel" even colder.

At any time of year, you may need to bundle up in a hat and wool coat in the morning, then strip down to a T-shirt and don your sunglasses in the afternoon. Layering is important. If you intend to be near the water or on a boat, bring a jacket and a hat—yes, even in summer! For biking, hiking, and boating, windbreakers are ideal.

Beaches can be extremely cold, and surfers and kite boarders wear full wet suits year-round.

are south of the Ferry Building on the eastern waterfront, right next to AT&T Park, *not* next to Pier 39.

If you prefer calm freshwater, you can rent rowboats ($19 per hour) and pedal boats ($24 per hour) at **Stow Lake** (⊠*Off John F. Kennedy Dr., ½ mi west of 10th Ave., Golden Gate Park* ☎*415/752–0347*), in Golden Gate Park. The lake is open daily for boating, weather permitting, but call for seasonal hours.

FOOTBALL

The **San Francisco '49ers** (⊠*Candlestick Park, 490 Jamestown Ave., Bayview Heights* ☎*415/656–4900* ⊕*www. sf49ers.com*) play at **Candlestick Park** near the San Mateo County border, just north of the airport. Single-game tickets, available via **Ticketmaster** (☎*415/421–8497* ⊕*www. ticketmaster.com*), almost always sell out far in advance.

HIKING

Hills and mountains—including Mt. Tamalpais in Marin County and Mt. Diablo in the East Bay, which has the second-longest sight lines anywhere in the world after Mt. Kilimanjaro—form a ring around the Bay Area. The **Bay Area Ridge Trail** (⊕*http://ridgetrail.org*) is an ongoing project to connect all of the region's ridgelines. The trail is currently 300 mi long, but when finished it will extend 500 mi, stretching from San Jose to Napa and encompassing all nine Bay Area counties.

But you don't have to leave the city for a nice hike. In the middle of San Francisco, you can climb to the top of Mt. Davidson, Bernal Heights, Corona Heights, or Buena Vista Park. Little more than undeveloped hilltops, they offer spectacular views of the city and beautiful shows of wildflowers in spring.

In the Presidio, hiking and biking trails wind through nearly 1,500 acres of woods and hills, past old redbrick military buildings and jaw-dropping scenic overlooks with bay and ocean views. Rangers and docents lead guided hikes and nature walks throughout the year. For a current schedule, pick up a copy of the quarterly *Park News* at the **Presidio Visitor Center** (⊠*Presidio Officers' Club, Bldg. 50, Moraga Ave., in Main Post area* ☎*415/561–4323* ⊕*www.nps. gov/prsf*) or go online. Stop by the **Warming Hut** (⊠*Bldg. 983, off Old Mason Rd., facing water just east of Fort Point* ☎*415/561–3040*) to refuel on snacks and to browse through the extensive selection of books (including good ones for kids) and the many ingenious gifts made from recycled materials.

★ Fodor'sChoice The Presidio is part of **Golden Gate National Recreation Area (GGNRA)** (☎*415/561–4700* ⊕*www.nps.gov/ goga*), which also encompasses the San Francisco coastline, the Marin Headlands, and Point Reyes National Seashore. It's veined with hiking trails, and guided walks are available. Current schedules are available at GGNRA visitor centers in the Presidio and Marin Headlands; you can also find them online at ⊕*www.nps.gov/goga/parknews*. For descriptions of each location within the recreation area—along with rich color photographs, hiking information, and maps—pick up a copy of *Guide to the Parks,* available in local bookstores or online from the **Golden Gate National Parks Conservancy** (☎*415/561–3000* ⊕*www.parksconservancy.org*).

☾ The **Golden Gate Promenade** is another great walk; it passes through Crissy Field, taking in marshlands, kite-flyers, the beachfront, and windsurfers, with the Golden Gate Bridge as a backdrop. The 3.3-mi walk is flat and easy—it should take about two hours round-trip. If you begin at Aquatic Park, you'll end up practically underneath the bridge at Fort Point Pier. ■TIP→**If you're driving, park at Fort Point and do the walk from west to east.** It can get blustery, even when it's sunny, so be sure to layer.

Hikers head to **Angel Island State Park** (☎415/435–1915 ⊕*www.angelisland*.org) for access to 13-plus mi of sometimes steep foot trails and fire roads that wind through the wildlife preserve. The Northridge/Sunset loop trail to the 788-foot summit of Mt. Livermore rewards with fantastic views; the Perimeter Road gives access to the island's beaches and historical sites. **Blue & Gold Fleet** (☎415/705–8200 ⊕*www.blueandgoldfleet.com*) operates a ferry to the island from Pier 41 at Fisherman's Wharf. The $15 round-trip fare ($850 for children 6–12; free for children 5 and under) includes park admission. Schedules change frequently, so call for specifics; at this writing, ferries leave at 10 AM weekdays and 10:35 AM weekends, returning around 3:20 PM weekdays, 3:50 PM weekends.

KAYAKING

Surrounded by water on three sides, San Francisco has plenty of opportunities for kayaking enthusiasts of all levels. **City Kayak** (✉*Pier 39, Embarcadero at Stockton St., Fisherman's Wharf* ✉*Pier 38, Embarcadero at Townsend St., SoMa* ☎415/357–1010 ⊕*www.citykayak.com*), the only kayak-rental outfit in the city, operates bay tours along the waterfront and beneath the Bay Bridge starting from $50 (children 12 and under are free); they also run full-moon night paddles and trips to Alcatraz for experienced kayakers. Rentals are $15 per hour for a single; $25 for a double; and $50 for a four-person kayak. Half-day trips depart at 10 AM daily. No prior experience is necessary, but you must watch an instructional video. Children must be at least 4 feet tall and able to swim 25 yards. ■TIP→**The Pier 39 location is for tours only, not rentals.** Trips run by **Outdoor Programs** (✉*500 Parnassus Ave., at 3rd Ave., Inner Sunset* ☎415/476–2078 ⊕*www.outdoors.ucsf.edu*) originate in either Sausalito or Mission Bay in San Francisco and range from moonlight paddles from Sausalito (with views of the San Francisco skyline) to daytime sea-kayaking classes for all levels.

Sea Trek Kayaking (☎415/488–1000 ⊕*www.seatrekkayak.com*) has trips around Angel Island and the Golden Gate Bridge, moonlight paddles, and many trips in Marin County. Half-day trips, some designed especially for families, are $65–$75 per person, $30–$45 for kids. Most excursions leave from Sausalito (just across the Golden Gate Bridge

A Shore Thing

Taking in a beachside sunset is the perfect way to end a busy day in the city (assuming the fog hasn't blown in for the afternoon). Always bring a sweater—even the sunniest of days can become cold and foggy without warning. Icy temperatures and treacherous currents make most waters too dangerous for swimming without a wet suit, but with a Frisbee, picnic, or some good walking shoes, you can have a fantastic day at the beach without leaving the city.

An urban beach, surrounded by Fort Mason, Ghirardelli Square, and Fisherman's Wharf, **Aquatic Park Beach** (⊕ *www. nps.gov/safr*) is a tiny, ¼-mi-long strip of sand with gentle water, bordered by docks and piers. The waters near shore are shallow, safe for kids to swim or wade, and fairly clean (admirably so, for a city). Facilities include restrooms and showers.

Baker Beach (✉ *Gibson Rd., off Bowley St., southwest corner of Presidio*), with gorgeous views of the Golden Gate Bridge and the Marin Headlands, is a local favorite. The pounding surf and strong currents make swimming a dangerous prospect, but the mile-long shoreline is ideal for fishing, building sand castles, or watching sea lions at play. On warm days, the entire beach is packed with bodies—including nudists, who hang out at the north end. Picnic tables, grills, restrooms, and drinking water are available.

Sheltered **China Beach,** one of the city's safest swimming beaches, was named for the poor Chinese fishermen who once camped here. (Some maps label it James D. Phelan Beach.) This 600-foot strip of sand, south of the Presidio and Baker Beach, has gentle waters as well as changing rooms, bathrooms, showers, grills, drinking water, and picnic tables.

The largest—and probably best—of San Francisco's city beaches, **Ocean Beach** stretches for more than 3 mi along the Great Highway south of the Cliff House, making it ideal for long walks and runs. It isn't the cleanest shore, but it's an easy-to-reach place to chill; spot sea lions sunning themselves atop Seal Rock, at the north end of the beach; or watch daredevil surfers riding the roiling waves. Because of extremely dangerous currents, swimming isn't recommended. After the sun sets, bonfires form a string of lights along the beach in summer. (Fires are prohibited north of Fulton Street or south of Lincoln Way, the northern and southern edges of Golden Gate Park.) Restrooms are at the north end.

5

in Marin County), but Angel Island tours leave from the island.

WHALE-WATCHING

Between January and April, hundreds of gray whales migrate along the coast; the rest of the year humpback and blue whales feed offshore at the Farallon Islands. The best place to watch them from shore is Point Reyes, in Marin County. In town, try the Coastal Trail at Lands End in Lincoln Park.

For a better view, head out on a whale-watching trip. Seas around San Francisco can be rough, so pack motion-sickness tablets. You should also dress warmly, wear sunscreen, and pack rain gear and sunglasses; binoculars come in handy, too. Tour companies don't provide meals or snacks, so bring your own lunch and water. Make reservations at least a week in advance. Most trips last a full day.

California Whale Adventures (☎415/760–8613 ⊕*www. californiawhaleadventures.com*) has year-round whale-watching trips ($95) Friday through Sunday. In October, you can take a great white shark tour, and seabird tours run July through October; these tours cost $150 per person and are operated on weekends only. All trips leave from Fisherman's Wharf.

The Oceanic Society (☎415/474–3385 ⊕*www.oceanicsociety. org*) operates year-round whale-watching excursions ($90 Friday, $100 weekends), minimum age 10 years, with top-notch interpretation; in winter they also run half-day trips ($45 adults, $40 ages 7–15) from Bodega Bay and Half Moon Bay (the minimum age is 7). The society also has a whale-watching hotline (☎415/474–0488) and publishes the excellent *Oceanic Society Field Guide to the Gray Whale*. Most trips leave from the San Francisco Yacht Harbor, outside the harbormaster's office in the Marina district.

Shopping

WORD OF MOUTH

"Saturday was the [Ferry Plaza] Farmers' Market. We knew it would be a happenin' place but were surprised when we looked out our window at 8 AM to see how busy it really was!"
—BeachGirl247

Updated
by Denise
M. Leto

FROM ITS SWANK BOUTIQUES TO its funky thrift stores, San Francisco is simply one of the best shopping destinations in the United States. Deep-pocketed browsers as well as window shoppers mob the dozens of pricey shops packed into a few blocks around Union Square, while bargain hunters dig through used-record and thrift shops in the Mission District and the Haight. From the anarchist bookstore to the mouthwatering specialty food purveyors at the gleaming Ferry Building, the local shopping opportunities strikingly reflect the city's character.

MAJOR SHOPPING DISTRICTS

Many San Francisco neighborhoods keep their own hours, and the shops in those neighborhoods follow suit. In the Castro and the Mission, for example, both filled with restaurants and nightspots, many of the shops are open until 8 PM or later, to take advantage of the evening foot traffic. More sedate residential neighborhoods like Noe Valley, Pacific Heights, and Union Street tend to close shop earlier, though, often by 6 PM and rarely past 7. (In these quieter neighborhoods, stores also tend to be closed Sunday, Monday, and sometimes even Tuesday.) Many Chinatown shops keep long hours, opening by 8 or 9 AM and staying open into the evening. And though the Union Square area attracts serious shoppers, you won't find anything to buy until around 10 AM, when most of the stores open. The neighborhoods below are profiled in alphabetical order.

THE CASTRO & NOE VALLEY

The Castro, often called the gay capital of the world, is filled with men's clothing boutiques and home-accessories stores geared to the neighborhood's fairly wealthy demographic. Just south of the Castro on 24th Street, largely residential Noe Valley is an enclave of fancy-food stores, bookshops, women's clothing boutiques, and specialty gift stores. "Stroller Valley," as it's also known, is dense with cute kid shops. The city's most adult-oriented neighborhood, the Castro, is nearly devoid of shops of interest to kids; be aware that window displays are sometimes explicit.

CHINATOWN

The intersection of Grant Avenue and Bush Street marks the gateway to Chinatown. The area's 24 blocks of shops, restaurants, and markets are a nonstop tide of activity. Dominating the exotic cityscape are the sights and smells of food: crates of bok choy, tanks of live crabs, cages of live

TOP 5 SHOPPING

Music Mecca, Haight, Union Square: Budding rock stars can spend all day in massive Amoeba, in the Haight, and still not get through all the CDs and vinyl. Loaded up on music, head to Union Square's Apple Store for the latest hot-pink iPod to store it.

Ahoy, Pirates!, Mission Prepare to board one of the city's most unique stores, 826 Valencia, where young buccaneers can pick up a Jolly Roger, a spyglass, and dig for treasure (really).

Go Fly a Kite, Chinatown: Wonder at brilliant dragons, swooping eagles, and a Darth Vader or two thrown in for good measure at the China-town Kite Shop, a Grant Avenue favorite for decades.

Toys for Little Kids, Noe Valley: Tots (and their parents) adore the high-quality toys a jumble at **Ark Toys, Books & Crafts.** You'll find everything from Thomas the Tank Engine and science kits to wooden European imports and ride-on toys.

Toys for Big Kids, Haight: Kids with a yen for Japanese pop-cultural gear and gadgets can stock up on Gama-Go Ninja Kitty bike messenger bags and Uglydoll keychains and figurines at superhip Giant Robot.

6

partridges, and hanging whole chickens. Racks of Chinese silks, colorful pottery, baskets, and carved figurines are displayed chockablock on the sidewalks, alongside fragrant herb shops where your bill might be tallied on an abacus. And if you need to knock off souvenir shopping for the kids and office-mates in your life, the dense and multiple selections of toys, T-shirts, mugs, magnets, decorative boxes, and countless other trinkets make it a quick, easy, and inexpensive proposition. Chinatown offers the city's most kid-friendly shopping; reasonably priced treasures await, from ninja swords to dragon-shaped kites.

FISHERMAN'S WHARF

A constant throng of sightseers crowds Fisherman's Wharf, and with good reason: Pier 39, the Anchorage, Ghirardelli Square, and the Cannery are all here, each with shops and restaurants, as well as outdoor entertainment—musicians, mimes, and magicians. Best of all is the Wharf's view of the bay and its proximity to cable-car lines, which can shuttle shoppers directly to Union Square. Many of the tourist-oriented shops border on tacky, slinging the requisite Golden Gate tees, taffy, and baskets of shells, but tucked into the mix are a few fine galleries, clothing shops, and groceries that even locals will deign to visit. If the kids want city souvenirs, you'll find the same ones in Chinatown for less money.

THE HAIGHT

Haight Street is a perennial attraction for visitors, if only to see the sign at Haight and Ashbury streets—the geographic center of the flower power movement during the 1960s. It's still possible to find high-quality vintage clothing, funky shoes, folk art from around the world, and used records and CDs galore in this always-busy neighborhood. For teens, the Haight can be a treasure trove, worth an entire day of browsing.

HAYES VALLEY

A community park called Patricia's Green breaks up a crowd of cool shops just west of the Civic Center. Here you can find everything from hip housewares to art galleries to handcrafted jewelry. The density of unique stores—as well as the lack of chains anywhere in sight—makes it a favorite destination for many San Francisco shoppers. Teens with flair and carryable little ones may enjoy Hayes Valley, but the offerings here are unlikely to grab young children (the refreshments are decidedly adult).

JAPANTOWN

Unlike the ethnic enclaves of Chinatown, North Beach, and the Mission, the 5-acre **Japan Center** (⊠*Bordered by Laguna, Fillmore, and Post Sts. and Geary Blvd.* ☎*No phone*) is under one roof. Especially worthwhile are the Kintetsu and Kinokuniya buildings, where shops sell things like bonsai trees, tapes and records, jewelry, antique kimonos, *tansu* (Japanese chests), electronics, and colorful glazed dinnerware and teapots. The *manga* (graphic novels), large design section, and funky Japanese pop-cultural offerings at the fantastic Kinokuniya Bookstores can occupy both kids and adults for hours.

THE MARINA DISTRICT

With the city's highest density of (mostly) nonchain stores, the Marina is an outstanding shopping nexus. But it's nobody's secret—those with plenty of cash and style to burn flood the boutiques to snap up luxe accessories and housewares. Union Street and Chestnut Street in particular cater to the shopping whims of the grown-up sorority sisters and frat boys who live in the surrounding pastel Victorians.

That population demands cute must-haves for babies, but there's not much of interest here for kids 5 and up.

THE MISSION

The aesthetic of the resident Pabst Blue Ribbon–downing hipsters and starving-artist types contributes to the affordability and individuality of shopping here. These night owls keep the city's best thrift stores, vintage-furniture shops, alternative bookstores, and, increasingly, small clothing boutiques afloat. As the Mission gentrifies, though, bargain hunters find themselves trekking the long blocks in search of truly local flavor. Thankfully, many of the city's best bakeries and cafés are sprinkled throughout the area. The same teens who dig the Haight will find plenty to love here.

NORTH BEACH

Although it's sometimes compared to New York City's Greenwich Village, North Beach is only a fraction of the size, clustered tightly around Washington Square and Columbus Avenue. Most of its businesses are small eateries, cafés, and shops selling clothing, antiques, and vintage wares. Once the center of the Beat movement, North Beach still has a bohemian spirit that's especially apparent at the rambling City Lights Bookstore, where Beat poetry lives on. Shops here may not cater to kids, but with so much eating going on, you can buy yourself some time for grownup browsing.

PACIFIC HEIGHTS

The rest of the city likes to deprecate its wealthiest neighborhood, but no one has any qualms about weaving through the mansions to come to Fillmore and Sacramento streets to shop. With grocery and hardware stores sitting alongside local clothing ateliers and international designer outposts, these streets manage to mix small-town America with big-city glitz. After you've splurged on a cashmere sweater or a handblown glass vase, an outdoor seat at Peet's or Coffee Bean is the perfect way to pass an afternoon watching the parade of Old Money, dogs, and strollers. The other half may shop *for* their kids here, but they don't shop *with* their kids here.

SOMA

High San Francisco rents mean there aren't many discount outlets in the city, but a few do exist in the renovated warehouses south of Market Street, called SoMa. Most outlets are along the streets and alleyways bordered by 2nd, Townsend, Howard, and 10th streets. At the other end of the spectrum is the gift shop of the San Francisco Museum of Modern Art, which sells handmade jewelry, upscale and offbeat housewares, and other great gift items. Distances here are long, so if you're planning to tackle the discount outlets, bring a stroller and plenty of diversions. With walkers, a stop at Metreon or Yerba Buena Gardens (and its carousel) may recharge their batteries.

UNION SQUARE

Serious shoppers head straight to Union Square, San Francisco's main shopping area and the site of most of its department stores, including Macy's, Neiman Marcus, Barney's, and Saks Fifth Avenue. Also here are the Virgin Megastore, Levi's, and Borders Books, Music & Cafe. Nearby are such platinum-card international boutiques as Yves Saint Laurent, Cartier, Emporio Armani, Gucci, Hermès of Paris, Louis Vuitton, and Gianni Versace. Break out the bribes, though, because about the only things here that kids will find cool are the tacky souvenirs.

The latest major arrival is the **Westfield San Francisco Shopping Centre** (⊠*865 Market St., between 4th and 5th Sts., Union Square* ☎*415/495–5656*), anchored by Bloomingdale's and Nordstrom. Besides the sheer scale of this mammoth mall, it's notable for its gorgeous atriums and its top-notch dining options (no typical food courts here—instead you'll find branches of a few top local restaurants.) If the kids need a break, head to one of the center's two family lounges (behind the food court and inside Bloomie's), with games, toys, a TV, and video console for them—and recliners and couches for you.

BOOKS

Alexander Book Co. The three floors of titles here are stocked with literature, poetry, and children's books, with a focus on hard-to-find works by men and women of color. ⊠*50 2nd St., between Market and Mission Sts., SoMa* ☎*415/495–2992.*

Book Passage. Windows at this modest-size bookstore frame close-up views of the Ferry Building docks and San Francisco Bay. Commuters snatch up magazines by the front door as they speed off to catch their ferries, while leisurely shoppers thumb through the thorough selection of cooking and travel titles. Author events typically take place several times a month. The store has a small but thoughtful selection of children's books, but alas, there's nowhere to sit. ✉ *1 Ferry Bldg., #42, Embarcadero at foot of Market St., Embarcadero* ☎ *415/835–1020.*

Booksmith. Founded in 1976, this fine bookshop sells current releases, children's titles, and offbeat periodicals. Authors passing through town often make a stop at this neighborhood institution. If there's a special event going on, keep walking; the kids' book section at the back will be impossible to reach. ✉ *1644 Haight St., between Cole and Clayton Sts., Haight* ☎ *415/863–8688.*

★ Fodor'sChoice **City Lights Bookstore.** The city's most famous bookstore is where the Beat movement of the 1950s was born. Neal Cassady and Jack Kerouac hung out in the basement and now regulars and tourists while hours away in this well-worn space. The upstairs room highlights impressive poetry and Beat literature collections. Poet Lawrence Ferlinghetti, the owner, remains active in the workings of this three-story place. Since publishing Allen Ginsberg's *Howl* in 1956, City Lights' press continues to publish a dozen new titles each year. But as famous as it is, somehow you just never see kids here. ✉ *261 Columbus Ave., at Broadway, North Beach* ☎ *415/362–8193.*

Dog Eared Books. An eclectic group of shoppers—gay and straight, fashionable and not—wanders the aisles of this pleasantly ramshackle bookstore. The diverse selection of publications, about 85% of them used, includes quirky selections like vintage children's books, remaindered art books, and local 'zines. A bin of free books just outside the front door is fun to browse, if only to see the odd assortment of out-of-date titles. ✉ *900 Valencia St., at 20th St., Mission* ☎ *415/282–1901.*

Modern Times Bookstore. Named after Charlie Chaplin's politically subversive film, the store stocks high-quality literary fiction and nonfiction, much of it with a political bent. There are also sections for children's books, Spanish-language titles, and magazines and local subversive 'zines. Author readings and public forums are held regularly. If you're looking to kill a little time in the Mission before hooking up with dinner companions, this is a low-key and inviting place to hide out in the stacks. Kids' books that are socially conscious and cute? It's definitely not the usual fare here. ✉ *888 Valencia St., between 19th and 20th Sts., Mission* ☎ *415/282–9246.*

CHILDREN'S CLOTHING

Dottie Doolittle. Pacific Heights mothers shop here for charming silk dresses and other special-occasion outfits for their little ones. Less pricey togs for infants, boys to size 12, and girls to size 16 are also on hand. ✉*3680 Sacramento St., at Spruce St., Pacific Heights* ☎*415/563–3244.*

Murik. Those with fashion-forward five-year-olds will be grateful to discover this tiny shop. From Petit Bateau jumpers for infants to linen pants and ruffled shirts for your grade-schooler, the pricey garments are so adorable you might wish you could wear them yourself. ✉*73 Geary St., between Grant Ave. and Kearny St., Union Square* ☎*415/395–9200.*

Small Frys. The colorful cottons carried here are mainly for infants, with some articles for older children. The mix includes OshKosh and many Californian and French labels. A few shelves of toys and whimsical finger puppets round out the collection. ✉*4066 24th St., between Castro and Noe Sts., Noe Valley* ☎*415/648–3954.*

Yountville. Tiny silk sweaters and flouncy pink swimsuits are among the Californian and European designs at this store for infants to eight-year-olds. ✉*2416 Fillmore St., between Jackson and Washington Sts., Pacific Heights* ☎*415/922–5050.*

DEPARTMENT STORES

Bloomingdales. The shiny newness (the store opened in late 2006), the black-and-white checkerboard theme, the abundance of glass, and the sheer size might remind you of Vegas. The store emphasizes American designers like Diane von Furstenberg and Jack Spade. Its well-planned layout defines individual departments without losing the grand and open feel. In the family lounge, tired little ones can play with toys and stuffed animals or watch Nickleodeon while you sink into a couch. Another lounge awaits in the kids' section, and there are PlayStations among the racks. ✉*845 Market St., between Grant Ave. and Kearny St., Union Square* ☎*415/856–5300.*

Macy's. Downtown has two behemoth branches of this retailer, where you can find almost anything you could want, if only you have the patience to find it. One—with entrances on Geary, Stockton, and O'Farrell streets—

CLOSE UP

Chocolate Rush

Domenico Ghirardelli started making chocolate in California in the mid-19th century. In the 1890s, he purchased the Pioneer Woolen Mill building, now part of San Francisco's Ghirardelli Square, and moved the **Ghirardelli Chocolate Company** there. Although production of its chocolate has since been moved across the bay, you can still visit the original factory, where you can purchase the famed confections, get a peek at some of the original chocolate-making equipment, and order an eight-scoop hot-fudge sundae at the adjacent soda fountain.

Scharffen Berger began making its world-renowned product in 1997, when a former winemaker and a colleague who had recently visited a chocolate maker in Lyons, France, teamed up to concoct chocolate by artisanal European methods. Reserve in advance to tour the factory, housed in a brick warehouse in Berkeley. (Yes, you'll get a taste at the end.) ✉ *914 Heinz Ave., Berkeley* ☎ *510/981–4066* ⊕ *www.scharffenbergertour.com.*

Joseph Schmidt Confections opened its small shop in the Castro in 1983. You can still shop here for the trademark egg-shaped truffles, as well as elaborate seasonal sculptures that have earned Schmidt the

title "the Rodin of chocolate." And because such works of art deserve better than a paper bag, chocolates can be packaged in hand-painted papier-mâché boxes. ✉ *3489 16th St., between Church and Sanchez Sts., Castro* ☎ *415/861–8682.*

Michael and Jacky Recchiuti take a different approach at **Recchiuti Confections,** established in 1997. Traditional French techniques are used to infuse chocolates with unusual flavors from around the globe. Chocolates subtly flavored with ingredients such as star anise and pink peppercorns, and caramels infused with rose geranium oil are delicate and complex. ✉ *1 Ferry Bldg. #30, Embarcadero at foot of Market St., Embarcadero* ☎ *415/834–9494.*

French confectioner Jean-Marc Gorce of **XOX Truffles** has won over San Francisco foodies and everyday chocoholics alike with his 27 varieties of the sweet treat. In 1998 he and his wife opened their first shop, a bright little storefront in North Beach suffused with the smell of their many liqueur-flavored truffles. ✉ *754 Columbus Ave., between Greenwich and Filbert Sts., North Beach* ☎ *415/421–4814.*

—Sharron Wood

6

houses the women's, children's, furniture, and housewares departments. With its large selection and its emphasis on American designers, like DKNY and Marc Jacobs, the department for young women stands out. The men's department occupies its own building across Stockton Street. During the holidays, the elaborate window displays (as well as the store's location across the street from Union Square and its massive Christmas tree) draw families from all around the Bay Area. ✉ *170 O'Farrell St., at Stockton St., Union Square* ☎ *415/397–3333 Men's branch:* ✉ *50 O'Farrell St., entrance on Stockton St., Union Square* ☎ *415/397–3333.*

Neiman Marcus. The surroundings, which include a Philip Johnson–designed checkerboard facade, gilded atrium, and stained-glass skylight, are as ritzy as the goods showcased in them. The mix includes designer men's and women's clothing and accessories as well as posh household wares. Although the prices may raise an eyebrow or two, Neiman's biannual Last Call sales—in January and July—draw a crowd. After hitting the vast handbag salon, ladies who lunch daintily order consommé and bread laden with strawberry butter in the Rotunda Restaurant. While you're browsing the very small children's department upstairs, your kids can dream about going home with that battery-operated, kid-size Ferrari. ✉ *150 Stockton St., at Geary Blvd., Union Square* ☎ *415/362–3900.*

Nordstrom. Somehow Nordstrom manages to be all things to all people, and this location, with spiral escalators circling a four-story atrium, is no exception. Whether you're an elegant lady of a certain age shopping for a new mink coat or a teen on the hunt for a Roxy hoodie, the salespeople are known for being happy to help. While still carrying the best selections in town of new designers like Tory Burch, their own Nordstom brands have loyal followings. The latest addition is a Nordstrom Spa. The shoe department is legendary for its customer service—even for the smallest feet. ✉ *San Francisco Shopping Centre, 865 Market St., between 4th and 5th Sts., Union Square* ☎ *415/243–8500.*

FARMERS' MARKET

★ Fodor'sChoice **Ferry Plaza Farmers' Market.** The most upscale and expensive of the city's farmers' markets, in front of the restored Ferry Building, places baked goods and fancy pots of jam alongside organic basil and heirloom tomatoes.

The Saturday market is the grandest, with about 100 vendors packed both in front of and behind the building. The Tuesday and Thursday markets are smaller. At the Sunday garden market, vegetable and ornamental plants crop up next to a small selection of food items. (The Thursday and Sunday markets don't operate in winter, generally December or January through March.) The Saturday market is quite an event, and keeping track of kids under 7 can be stressful here. Happily, chasing pigeons and watching boats on the bay behind the building offers a nearby (and free) break. ✉*Ferry Plaza, Embarcadero at north end of Market St., Financial District* 🕾*415/291–3276* ⊕*www.ferryplazafarmersmarket. com* 🕙*Tues. and Sun. 10–2, Thurs. 4–8, Sat. 8–2.*

MUSIC

★ Fodor'sChoice **Amoeba Music.** With more than 2.5 million new and used CDs, DVDs, and records, this warehouselike store (and the original Berkeley location) carries titles you can't find on Amazon at bargain prices. No niche is ignored—from electronica and hip-hop to jazz and classical—and the stock changes daily. Weekly in-store performances attract large crowds. Teens and tweens laden with the store's trademark yellow bags glide dreamily down Haight Street, broke and happy. ✉*1855 Haight St., between Stanyan and Shrader Sts., Haight* 🕾*415/831–1200.*

Recycled Records. A Haight Street landmark, the store buys, sells, and trades a vast selection of used records, including hard-to-find imports and those of obscure alternative bands. The CD collection is large, but the vinyl is the real draw. ✉*1377 Haight St., between Masonic and Central Aves., Haight* 🕾*415/626–4075.*

Virgin Megastore. The huge, glitzy music store near Union Square has dozens of listening stations, extensive DVD and video-game collections, and many music and pop-culture-related books. The third-floor Citizen Cupcake serves panini, sweet treats, and even sake cocktails. ✉*2 Stockton St., at Market St., Union Square* 🕾*415/397–4525.*

TOYS & GADGETS

Apple Store San Francisco. A shiny, stainless-steel box is the setting for San Francisco's flagship Apple store, a high-tech temple to Macs and the people who use them. Play around with iPods, laptops, and hundreds of geeky accessories; then watch a theater presentation or attend an educational workshop. There is, naturellement, an Internet café, while the "Genius Bar" help those with computer woes. ✉1 Stockton St., at Market St., Union Square ☎415/392–0202.

Ark Toys, Books & Crafts. The store emphasizes high-quality toys, many of which have an educational bent (books, science kits) or encourage imaginative play (dress-up costumes, paper dolls). The stock includes numerous toys manufactured in Europe. Most of the items are for toddlers through 12-year-olds. ✉3845 24th St., between Church and Sanchez Sts., Noe Valley ☎415/821–1257.

Chinatown Kite Shop. Kites at this family-owned business (operating since 1969) range from basic diamond shapes to box- and animal-shaped configurations. Colorful dragon kites make great Chinatown souvenirs. ✉717 Grant Ave., between Clay and Sacramento Sts., Chinatown ☎415/989–5182.

826 Valencia. The brainchild of author Dave Eggers is primarily a center established to help kids with their writing skills via tutoring and storytelling events. But the storefront is also "San Francisco's only independent pirate supply store," a quirky space filled with eye patches, spyglasses, and other pirate-theme paraphernalia. Eggers's quarterly journal, McSweeney's, and other publications are available here. Proceeds benefit the writing center. Kids can dig for buried treasure, search for secret compartments, and stock up on pirate gear. ✉826 Valencia St., between 18th and 19th Sts., Mission ☎415/642–5905.

Exploratorium. The educational gadgets and gizmos sold here are so much fun that your kids—whether they're in grade school or junior high—might not realize they're learning while they're playing with them. Space- and dinosaur-related games are popular, as are science videos and CD-ROMs. ✉3601 Lyon St., at Marina Blvd., Marina ☎415/561–0360.

Giant Robot. This superhip spot feeds San Franciscans' passion for Asian pop cultural fluff, from Gama-Go Ninja Kitty bike messenger bags and Uglydoll keychains and figurines to Astro Boy stationery sets. Of course, the store also carries Giant Robot magazine, as well as a large selection of T-shirts. ✉618 Shrader St., at Haight St., Haight ☎415/876–4773.

FAMILY FUN

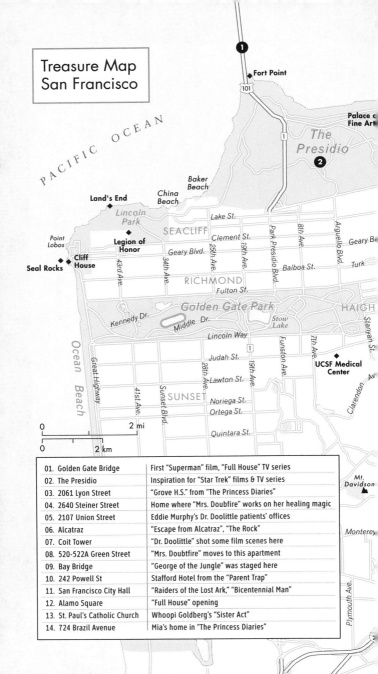

Treasure Map
San Francisco

01. Golden Gate Bridge	First "Superman" film, "Full House" TV series
02. The Presidio	Inspiration for "Star Trek" films & TV series
03. 2061 Lyon Street	"Grove H.S." from "The Princess Diaries"
04. 2640 Steiner Street	Home where "Mrs. Doubtfire" works on her healing magic
05. 2107 Union Street	Eddie Murphy's Dr. Doolittle patients' offices
06. Alcatraz	"Escape from Alcatraz", "The Rock"
07. Coit Tower	"Dr. Doolittle" shot some film scenes here
08. 520-522A Green Street	"Mrs. Doubtfire" moves to this apartment
09. Bay Bridge	"George of the Jungle" was staged here
10. 242 Powell St	Stafford Hotel from the "Parent Trap"
11. San Francisco City Hall	"Raiders of the Lost Ark", "Bicentennial Man"
12. Alamo Square	"Full House" opening
13. St. Paul's Catholic Church	Whoopi Goldberg's "Sister Act"
14. 724 Brazil Avenue	Mia's home in "The Princess Diaries"

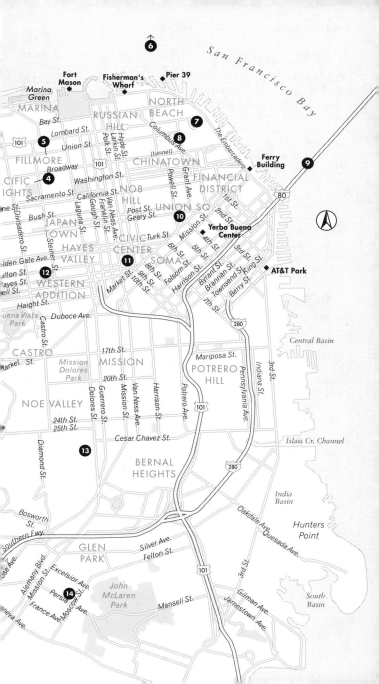

THE CLASSICS

"I'm thinking of an animal . . ."

With older kids you can play 20 Questions: Have your leader think of an animal, vegetable, or mineral (or, alternatively, a person, place, or thing) and let everybody else try to guess what it is. The correct guesser takes over as leader. If no one figures out the secret within 20 questions, the first person goes again. With younger children, limit the guessing to animals and don't put a ceiling on how many questions can be asked. With rivalrous siblings, just take turns being leader. Make the game's theme things you expect to see at your day's destination.

"I see something you don't see and it is blue."

Stuck for a way to get your youngsters to settle down in a museum? Sit them down on a bench in the middle of a room and play this vintage favorite. The leader gives just one clue—the color—and everybody guesses away.

FUN WITH THE ALPHABET

Family Ark

Noah had his ark—here's your chance to build your own. It's easy: Just start naming animals and work your way through the alphabet, from antelope to zebra.

"I'm going to the grocery . . ."

The first player begins, "I'm going to the grocery and I'm going to buy . . ." and finishes the sentence with the name of an object, found in grocery stores, that begins with the letter "A." The second player repeats what the first player has said, and adds the name of another item that starts with "B." The third player repeats everything that has been said so far and adds something that begins with "C" and so on through the alphabet. Anyone who skips or misremembers an item is out (or decide up front that you'll give hints to all who need 'em). You can modify the theme depending on where you're going that day, as "I'm going to X and I'm going to see . . ."

"I'm going to Asia on an ant to act up."

Working their way through the alphabet, players concoct silly sentences stating where they're going, how they're traveling, and what they'll do.

What I See, from A to Z

In this game, kids look for objects in alphabetical order—first something whose name begins with "A," next an item whose name begins with "B," and so on. If you're in the car, have children do their spotting through their own window. Whoever gets to Z first wins. Or have each child play to beat his own time. Try this one as you make your way through zoos and museums, too.

JUMP-START A CONVERSATION

What if . . . ?

Riding in the car and waiting in a restaurant are great times to get to know your youngsters better. Begin with imaginative questions to prime the pump.

■ If you were the tallest man on earth, what would your life be like? The shortest?

■ If you had a magic carpet, where would you go? Why? What would you do there?

■ If your parents gave you three wishes, what would they be?

■ If you were elected president, what changes would you make?

■ What animal would you like to be and what would your life be like?

■ What's a friend? Who are your best friends? What do you like to do together?

■ Describe a day in your life 10 years from now.

Druthers

How do your kids really feel about things? Just ask. "Would you rather eat worms or hamburgers? Hamburgers or candy?" Choose serious and silly topics—and have fun!

Faker, Faker

Reveal three facts about yourself. The catch: One of the facts is a fake. Have your kids ferret out the fiction. Take turns being the faker. Fakers who stump everyone win.

KEEP A STRAIGHT FACE

"Ha!"

Work your way around the car. First person says "Ha." Second person says "Ha, ha." Third person says "Ha" three times. And so on. Just try to keep a straight face. Or substitute "Here, kitty, kitty, kitty!"

Wiggle & Giggle

Give your kids a chance to stick out their tongues at you. Start by making a face, then have the next person imitate you and add a gesture of his own—snapping fingers, winking, clapping, sneezing, or the like. The next person mimics the first two and adds a third gesture, and so on.

Junior Opera

During a designated period of time, have your kids sing everything they want to say.

Igpay Atinlay

Proclaim the next 30 minutes Pig Latin time, and everybody has to talk in this fun code. To speak it, move the first consonant of every word to the end of the word and add "ay." "Pig" becomes "igpay," and "Latin" becomes "atinlay." For words that begin with a vowel, just add "ay" as a suffix.

MORE GOOD TIMES

Build a Story

"Once upon a time there lived . . ." Finish the sentence and ask the rest of your family, one at a time, to add another sentence or two. Bring a tape recorder along to record the narrative—and you can enjoy your creation again and again.

Not the Goofy Game

Have one child name a category. (Some ideas: first names, last names, animals, countries, friends, feelings, foods, hot or cold things, clothing.) Then take turns naming things that fall into that category. You're out if you name something that doesn't belong in the category—or if you can't think of another item to name. When only one person remains, start again. Choose categories depending on where you're going or where you've been—historic topics if you've seen a historic sight, animal topics before or after the zoo, upside-down things if you've been to the circus, and so on. Make the game harder by choosing category items in A-B-C order.

Color of the Day

Choose a color at the beginning of your outing and have your kids be on the lookout for things that are that color, calling out what they've seen when they spot it. If you want to keep score, keep a running list or use a pen to mark points on your kids' hands for every item they spot.

Click

Say "Click!" Then give each one of your kids a full minute to study a page of a magazine. After everyone has had a turn, go around the car naming items from the page. Players who can't name an item or who make a mistake are out.

The Quiet Game

Need a good giggle—or a moment of calm to figure out your route? The driver sets a time limit and everybody must be silent. The last person to make a sound wins.

Travel Smart
Family San
Francisco with
Kids

WORD OF MOUTH

"I keep this number in my cell phone: 415/673–MUNI. They're great! If I get lost, I just call and I relay to them where I am (or if I don't really know, I tell them what I see around me) and the operator might say, 'Oh, you're on the wrong side. Cross the street and catch the ___ bus.'"

—MelissaHl

GETTING HERE & AROUND

▌ BY AIR

Nonstop flights from New York to San Francisco take about 5½ hours, and with the 3-hour time change, it's possible to leave JFK by 8 AM and be in San Francisco by 10:30 AM. Some flights may require a midway stop, making the total excursion between 8 and 9½ hours. Nonstop times are approximately 1½ hours from Los Angeles, 3 hours from Dallas, 4½ hours from Chicago, 4½ hours from Atlanta, 11 hours from London, 12 hours from Auckland, and 13½ hours from Sydney. Travel time from Melbourne is about 16 hours. There is no nonstop service from Melbourne to San Francisco.

Airlines & Airports **Airline and Airport Links.com** (⊕www.airlineandairportlinks.com) has links to many of the world's airlines and airports.

Airline Security Issues **Transportation Security Administration** (⊕www.tsa.gov) has answers for almost every question that might come up.

AIRPORTS

The major gateway to San Francisco is San Francisco International Airport (SFO), 15 mi south of the city. It's off U.S. 101 near Millbrae and San Bruno. Oakland International Airport (OAK) is across the bay, not much farther away from downtown San Francisco (via I–80 east and I–880 south), but rush-hour traffic on the Bay Bridge

may lengthen travel times considerably. San Jose International Airport (SJC) is about 40 mi south of San Francisco; travel time depends largely on traffic flow, but plan an hour and a half with moderate traffic.

At all three airports security check-in can take 15–30 minutes at peak travel times.

Airport Information **San Francisco International Airport** ([SFO] ☎650/761-0800 ⊕www.flysfo.com). **Oakland International Airport** ([OAK] ☎510/577-4000 ⊕www.flyoakland.com). **San Jose International Airport** ([SJC] ☎408/277-4759 ⊕www.sjc.org).

GROUND TRANSPORTATION

FROM SAN FRANCISCO INTERNATIONAL AIRPORT
Transportation signage at the airport is color-coded by type and is quite clear. A taxi ride to downtown costs $35–$40. Airport shuttles are inexpensive and generally efficient. Lorrie's Airport Service and SuperShuttle both stop at the lower level near baggage claim, and take you anywhere within the city limits of San Francisco. They charge $15–$17, depending on where you're going. Lorrie's also sells tickets online, at a $2 discount each way; you can print them out before leaving home. SuperShuttle offers discounts for more than one person traveling in the same party ($16 for the first passenger, $16 each additional), but only if

you're traveling to a residential address.

You can take BART directly to downtown San Francisco; the trip takes about 30 minutes and costs less than $5.50. (There are both manned booths and vending machines for ticket purchases.) Trains leave from the international terminal every 15 minutes on weekdays and every 20 minutes on weekends.

Another inexpensive way to get to San Francisco is via two SamTrans buses: No. 292 (55 minutes, $1.50 from SFO, $3 to SFO) and the KX (35 minutes, $4; only one small carry-on bag permitted). Board the SamTrans buses on the lower level.

To drive to downtown San Francisco from the airport, take U.S. 101 north to the Civic Center/9th Street, 7th Street, or 4th Street/Downtown exit. If you're headed to the Embarcadero or Fisherman's Wharf, take I–280 north (the exit is to the right, just north of the airport, off U.S. 101) and get off at the 4th Street/King Street exit. King Street becomes the Embarcadero a few blocks east of the exit. The Embarcadero winds around the waterfront to Fisherman's Wharf.

FROM OAKLAND INTERNATIONAL AIRPORT

A taxi to downtown San Francisco costs $35–$40. By airport regulations, you must make reservations for shuttle service. BayPorter Express and other shuttles serve major hotels and provide door-to-door service to the East Bay and San Francisco. SuperShuttle operates vans to San Francisco and Oakland.

The best way to get to San Francisco via public transit is to take the AIR BART bus ($3) to the Coliseum/Oakland International Airport BART station (BART fares vary depending on where you're going; the ride to downtown San Francisco costs $3.55).

If you're driving from Oakland International Airport, take Hegenberger Road east to I–880 north to I–80 west over the Bay Bridge. This will likely take at least an hour.

Contacts **BayPorter Express** (☎415/467–1800 ⊕www.bayporter. com). **Lorrie's Airport Service** (☎415/334–9000 ⊕www.gosfovan. com). **SamTrans** (☎800/660–4287 ⊕www.samtrans.com). **SuperShuttle** (☎800/258–3826 or 415/558–8500 ⊕www.supershuttle.com).

FLIGHTS

Of the major carriers, Alaska, American, Continental, Delta, Mexicana, Southwest, and United all fly into San Francisco, Oakland, and San Jose airports. Harmony Airways, jetBlue, Primaris, and US Airways service Oakland. Frontier, Hawaiian, Horizon Air, and Northwest fly into SFO and San Jose. Virgin Atlantic and the budget-conscious Midwest Express fly into SFO.

Airline Contacts **Alaska Airlines** (☎800/252–7522 or 206/433–3100 ⊕www.alaskaair.com). **American Airlines** (☎800/433–7300 ⊕www. aa.com). **Continental Airlines** (☎800/523–3273 for U.S. and Mexico reservations, 800/231–0856 for international reservations ⊕www. continental.com). **Delta Airlines** (☎ 800/221–1212 for U.S. reservations, 800/241–4141 for international reservations ⊕www.delta. com). **jetBlue** (☎800/538–2583 ⊕www.jetblue.com). **Northwest Airlines** (☎800/225–2525 ⊕www. nwa.com). **Southwest Airlines** (☎ 800/435–9792 ⊕www. southwest.com). **United Airlines** (☎ 800/864–8331 for U.S. reservations, 800/538–2929 for international reservations ⊕www.united. com). **US Airways** (☎800/428–4322 for U.S. and Canada reservations, 800/622–1015 for international reservations ⊕www.usairways.com).

Smaller Airlines **Frontier Airlines** (☎800/432–1359 ⊕www. frontierairlines.com). **Midwest Airlines** (☎800/452–2022 ⊕www. midwestairlines.com).

▌ BY BART

Bay Area Rapid Transit (BART) trains, which run until midnight, travel under the bay via tunnel to connect San Francisco with Oakland, Berkeley, Pittsburgh/Bay Point, Richmond, Fremont, Dublin/ Pleasanton, and other small cities and towns in between. Within San Francisco, stations are limited to downtown, the Mission, and a couple of outlying neighborhoods.

Trains travel frequently from early morning until evening on weekdays—after 8 PM weekdays—and on weekends there's often a 20-minute wait between trains on the same line. Trains also travel south from San Francisco as far as Millbrae. BART trains connect downtown San Francisco to San Francisco International Airport; a ride is $5.35.

Intracity San Francisco fares are $1.50; intercity fares are $2.65–$5.60. BART bases its ticket prices on miles traveled and does not offer price breaks by zone. A monthly ticket, called a Fast Pass, is available for $48 and can be used on BART and on all Muni lines (including cable cars) within city limits. The easy-to-read maps posted in BART stations list fares based on destination, radiating out from your starting point of the current station.

During morning and evening rush hour, trains within the city are crowded—even standing room can be hard to come by. Cars at the far front and back of the train are less likely to be filled to capacity. Smoking, eating, and drinking are prohibited on trains and in stations.

Contacts **Bay Area Rapid Transit** ([BART] ☎415/989–2278 or 650/992–2278 ⊕www.bart.gov).

▌ BY BOAT

Several ferry lines run out of San Francisco. Blue & Gold Fleet operates a number of lines, including service to Sausalito ($9 one-way) and Tiburon ($9 one-way). Tickets are sold at Pier 41 (between Fisherman's Wharf and Pier 39), where the boats depart. There are also weekday Blue & Gold commuter ferries to Tiburon ($9) and Vallejo ($12.50) from the San Francisco Ferry Building. Alcatraz Cruises, owned by Hornblower Yachts, operates the ferries to Alcatraz Island ($24.50 including audio tour and National Park Service ranger–led programs) from Pier 33, about a half-mile east of Fisherman's Wharf ($2 shuttle buses serve several area hotels and other locations). Boats leave 10 times a day (14 times a day in summer) and the journey itself is 30 minutes. Allow roughly 2½ hours for a round-trip jaunt. Golden Gate Ferry runs daily to and from Sausalito and Larkspur (each costs $7.10 one-way), leaving from Pier 1, behind the San Francisco Ferry Building. The Alameda/Oakland Ferry operates daily between Alameda's Main Street Ferry Building, Oakland's Jack London Square, and San Francisco's Pier 41 and the Ferry Building ($6 one-way); some ferries go only to Pier 41 or the Ferry Building, so ask when you board. Purchase tickets on board.

Information **Alameda/Oakland Ferry** (☎510/522–3300 ⊕www.eastbayferry.com). **Alcatraz Cruises** (☎415/981–7625 ⊕www.alcatrazcruises.com). **Blue & Gold Fleet** (☎415/705–5555 ⊕www.blueandgoldfleet.com). **Golden Gate Ferry** (☎415/923–2000 ⊕www.goldengateferry.org). **San Francisco Ferry Building** (⊠Foot of Market St. on Embarcadero).

▌ BY BUS

Greyhound, the only long-distance bus company serving San Francisco, operates buses to and from most major cities in the country, terminating at the bus depot on Mission Street, near the Financial District. Service in California is limited to hub towns and cities only. Reservations are not accepted; seating is on a first-come, first-served basis. Cash, traveler's checks, and credit cards are accepted. Smoking is prohibited on all buses in California.

Bus Information **Greyhound** (⊠425 Mission St., between Fremont and 1st Sts., SoMa ☎800/231–2222 or 415/495–1569 ⊕www.greyhound.com).

MUNI

The San Francisco Municipal Railway, or Muni, operates light-rail vehicles, the historic F-line streetcars along Fisherman's Wharf and Market Street, trolley buses, and the world-famous cable cars. Light rail travels along Market Street to the Mission District and Noe Valley (J line), the Ingleside District (K line), and the Sunset District (L, M, and N lines); during peak hours (Mon.–Fri., 6 AM–9 AM and 3 PM–7 PM) the J line continues around the Embarcadero to the Caltrain station at 4th and King streets. The new T line light rail runs from the Castro, down Market Street, around the Embarcadero, and south past Hunters Point and Monster Park to Sunnydale Avenue and Bayshore Boulevard. Muni provides 24-hour service on select lines to all areas of the city.

On buses and streetcars, the fare is $1.50. Exact change is required, and dollar bills are accepted in the fare boxes. For all Muni vehicles other than cable cars, 90-minute transfers are issued free upon request at the time the fare is paid. Transfers are valid for two additional transfers in any direction. Cable cars cost $5 and include no transfers (*see By Cable Car, below*).

One-day ($11), three-day ($18), and seven-day ($24) Passports valid on the entire Muni system can be purchased at several outlets, including the cable-car ticket booth at Powell and Market streets and the visitor information center downstairs in Hallidie Plaza. A monthly ticket, called a Fast Pass, is available for $45 and can be used on all Muni lines (including cable cars) and on BART within city limits. The San Francisco CityPass, a discount ticket booklet to several major city attractions, also covers all Muni travel for seven consecutive days.

The San Francisco Municipal Transit and Street Map ($2.50) is a useful guide to the extensive transportation system. You can buy the map at most bookstores and at the San Francisco Visitor Information Center, on the lower level of Hallidie Plaza at Powell and Market streets.

■TIP→**During football season, Muni runs a special weekend shuttle to Candlestick Park for $7 round-trip.**

Outside the city, AC Transit serves the East Bay, and Golden Gate Transit serves Marin and Sonoma counties.

Bus & MUNI Information **AC Transit** (☎510/839–2882 ⊕www.actransit.org). **Golden Gate Transit** (☎415/923–2000 ⊕www.goldengate.org). **San Francisco Municipal Railway System** ([Muni] ☎415/673–6864 ⊕www.sfmuni.com).

■ **BY CABLE CAR**

Don't miss the sensation of moving up and down some of San Francisco's steepest hills in a clattering cable car, the only moving thing listed on the National Register of Historic Places. As it pauses at a designated stop, jump aboard and wedge yourself into any available space. Then just hold on.

The fare (for one direction) is $5 (Muni Passport holders pay a $1 supplement). You can buy tickets on board (exact change isn't necessary) or at the kiosks at the cable-car turnarounds at Hyde and Beach streets and at Powell and Market streets.

The heavily traveled Powell–Mason and Powell–Hyde lines begin at Powell and Market streets near Union Square and terminate at Fisherman's Wharf; lines for these routes can be long, especially in summer. The California Street line runs east and west from Market and California streets to Van Ness Avenue; there is often no wait to board this route.

■ **BY CAR**

Driving in San Francisco can be a challenge because of the one-way streets, snarly traffic, and steep hills. The first two elements can be frustrating enough, but those hills are tough for unfamiliar drivers.

Be sure to leave plenty of room between your car and other vehicles when on a steep slope. This is especially important when you've braked at a stop sign on a steep incline. Whether with a stick shift or an automatic transmission, every car rolls backward for a moment once the brake is released. So don't pull too close to the car ahead of you. When it's time to pull forward, keep your foot on the brake while tapping lightly on the accelerator. Once the engine is engaged, let up on the brake and head uphill.

■TIP➔Remember to curb your wheels when parking on hills—turn wheels away from the curb when facing uphill, toward the curb when facing downhill. You can get a ticket if you don't do this.

San Francisco is built on the grid system. Market Street, which runs diagonally southwest to northeast, divides several neighborhoods. If a street begins at Market, that's where the numbering of its addresses begins.

Throughout the city, as you move from one block to the next, the addresses on most streets increase by 100. To find the block number you're in, look at the top of the white street signs at intersections. You'll see a multiple of 100, with an arrow pointing to the next-highest block.

With a numbered road, you need to know whether it's called an avenue or a street. "The Avenues" begin one block west of Arguello Boulevard and run north–south through the Richmond and Sunset districts, in the western part of the city. Numbered *streets,* however, begin downtown, south of Market Street, and continue south and west through Potrero Hill, the Mission, the Castro, and Noe Valley.

Market Street runs southwest from the Ferry Building, then becomes Portola Drive as it nears Twin Peaks (which lie beneath the giant radio-antennae structure, Sutro Tower). It can be difficult to drive across Market. The major east–west streets north of Market are Geary Boulevard (it's called Geary Street east of Van Ness Avenue), which runs to the Pacific Ocean; Fulton Street, which begins at the back of the Opera House and continues along the north side of Golden Gate Park to Ocean Beach; Oak Street, which runs east from Golden Gate Park toward downtown, then flows into northbound Franklin Street; and Fell Street, the left two lanes of which cut through Golden Gate Park and empty into Lincoln Boulevard, which continues to the ocean.

Among the major north–south streets are Divisadero, which becomes Castro Street at Duboce Avenue and continues to just past César Chavez Street; Van Ness Avenue, which becomes South Van Ness Avenue when it crosses Market Street; and Park Presidio Boulevard, which empties into 19th Avenue.

PARKING

San Francisco is a terrible city for parking. In the Financial District and Civic Center neighborhoods, parking is forbidden on most streets between 4 PM and 6 PM. Check street signs carefully to confirm, because illegally parked cars are towed immediately. Downtown parking lots are often full, and most are expensive. The city-owned Sutter-Stockton, Ellis-

O'Farrell, and 5th-and-Mission garages have the most reasonable rates in the downtown area. Large hotels often have parking available, but it doesn't come cheap; many charge in excess of $40 a day for the privilege.

Garages **Ellis-O'Farrell Garage** (⌧123 O'Farrell St., at Stockton St., Downtown ☎415/986–4800 ⊕www.eofgarage.com). **Embarcadero Center Garage** (⌧1–4 Embarcadero Center, between Battery and Drumm Sts., Financial District ☎800/733–6318 ⊕www.embarcaderocenter.com). **5th-and-Mission Garage** (⌧833 Mission St., at 5th St., SoMa ☎415/982–8522 ⊕www.fifthandmission.com). **Opera Plaza Garage** (⌧601 Van Ness Ave., at Turk St., Civic Center ☎415/771–4776). **Pier 39 Garage** (⌧Embarcadero at Beach St., Fisherman's Wharf ☎415/705–5418 ⊕www.pier39.com). **Portsmouth Square Garage** (⌧733 Kearny St., at Clay St., Chinatown ☎415/982–6353 ⊕www.portsmouthsquaregarage.com). **766 Vallejo Garage** (⌧766 Vallejo St., at Powell St., North Beach ☎415/989–4490). **Sutter-Stockton Garage** (⌧444 Stockton St., at Sutter St., Downtown ☎415/982–7275). **Wharf Garage** (⌧350 Beach St., at Taylor St., Fisherman's Wharf).

ROAD CONDITIONS
Although rush "hour" is 6–10 AM and 3–7 PM, you can hit gridlock on any day at any time, especially over the Bay Bridge and leaving and/or entering the city from the south. Sunday-afternoon traffic can be heavy as well, especially over the bridges.

The most comprehensive and immediate traffic updates are available through the city's 511 service, either online at *www.511.org* (where Web cams show you the traffic on your selected route) or by calling 511. On the radio, tune into an all-news radio station such as KSFO 560 AM, KCBS 740 AM, and KNBR 680/1050 AM.

Be especially watchful of nonindicated lane changes. There's a lot of construction going on in the SoMa neighborhood and the waterfront area in the southeast, but this doesn't create too many traffic problems.

San Francisco is the only major American city uncut by freeways. To get from the Bay Bridge to the Golden Gate Bridge, you'll have to take surface streets, specifically Van Ness Avenue, which doubles as U.S. Hwy 101 through the city.

ROADSIDE EMERGENCIES
Dial 911 to report accidents on the road and to reach police, the highway patrol, or the fire department.

Emergency Services **AAA** (☎415/565–2012).

RULES OF THE ROAD
To encourage carpooling during heavy traffic times, some freeways have special lanes for so-called high-occupancy vehicles (HOVs)—cars carrying more than one or two passengers. Look for the white-painted diamond in the middle of the lane. Road signs next to or above the lane indicate the hours that carpooling is in effect. If you're stopped by the police because you

don't meet the criteria for travel in these lanes, expect a fine of more than $200.

In July 2008, state law banned drivers from using handheld mobile telephones while operating a vehicle (but that bad habit will surely be hard to shake). The use of seat belts in both front and back seats is required in California. The speed limit on city streets is 25 MPH unless otherwise posted. A right turn on a red light after stopping is legal unless posted otherwise, as is a left on red at the intersection of two one-way streets. Always strap children under 80 pounds or age eight into approved child-safety seats.

RENTAL CARS

Unless you plan on making excursions into Marin County, the Wine Country, or beyond, avoid renting a car in San Francisco. Driving in the city is difficult and there are several other ways of getting around town. If you do have a day trip on your agenda, it's easy to organize a single day rate with a car rental agency (although you should check to see whether they mean a 24-hour time period or less).

When you reserve a car, ask about cancellation penalties, taxes, drop-off charges (if you're planning to pick up the car in one city and leave it in another), and surcharges (for being under or over a certain age, for additional drivers, or for driving across state or country borders or beyond a specific distance from your point of rental). All these things can add substantially to your costs. Request car seats and extras such as GPS when you book.

Rates are sometimes—but not always—better if you book in advance or reserve through a rental agency's Web site. There are other reasons to book ahead, though: for popular destinations, during busy times of the year, or to ensure that you get certain types of cars (vans, SUVs, exotic sports cars).

■TIP→**Make sure that a confirmed reservation guarantees you a car. Agencies sometimes overbook, particularly for busy weekends and holiday periods.**

Car rental costs in San Francisco vary seasonally but generally begin at $30 a day and $150 a week for an economy car with air-conditioning, automatic transmission, and unlimited mileage. This doesn't include tax on car rentals, which is 8.5%. If you dream of driving with the top down, or heading out of town to ski the Sierra, consider renting a specialty vehicle. Most major agencies have a few on hand, but the best overall service is with two locally owned agencies: Specialty Rentals and City Rent-a-Car. The former specializes in high-end vehicles and arranges for airport pickup and drop-off. City Rent-a-Car also arranges airport transfers but also delivers cars to Bay Area hotels. Both agencies also rent standard vehicles at prices competitive with those of the majors.

ALTERNATIVE RENTALS

City Car Share, Flex Car, and Zip Car are membership organizations for residents who need a car only for short-term use. They're especially useful if you only want to rent a car for part of the day (say four to six hours), find yourself far from the airport, or if you're younger than most rental agencies' 25-years-or-older requirement. The membership fee often allows you to use their service in several metropolitan areas. If using such a service, you can rent a car by the hour as well as by the day.

Two companies, Electric Time Car Rentals and GoCar, rent electric vehicles at Fisherman's Wharf and Union Square. These cars can travel between 25 and 35 MPH and are very handy for neighborhood-based sightseeing, but they're not allowed on the Golden Gate Bridge.

Electric Time Car Rentals has two-seat and four-seat cars with detachable roofs, locked storage boxes, and GPS audio tours of the city. They're at Anchorage Alley in Fisherman's Wharf. The GoCars are electric, two-seater, three-wheeled, open convertibles with roll bars (so drivers must wear helmets). Their vehicles also have computerized navigation and audio guides. You can pick up a GoCar at two locations: Fisherman's Wharf and Union Square.

Automobile Associations U.S.: **American Automobile Association** ([AAA] ☎415/565–2141 ⊕www.aaa.com); most contact with the organization is through state and regional members. **National Automobile Club** (☎800/622–2136 ⊕www.thenac.com); membership is open to California residents only.

Local Agencies A-One Rent-a-Car (☎415/771–3978). **City Car Share** (☎415/995–8588 or 510/352–0323

⊕www.citycarshare.org). **City Rent-a-Car** (☎415/861–1312 or 415/359–1331). **Electric Time Car Rentals** (☎415/674–8800 ⊕www.etcars.com). **Flex Car** (☎415/282–3539 ⊕www.flexcar. com). **GoCar** (☎800/914–6227 ⊕www.gocarsf.com). **Specialty Rentals** (☎415/701–1600 or 800/400–8412 ⊕www. specialtyrentals.com). **Super Cheap Car Rental** (☎650/777–9993 ⊕www.supercheapcar.com). **Zip Car** (☎415/495–7478 ⊕www.zipcar. com).

Major Agencies Alamo (☎800/462–5266 ⊕www.alamo. com). **Avis** (☎800/331–1212 ⊕www.avis.com). **Budget** (☎800/527–0700 ⊕www.budget. com). **Hertz** (☎800/654–3131 ⊕www.hertz.com). **National Car Rental** (☎800/227–7368 ⊕www. nationalcar.com).

CAR-RENTAL INSURANCE
If you own a car and carry comprehensive car insurance for both collision and liability, your personal auto insurance will probably cover a rental, but read your policy's fine print to be sure. If you don't have auto insurance, then you should probably buy the collision- or loss-damage waiver (CDW or LDW) from the rental company. This eliminates your liability for damage to the car. Some credit cards offer CDW coverage, but it's usually supplemental to your own insurance and rarely covers SUVs, minivans, luxury models, and the like. If your coverage is secondary, you may still be liable for loss-of-use costs from the car-rental company (again, read the fine print).

But no credit-card insurance is valid unless you use that card for *all* transactions, from reserving to paying the final bill.

■TIP→**Diners Club offers primary CDW coverage on all rentals reserved and paid for with the card. This means that Diners Club's company—not your own car insurance—pays in case of an accident. It** *doesn't* **mean that your car-insurance company won't raise your rates once it discovers you had an accident.**

You may also be offered supplemental liability coverage; the car-rental company is required to carry a minimal level of liability coverage insuring all renters, but it's rarely enough to cover claims in a really serious accident if you're at fault. Your own auto-insurance policy will protect you if you own a car; if you don't, you have to decide whether you are willing to take the risk.

U.S. rental companies sell CDWs and LDWs for about $15 to $25 a day; supplemental liability is usually more than $10 a day. The car-rental company may offer you all sorts of other policies, but they're rarely worth the cost. Personal accident insurance, which is basic hospitalization coverage, is an especially egregious rip-off if you already have health insurance.

■TIP→**You can decline the insurance from the rental company and purchase it through a third-party provider such as Travel Guard (www.travelguard.com)—$9 per day for $35,000 of coverage. That's sometimes just under half the price of the CDW offered by some car-rental companies.**

Rental agencies in California aren't required to include liability insurance in the price of the rental. If you cause an accident, you may expose your assets to litigation. When in doubt about your own policy's coverage, take the liability coverage that the agency offers. If you plan to take the car out of California, ask if the policy is valid in other states or countries. Most car-rental companies won't insure a loss or damage that occurs outside of their coverage area—particularly in Mexico, though some offer supplemental policies for Mexico.

■ BY TAXI

Taxi service is notoriously bad in San Francisco, and hailing a cab can be frustratingly difficult in some parts of the city, especially on weekends. Popular nightspots such as the Mission, SoMa, North Beach, the Haight, and the Castro have a lot of cabs but a lot of people looking for taxis, too. Midweek, and during the day, you shouldn't have much of a problem—unless it's raining. In a pinch, hotel taxi stands are an option, as is calling for a pick-up. But be forewarned: taxi companies frequently don't answer the phone in peak periods. The absolute worst time to find a taxi is Friday afternoon and evening; plan well ahead, and if you're going to the airport, make a reservation or book a shuttle instead. Most taxi companies take advance reservations for airport and out-of-town runs but not in-town transfers.

Taxis in San Francisco charge $3.10 for the first .2 mi (one of the highest base rates in the United States), 45¢ for each additional .2 mi, and 45¢ per minute in stalled traffic. There is no charge for additional passengers; there is no surcharge for luggage. For trips outside city limits, multiply the metered rate by 1.5.

Taxi Companies **City Wide Cab** (☎415/920–0700). **DeSoto Cab** (☎415/970–1370). **Luxor Cab** (☎415/282–4141). **Veteran's Taxicab** (☎415/648–1313). **Yellow Cab** (☎415/333–3333).

Complaints **San Francisco Police Department Taxi Detail** (☎415/553–1447).

▌ BY TRAIN

Amtrak trains travel to the Bay Area from some cities in California and the United States. The *Coast Starlight* travels north from Los Angeles to Seattle, passing the Bay Area along the way, but contrary to its name, the train runs inland through the Central Valley for much of its route through Northern California; the most scenic stretch is in Southern California, between San Luis Obispo and Los Angeles. Amtrak also has several routes between San Jose, Oakland, and Sacramento. The *California Zephyr* travels from Chicago to the Bay Area and has spectacular alpine vistas as it crosses the Sierra Nevada mountains. San Francisco doesn't have an Amtrak train station but does have an Amtrak bus station, at the Ferry Building, which provides service to trains in Emeryville, just over the Bay

Bridge. Shuttle buses also connect the Emeryville train station with downtown Oakland, the Caltrain station, and other points in downtown San Francisco.

Caltrain connects San Francisco to Palo Alto, San Jose, Santa Clara, and many smaller cities en route. In San Francisco, trains leave from the main depot, at 4th and Townsend streets, and a rail-side stop at 22nd and Pennsylvania streets. One-way fares are $2.25–$11, depending on the number of zones through which your travel tickets are valid for four hours after purchase time. A ticket is $5.75 from San Francisco to Palo Alto, at least $7.50 to San Jose. You can also buy a day pass ($4.50–$22) for unlimited travel in a 24-hour period. Trips last 1 to 1¾ hours; it's worth waiting for an express train. On weekdays, trains depart three or four times per hour during the morning and evening, twice per hour during daytime noncommute hours, and as little as once per hour in the evening. Weekend trains run once per hour. The system shuts down at midnight. There are no onboard ticket sales. You must buy tickets before boarding the train or potentially pay a $250 fine for fare evasion.

INFORMATION
Amtrak (☎800/872–7245 ⊕www.amtrak.com). **Caltrain** (☎800/660–4287 ⊕www.caltrain.com). **San Francisco Caltrain Station** (✉700 4th St., at King St. ☎ 800/660–4287).

ESSENTIALS

▮ ACCOMMODATIONS

Most hotels allow children under a certain age to stay in their parents' room at no extra charge, but others charge for them as extra adults; find out the cutoff age for discounts.

▮TIP→Assume that hotels operate on the European Plan (EP, no meals) unless we specify that they use the Breakfast Plan (BP, with full breakfast), Continental Plan (CP, continental breakfast), Full American Plan (FAP, all meals), Modified American Plan (MAP, breakfast and dinner) or are all-inclusive (AI, all meals and most activities).

Contacts **Interhome** (☎ 954/791-8282 or 800/882-6864 ⊕www.interhome.us). **San Francisco Reservations** (✉360 22nd St., Suite 300, Oakland 94612 ☎800/677-1500 or 510/628-4450 ⊕www.hotelres.com). **Vacation Home Rentals Worldwide** (☎201/767-9393 or 800/633-3284 ⊕www.vhrww.com). **Villas International** (☎415/499-9490 or 800/221-2260 ⊕www.villasintl.com).

BED & BREAKFASTS

Here's your chance to inhabit one of the city's lovely Victorian homes. San Francisco has plenty of bed-and-breakfasts, small inns, and romantic cottages. For a full list of options plus photographs, check Bed & Breakfast San Francisco. The company has the most uncluttered Web site and the clearest map of San Francisco neighborhoods.

Reservation Services **Bed & Breakfast.com** (☎512/322-2710 or 800/462-2632 ⊕www.bedandbreakfast.com) also sends out an online newsletter. **Bed & Breakfast Inns Online** (☎615/868-1946 or 800/215-7365 ⊕www.bbonline.com). **Bed & Breakfast San Francisco** (☎415/899-0060 or 800/452-8249 ⊕www.bbsf.com). **BnB Finder.com** (☎212/432-7693 or 888/547-8226 ⊕www.bnbfinder.com).

▮ EATING OUT

MEALS & MEALTIMES

Unless otherwise noted, the restaurants listed in this guide are open daily for lunch and dinner.

San Francisco is a city that loves its restaurants—it literally has enough restaurant seats for the city's entire population to sit down en masse simultaneously. That said, you may have to wait in line for a table at breakfast on the weekends or dinner on Friday or Saturday evenings. Breakfast hours range from 7 AM to 11 AM with the majority of Bay Area residents waking up late and forming lines around 10 AM. Arrive before 9 AM if you want to get a table quickly. Likewise, most Bay Area residents make dinner reservations between 7 PM and 9 PM. A willingness to eat dinner between 5:30 PM and 6:30 PM will help you get a reservation at even the most trendy local restaurants.

RESERVATIONS & DRESS

Regardless of where you are, it's a good idea to make a reservation if you can. In some places (Hong Kong, for example), it's expected. We only mention them specifically when reservations are essential (there's no other way you'll ever get a table) or when they are not accepted. For popular restaurants, book as far ahead as you can (often 30 days), and reconfirm as soon as you arrive. (Large parties should always call ahead to check the reservations policy.) We mention dress only when men are required to wear a jacket or a jacket and tie.

Online reservation services make it easy to book a table before you even leave home. OpenTable covers most states, including 20 major cities, and has limited listings in Canada, Mexico, the United Kingdom, and elsewhere. DinnerBroker has restaurants throughout the United States as well as a few in Canada.

Contacts **OpenTable** (⊕www. opentable.com). **DinnerBroker** (⊕www.dinnerbroker.com).

WINES, BEER & SPIRITS

With some of the world's best vineyards within 100 mi of the city, it's little wonder that San Francisco's restaurants and bars often have notable wines available—whether high-profile or under-the-radar labels. There are plenty of locally made beers and liquors, too. Hometown microbreweries include Magnolia Pub & Brewery (ales), Gordon Biersch (mostly lager), San Francisco Brewing Company, and Speakeasy (ales and lagers). Anchor Brewing Company has been going strong since 1896 and its popular Anchor Steam gets distributed all over the country. Anchor also owns the Hotaling's label—the whiskey best known for the warehouse that survived the 1906 quake and fire.

▌ HEALTH

For detailed information on San Francisco's most current public health issues, visit the Department of Public Health's Web site (*www. sfdph.org*).

▌ PACKING

When packing for a vacation in the Bay Area, prepare for major temperature swings. An hour's drive can take you up or down as much as 30°F in summer, and the variation from day to night in a single location is often very noticeable. Take along sweaters, jackets, and clothes for layering as your best insurance for coping with temperature differences. Include shorts or cool cottons for summer, and pack a bathing suit (many lodgings have pools and hot tubs). Bear in mind, however, that the city can be chilly any time of year but especially in summer, when the fog rolls and descends and the wind kicks up in the afternoon. People aren't kidding when they talk about putting on their coats in June.

Although casual dressing is a hallmark of the California lifestyle, in cities, including San Francisco, many men wear jackets for dinner at the more expensive restaurants. Women should wear something dressier than regulation sightseeing garb. However, the Bay Area does respect eccentricity. No restaurant has ever turned away a customer based on the loudness of their clothing choices or the unusual color of their hair.

▌ RESTROOMS

Public facilities are in forest-green kiosks at Pier 39, on Market Street at Powell Street, at Castro and Market streets, and at the Civic Center. The fee to use the facilities is 25¢, although it's free at some places. Since they're self-cleaning, they're usually tolerable. Most public garages have restrooms, and large hotels usually have lobby-level facilities.

Find a Loo **The Bathroom Diaries** (⊕www.thebathroomdiaries.com) is flush with unsanitized info on restrooms the world over—each one located, reviewed, and rated.

▌ SAFETY

San Francisco is generally a safe place for travelers who observe all normal urban precautions. First, avoid looking like a tourist. Dress inconspicuously, remove badges when leaving convention areas, and know the routes to your destination before you set out. Use common sense and, unless you know exactly where you're going, steer clear of certain neighborhoods late at night: the Tenderloin, Civic Center plaza, parts of the Mission (around 14th Street, for example, or south of 24th to César Chavez Street), and the Lower Haight should be avoided, especially if you're walking alone.

Like many larger cities, San Francisco has many homeless people. Although most are no threat, some are more aggressive and can persist in their pleas for cash until it feels like harassment. If you feel uncomfortable, don't reach for your wallet.

▌ HOURS OF OPERATION

Most museums are open daily from 9 or 10 in the morning until 5 or 6 and are closed one day a week (usually Monday or Wednesday). Most stay open late one day of the week, and many offer free admission once a month.

Most pharmacies are open weekdays 9:30–8 and weekends 9:30–5. Walgreens drugstores in the Marina and the Castro have 24-hour pharmacies.

Store hours vary slightly, but standard shopping times are between 10 AM and 5 or 6 PM Monday through Wednesday and Friday and Saturday; between 10 and 8 or 9 on Thursday; and from noon to 5 on Sunday. Stores on and around Fisherman's Wharf often have longer hours in summer.

Contacts **Walgreens** (⊠498 Castro, at 18th St., Castro ☎415/861–3136 ⊠3201 Divisadero St., at Lombard St., Marina ☎415/931–6417 ⊠135 Powell St., at O'Farrell St., Downtown ☎415/391–7222).

▌ CREDIT CARDS

Throughout this guide, the following abbreviations are used: **AE,** American Express; **D,** Discover; **DC,** Diners Club; **MC,** MasterCard; and **V,** Visa.

Reporting Lost Cards **American Express** (☎800/528–4800 in U.S. ⊕www.americanexpress.com). **Diners Club** (☎800/234–6377 in U.S. ⊕www.dinersclub.com). **Discover** (☎800/347–2683 in U.S. ⊕www.discovercard.com). **MasterCard** (☎800/627–8372 in U.S. ⊕www.mastercard.com). **Visa** (☎800/847–2911 in U.S. ⊕www. visa.com).

▌ TAXES

The sales tax in San Francisco is 8.5%. Nonprepared foods (from grocery stores) are exempt. The tax on hotel rooms is 14%.

▌ DAY TOURS & GUIDES

For walking tour recommendations, *see* the Experience San Francisco chapter.

BOAT TOURS

Blue & Gold Fleet operates a bay cruise that lasts about an hour. Tickets may be purchased at Pier 39, near Fisherman's Wharf. The tour, on a ferryboat with outside seating on the upper deck, loops around the bay, taking in the Bay Bridge, Alcatraz Island, and the Golden Gate Bridge. An audiotape tells you what you're seeing. Discounts are available for tickets purchased online.

Information **Blue & Gold Fleet** (☎415/705–5555 ⊕www. blueandgoldfleet.com).

BUS & VAN TOURS

In addition to bus and van tours of the city, most tour companies run excursions to various Bay Area and Northern California destinations, such as Marin County and the Wine Country, as well as to farther-flung areas, such as Monterey and Yosemite. City tours generally last 3½ hours and cost $40–$45. The bigger outfits operate large buses, which tend to be roomy. Service is more intimate with the smaller companies, however, because they can fit only about 10 people per vehicle; the vans can be a little tight, but with the driver-guide right in front of you, you're able to ask questions easily and won't have to worry about interrupting someone on a microphone, as is the case with the big companies.

Great Pacific Tours is the best small company and conducts city tours in passenger vans (starting at $44). Super Sightseeing is also locally owned and operates tours in 28- and 50-passenger buses. For about $15 to $20 more, both companies can supplement a city tour with a bay cruise. Super Sightseeing can also add a trip to Alcatraz for $16.

Information **Great Pacific Tours** (☎415/626–4499 ⊕www. greatpacifictour.com). **Super Sightseeing** (☎415/777–2288 or 888/868–7788 ⊕www. supersightseeing.com).

▌ TRIP INSURANCE

What kind of coverage do you honestly need? Do you even need trip insurance at all? Take a deep breath and read on.

We believe that comprehensive trip insurance is especially valuable if you're booking a very expensive or complicated trip (particularly to an isolated region) or if you're booking far in advance. Who knows what could happen six months down the road? But whether or not you get insurance has more to do with how comfortable you are assuming all that risk yourself.

Comprehensive travel policies typically cover trip-cancellation and interruption, letting you cancel or cut your trip short because of a personal emergency, illness, or, in some cases, acts of terrorism in your destination. Such policies also cover evacuation and medical care. Some also cover you for trip delays because of bad weather or mechanical problems as well as for lost or delayed baggage. Another type of coverage to look for is financial default—that is, when your trip is disrupted because a tour operator, airline, or cruise line goes out of business. Generally you must buy this when you book your trip or shortly thereafter, and it's only available to you if your operator isn't on a list of excluded companies.

If you're going abroad, consider buying medical-only coverage at the very least. Neither Medicare nor some private insurers cover medical expenses anywhere outside of the United States (including time aboard a cruise ship, even if it leaves from a U.S. port). Medical-only policies typically reimburse you for medical care (excluding that related to preexisting conditions) and hospitalization abroad,

and provide for evacuation. You still have to pay the bills and await reimbursement from the insurer, though.

Expect comprehensive travel insurance policies to cost about 4% to 7% or 8% of the total price of your trip (it's more like 8%–12% if you're over age 70). A medical-only policy may or may not be cheaper than a comprehensive policy. Always read the fine print of your policy to make sure that you are covered for the risks that are of most concern to you. Compare several policies to make sure you're getting the best price and range of coverage available.

▌ VISITOR INFORMATION

The San Francisco Convention and Visitors Bureau can mail you brochures, maps, and festivals and events listings. Once you're in town, you can stop by their info center near Union Square. Information about the Wine Country, redwood groves, and northwestern California is available at the California Welcome Center on Pier 39.

City **San Francisco Convention and Visitors Bureau** (✉201 3rd St., Suite 900, San Francisco ☎415/391–2000, 415/392–0328 TDD ⊕www.onlyinsanfrancisco.com). **San Francisco Visitor Information Center** (✉ Hallidie Plaza, lower level, 900 Market St., Union Sq. ☎415/391–2000, 415/392–0328 TDD ⊕www.onlyinsanfrancisco.com).

State **California Travel and Tourism Commission** (✉980 9th St., Suite 480, Sacramento ☎800/862–2543 or

916/444-4429 ⊕www.visitcalifornia. com); free visitor's information and itinerary planners. **California Welcome Center** (✉2nd level, Pier 39, San Francisco ☎415/981-1280 ⊕www.visitcwc.com).

ONLINE RESOURCES
Start your search for all things San Francisco by following the links option from **www.sfcityscape.com.** This comprehensive Web site posts a link to every local publication, cultural institution, and government agency in the Bay Area.

For a snappy view of city trends, with gossip on everything from the city's best ice cream to concerts, check out **www.sfist.com.** For local politics and news, there's the online presence of the major daily newspaper, **www.sfgate.com/chronicle** as well as **www.fogcityjournal.com.**

Current arts and cultural events are detailed on the extensive events calendar of **www.sfstation.com** or the *San Francisco Chronicle* newspaper's online entertainment Web site, **www.sfgate.com/eguide.**

You can browse articles from *San Francisco*, a monthly glossy, at **www.sanfran.com.** The annual summer issues on "bests" (restaurants, activities, and so on) are handy overviews. *SF Weekly*'s site, **www.sfweekly.com,** makes for good browsing.

Where's the Wi-Fi? Although San Francisco's mayor, Gavin Newsom, promised to establish free, citywide wireless Web connections, he hasn't set a deadline. Click on **www.wififreespot.com/ca.html** to see where you can log on in the Bay Area for free.

INDEX

ABOUT OUR WRITER

Denise M. Leto has been mining San Francisco's back streets for more than a decade to share the city's ever-changing flavor and hidden gems with travelers. A longtime contributor to and editor of many Fodor's guidebooks, she shares her love of local lore with her two young, homeschooled sons, who can tell you the story behind Coit Tower and point out the city's original shoreline.

She dedicates this book to Jasper and Lukas, who are always up for another San Francisco experience, especially if it involves a bakery.